WALT WHITMAN
BUILDER FOR AMERICA

OTHER BOOKS BY BABETTE DEUTSCH

Poetry

BANNERS

HONEY OUT OF THE ROCK

FIRE FOR THE NIGHT

EPISTLE TO PROMETHEUS

ONE PART LOVE

Novels

A BRITTLE HEAVEN

IN SUCH A NIGHT

MASK OF SILENUS

Criticism

POTABLE GOLD:
An Essay on Poetry and This Age

THIS MODERN POETRY

Juvenile

HEROES OF THE KALEVALA:
Finland's Saga

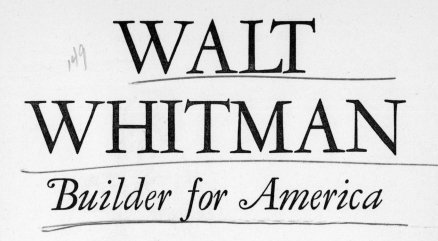

WALT
WHITMAN
Builder for America

By BABETTE DEUTSCH

ILLUSTRATED BY RAFAELLO BUSONI

NEW YORK · Julian Messner, Inc.

PUBLISHED BY JULIAN MESSNER, INC.
8 WEST 40TH STREET, NEW YORK

PRINTED IN THE UNITED STATES OF AMERICA
By Montauk Book Manufacturing Co., New York

FOR ADAM
expecting the main things from him

CONTENTS

As a young woman I came upon these words of Walt Whitman:

"Go, dear friend, if need be give up all else, and commence to-day to inure yourself to pluck, reality, self-esteem, definiteness, elevatedness,
Rest not till you rivet and publish yourself of your own Personality."

These lines stirred me so that I started reading Whitman from cover to cover, and have done so over and over again for more than fifty years, finding in him courage to stand for my own truth, my personality, and all that I hold dear in life.

It is therefore for me a profound satisfaction that this remarkable biography of him has won my award.

JULIA ELLSWORTH FORD.

WALT WHITMAN
BUILDER FOR AMERICA

O America because you build for mankind
    I build for you,

O well-beloved stone-cutters, I lead them
    who plan with decision and science,

Lead the present with friendly hand
    toward the future.

1. STARTING FROM PAUMANOK

W ALT WAS the son of a carpenter. But his adventures began on a farm, within sound and smell of the sea.

His grandmother Van Velsor was a sea-captain's daughter. Walt liked to hear her tell the story of Old Salt Kossabone, his great-great-grandfather, who

3

used to sit in his huge arm-chair at the window of his house on the hill, when he was too old for sailing, facing the bay and the cape beyond and the stretch of water that led to the ocean. One evening he sat there, a shaggy sea-dog of ninety, muttering to himself as he watched the vessels, and especially one outbound brig that struggled for hours, fighting the wind and the tide. Through sunset and dusk Old Salt Kossabone watched, grumbling. As night fell, suddenly the brig's luck turned, the breeze struck her sails and she veered, rounding the cape. "She's free! She's for her destination!" muttered the old Dutchman, in high content. They were the last words he spoke. When his granddaughter came over to him, she found him dead, his eyes fixed upon the open sea.

There were vigorous folk among his father's people, too. Walt never saw his great-grandmother Sarah Whitman, though she lived to be ninety. But he heard tell of her so often that he felt as if he knew her: a tall straight figure, dark of skin and brusque of speech, grim toward strangers and gentle only with the pickaninnies who swarmed about her skirts. When she was left widowed, she acted as master of the farm, riding out every day to see to her land and boss her slaves, chewing tobacco like a man, and swearing like a man at the idlers.

There were about a dozen slaves on the Whitman farm on Long Island when Walt was a small boy. During the day they were scattered, tending the animals or working in the fields, but the boy would see the younger darkies every evening in the firelit kitchen, squatting on the floor over their bowls of Indian corn mush and milk. Walt's

4

special friend was the freedman, old Mose, full of old-fashioned courtesy but a jolly companion.

The kitchen, at home, and at his grandfather Van Velsor's, was a good place to be. There were roaring wood fires in the winter, and always plenty of pork and beef and poultry, platters piled with steaming vegetables fresh from the garden, and home-brewed cider to wash it all down. The furniture was plain. The floors were bare. The clothes were homespun. The work was endless, for both the men and the women of the household, indoors and out. But there was comfort of a homely sort, and constant activity.

There were frequent visits to the Van Velsor homestead, where the sturdy blue-eyed black-haired boy was made much of by his grandmother Naomi, a soft-spoken woman smiling from under her modest Quaker cap, and by his stout ruddy grandfather, Major Cornelius. There must have been pony rides, for the Van Velsors bred and trained blooded horses, and both men and women made all journeys across the island on horseback.

Walt was too little to do more than tag after the small pink pigs or admire the strong fingers that pumped the hissing milk into the pail so steadily, or patter up and down the sand, smooth and cool to his bare feet, when they all gathered on the beach for a clam-bake, or stop in the door-yard a minute in spring to get the full sweetness of the lilac blossoming there. But everything he saw and touched, everything he smelt and tasted, the scent of the salt hay in the sun, the melancholy clank of the cow-bells at evening, fed him and delighted him and became part of him for always.

5.

There were few books. The annual copy of the Almanac, with its account of tides and eclipses, its advice on crops and cider-making, its occasional broad jokes, was not calculated to entertain a small boy. For the most part Walt's hunger for stories had to be satisfied with tales of his kinsmen: the Whitman who had come over in the "True Love" from England nearly two hundred years before Walt was born, the Van Velsor who had sailed from Holland to people Long Island with sturdy Quaker stock, the sailors and artisans and farmers, the soldiers who had fought in the Revolutionary War. When Walt was born, on the last day of May, 1819, John Adams and Thomas Jefferson were still living.

There was one yarn about those war-days that Walt especially relished. He had it directly from his great-grandfather the seaman.

"The enemy was no skulk," said the old man. "He had tough British pluck. It was toward evening he came on us, raking us horribly. My captain lashed fast with his own hands. The yards were tangled. It was no joke.

"We closed with him. Got some eighteen-pound shots under water. At the first fire two big pieces burst on our lower gun-deck. All hands were killed, the men above blown up.

"At sundown we were still fighting. It got dark. There was a full moon, and we fought by moonlight. Eight, nine, ten o'clock. Our leaks were gaining. They reported five feet of water. The master-at-arms loosed the prisoners in the aft'-hold to give them a chance to save themselves. We couldn't get to the magazines: sentinels were posted to

6

stop us; there were so many strange faces they didn't know whom to trust. Our frigate was afire.

"The enemy ship asked if we demanded quarter. Would we strike our colors and surrender? Do you know what our little captain said to that?" The old man laughed. " 'We have not struck,' he said. 'We have just begun to fight.'

"Yes, but we had only three guns in use. The captain himself directed one against the enemy's mainmast. The two others kept unloading grape-shot to clear his decks. The tops, specially the main-top, held out well. There wasn't a break in the firing.

"One of the pumps had been shot away. The leaks were gaining. We had no doubt we were sinking. The fire was eating toward the powder-magazine.

"Our captain gave his orders in an ordinary voice. His eyes were as bright as battle-lanterns.

"I remember the cabin-boy, he was only a child, lying dead on the quarter-deck. And near him lay an old salt with long white hair and carefully curled whiskers. The rigging dangled. The flames were licking, below and above. The couple of officers still fit for duty were 'most too hoarse to shout orders. We were sinking right enough. We fought on.

"It was near midnight they surrendered to us."

The old man paused, remembering more than he had told: the heaps of bodies flung any whichway, the dabs of flesh on the broken spars, the sharp powder-smell mixed with the smell of the sea, the heave of the ship, the short scream of the wounded, the roar of flame in the

7

wind and the stars dead quiet above, the white-faced captain giving orders to pass from their sinking vessel to the conquered Britisher.

" 'We have not struck,' " repeated the old seaman, savoring the words: " 'We have just begun to fight.' "

When the stories were finished, Walt would seek out his mother. Even if she had nothing to say, it was good to be near her, watching her stir the pot or set the dishes for supper, or smile at him over her mending. He was not so sure of his father. Walter Whitman was a giant of a man, slow of speech, but terrible as a tornado when he was angry. Walt was on the lookout for a loud quick word or a smart cuff.

Either because of his short temper or because his neighbors found him driving too sharp a bargain, the carpenter was not prospering at West Hills. He had to provide for his wife and three small children—Walt was the second son—and soon there would be another baby in the family. The Whitmans had occupied the West Hills farm for generations. But times were changing. Walt's father decided to move on.

He did not go far. Long Island still held him. But it was a big change from the salty acres near Cold Spring Harbor to the village of Brooklyn. Long Island is shaped like a fish, and Brooklyn is near the jaws that snap at Manhattan. Walt was only five years old when the family settled in Brooklyn, but as he grew, his appetite for the city: its swarming crowds, its thundering wagons pulled by heavy dray-horses, its great warehouses and smoking chimneys, its flaring lights and reaching shadows, grew with him.

8

Even a little boy had fine things happen to him in these parts.

"Guess who's coming to Brooklyn for the Fourth of July!"

Grandfather Van Velsor? Walt missed the genial old Major, as he missed the rich aroma of the stables at the homestead. No, somebody more important than that. Walt tried to guess, and gave it up.

"General Lafayette!"

"Will I see him?"

It would be wonderful to see the man who had helped General Washington. To a grandchild of the Revolution, Washington was less the first President of the Republic than the fighter who had driven out the British. Walt didn't know much about the French Revolution, but the thought of seeing Lafayette made the War seem close and real.

"All the school children will see him. You'll be lined up to greet him when he drives from Fulton Ferry. He's promised to lay the cornerstone of the Apprentice's Library."

To the carpenter's son the laying of a cornerstone was something of a commonplace. But a library was not. And certainly General Lafayette was not.

Walt was up early on that bright Fourth, and standing in line to watch the General's yellow coach pass through the aisle of children and the women with waving handkerchiefs and the scattered white-haired veterans of the Revolution. Then he ran with the crowd to the corner of Henry and Cranberry Streets where the speeches were to be made.

9

There was such a press of people that a small boy had to push against trouser-legs and peer around skirts to catch a glimpse of the gaping excavation piled about with stones. Walt managed to squeeze into the inner circle but it was still hard to get a good view of what was going forward. Friendly onlookers were lifting children onto their shoulders or setting them up on the heaps of stone. There must have been something attractive about the chubby black-haired boy staring at the spectacle with wide grey-blue eyes. For suddenly Lafayette, in his splendid regalia, stooped down to little Walt, hugged him briefly, kissed the round cheek burning with excitement, and set the boy down on a safe spot to watch the ceremony.

That red-letter day stood out against the dull background of the schoolroom and an unsettled home. The family moved almost every year. There was the house on Front Street, and then the house on Cranberry Street, and then the carpenter built his own house on Johnson Street. But he could not meet the mortgage, and they had to move again. This time he built on Tillary Street, but again there was a foreclosure and they had to get out.

Walt, with a small boy's big appetite for adventure, had his own ways of finding it.

2. DROPPED IN THE STREET

Mᴏʀᴇ ᴏғᴛᴇɴ than not, he escaped into Catherine
Street. Where it met Front Street there was a
corner grocery kept by one of his friends.

"Hello, Mr. Copeland."

"Hello, Walt."

Then perhaps the grocer would shove a handful of

11

crackers across the counter or reach into the briny barrel to fetch up a pickle for the boy to bite into crisply. The grocer had the politician's gift for friendliness: in good time he became Mayor Copeland.

The New Ferry at the foot of Catherine Street was Walt's special haunt. The deckhands liked to joke with the little shaver who watched them admiringly. The gatekeepers were on the lookout for him, and dead-headed him with a wink, letting him ride from Brooklyn to Manhattan and back without a ticket. Walt spent hours fascinated by the stallions that trudged round the central houses of the boats, before steam replaced horse-power. The grandson of Major Cornelius loved horses, the clumsy powerful creatures as much as and maybe more than the high-stepping fine-ankled thoroughbreds that had the run of the Van Velsor pastures.

He threw stones and brick-bats at the mulberry trees on Nassau Street, to the peril of passers-by, when the fruit hung heavy and sweet on the boughs. He fished in the scummy ponds and black creeks with a bent pin on a string of tow in the neighborhood of Wallabout. This district—so much of Brooklyn—was thick with Revolutionary memories.

Yonder the British transports had landed. On these hills the boys and young men, a brigade of two thousand, had stood to their guns in the fierce Battle of Long Island. It had ended in dismal rain and retreat by torchlight across the river. In that old vault lay the huddled bones of the Revolutionary soldiers who had languished in the horrible British prison ships and whose dead bodies had been flung there to rot. Cartloads of old charnel ashes, once living men, the stepping stones to Walt's America.

He witnessed a military funeral himself when he was ten years old. Sitting in the school-room one spring day he had felt a dull shock like the explosion of an earthquake. A disgruntled sailor had fired the powder magazine of the frigate "Fulton," killing some fifty men. Walt was one of the boys who followed the procession of sailors, marching two by two, when the officers' coffins were carried to the cemetery. He had stared at the banners tied with crape, heard the muffled drums, the bugles wailing the dead march, the guns fire a salute over the graves, and trotted back again to the rousing music of a sailors' jig.

Once a week Walt went to Sunday School at St. Ann's. He seems to have liked it neither less nor better than public school every day. The Whitmans' religion was not a matter of fasts and feasts, but a sound workaday morality, plain and good as bread. But there was one preacher, the boyhood friend of Walt's great-grandfather, whose name was a household word: the old Quaker, Elias Hicks.

He had been a storm-center in Quakerdom since the memorable meeting in Philadelphia when he had stood up before the Friends to speak, as always, of the "inner light" that was to fill the world with Godliness.

"It is not only light, but love—the love which casts out all fear," said Elias. And he went on to speak of the fellowship of those who dwell in God, and of the blood of Jesus Christ His Son that cleanses men from all sin.

"But what blood, my friends?" cried Elias. "Did Jesus Christ, the Saviour, ever have any material blood? Not a drop of it, my friends, not a drop of it. That blood which cleanseth from all sin was the life of the soul of Jesus."

13

The Friends, who had sat quietly through the beginning of Elias's discourse, stirred in their seats.

"The blood of Christ—the blood of Christ," Elias repeated. "Why, my friends, the actual blood of Christ in itself was no more effectual than the blood of bulls and goats—not a bit more—not a bit."

There was an appalled silence. Then the meeting-house shook with the thumping of canes, angry mutterings, the noise of shuffling feet, as men and women rose and stamped out of the hall. The greater number remained, with flushed faces and bright eyes, waiting to hear what terrible thing Elias would say next. If he was disturbed by the commotion, he did not show it. He was on fire with his own thought.

The soul of man, he insisted, has no material blood. But what such blood is to the life of the body, the spirit of Jesus is to the immortal soul. It was not only of the dust of the ground that God had made man: He had breathed into him the breath of life. That was the true blood of Jesus. That was how man became alive with God.

Not since Mary Dyer had been hanged for heresy on Boston Common fifty years earlier had there been such violent dissension. The placid meetings of the Friends were turned into something approaching mob riots. Elias Hicks set brother against brother, wife against husband, child against father. But the Hicksites held firm. These peace-loving Quakers knew how to stand up under persecution. Had not the founder of the sect, the indomitable George Fox, gone into court-rooms and taverns, into marketplaces and "steeplehouses" to bear testimony, and been dragged out and flogged till he was bruised and bleeding,

14

yet while he had breath to cry out still proclaimed his faith? Had not the early Friends who took refuge in America been whipped and maimed and burned alive for their beliefs? Nothing could move them. Nothing could move Elias.

Walt was too young to understand the controversy. He knew only that old Elias was a wonderfully good man and a fiery preacher. It would be a fine thing to see him face to face and to hear him speak.

One winter evening toward sunset the carpenter came home from work, and threw an armful of kindling on the floor near the kitchen stove with a kind of jauntiness, like a man who has come home with a pair of theatre tickets.

"Come, mother," he said. "Elias preaches tonight."

Mrs. Whitman needed no urging to hurry the supper and the dish-washing and put the smaller boys to bed. Then she ran to ask a neighbor to mind the young ones in her absence, and straightened her bonnet and cape.

But Walt? What about him? He had been unusually good all day. And it was a rare chance for him to see the great old man. Yes, Walt might come along!

Elias preached in odd places, schoolrooms and parlors and barns, it made no difference to him, so long as he could spread the word. This time the meeting was in the ballroom of Morrison's Hotel on Brooklyn Heights. Walt marched through the streets—the harbor looked strange at night but no less wonderful—in a kind of daze. He had never been anywhere like this. A velvet divan ran all round the walls of the crowded ballroom. Splendid chandeliers, the gas-light sparkling on their crystal pendants,

15

hung from the ceiling. There were richly gowned ladies on the settees, attended by fashionable gentlemen. Walt's father pointed out the notables from New York. One corner was occupied by a group of uniformed officers. On the platform sat a dozen of the faithful: grim elderly men in broad-brimmed hats, grave women in modest Quaker dress.

The glittering ballroom was as still as a meeting-house. Just when Walt thought he could not bear the silence a minute longer, a tall erect old man in a drab coat and the broad-brimmed Quaker hat rose to his feet. His lined face was clean-shaven, and for all his eighty years, his eyes shone piercingly as black diamonds. In perfect stillness that dark burning glance traveled from face to face: the Friends, the fashionables, the curiosity-seekers. Then in a rich grave voice he asked slowly:

"What is the chief end of man? I was told in my early youth, it was to glorify God, and seek and enjoy Him forever."

As he went on speaking, the old man's fervor mounted. He took his broad-brimmed hat from his head and all but dashed it on the seat behind him. His voice, that had been serious and tender, rose to the pitch of passion. Some of his listeners found their eyes wet with tears. Walt could not follow all the words, nor even half of what they meant. But the terrible sincerity of the old man, his faith in the guiding love that was above and beyond all rituals and observances, the God in man that was the light of the world, struck the boy to the heart.

Walt, who was curious about everything and everyone: the traffic hurtling over the cobbles, the stevedores on the

16

wharves, the animals on the farm, the lonely herdsman, the fisherman at his nets, the shouting auctioneer and the dumb slave on the block, was not curious about God. He saw something of God every hour of the twenty-four, in the faces of men and women, in his own face in the glass. He found letters from God dropped in the street—every object he saw was a direct message—and he left them where they were, for he knew others would come, "punctually come for ever and ever."

Perhaps those letters came thickest in the summer, for then he would go back to West Hills, to the old homestead at Paumanok—he liked to give Long Island its Indian name: "the island with its breast long-drawn-out and laid against the sea"—to the haunts where all was at once familiar and fresh.

There was no end to the joys of the bay. You could walk through sweet-smelling apple orchards and a tangle of blackberry vines, munching as you went, to the meadows on the south side. There you went out with the men to cut swathes of salt hay, or with rolled-up trousers and bare feet, dug in the wet sand for clams, and built bonfires for a chowder-feast on the beach. There was good fishing too, especially on the eastern end of the island. Here Walt met up with the half-savage bay-men, who herded droves of horses and sheep for the farmers, and were almost as uncouth as the Indians at Montauk Point. Walt had enough of their own simplicity to make friends with these men, and with the sea-bass fishers, who took him sailing with them, and filled him with wild stories of gales and wrecks.

He knew every secret of Paumanok: the dunes where

17

he could gather sea-gulls' eggs, left lying in clusters of two or three for the hot sun to hatch; the old light-house on Turtle Hill, where he spent hours watching the roll of the combers, listening to the roar of the surf that was more full of mystery than any man-made music; the prairies that spread out in the midst of the island, where the great herds were pastured, and where Walt, after a long ramble, on which he had stuffed himself well with huckleberries, would stand to watch them being led off in the sunset. It was good just to stand there, drinking in the saffron light, the spicy air, the solemn clank of a thousand cow-bells.

He circled the island in fishing-boats, sailing craft, and pilot-boats. He galloped over every road on horseback. But he liked best to explore afoot, at odd hours, at all seasons, for sometimes there were winter holidays on Long Island too, the chief delight of which was to go down to the South Bay with another fellow, dragging a sled and a basket, armed with axe and spear, to cut holes in the thick ice and spear the eels that lurked just under the surface. You could make a delicious supper of their fat white meat. Walt was apt to take his meals where he found them. He was too much of a vagrant to remember to come home on time.

"What are you going to be, Walt, when you grow up?"

The boy would have been stumped for an answer to that question. Nothing that took much schooling, certainly. A builder, like his father, perhaps. But it was a poor trade, or else Walter Whitman was a bad businessman. The family lived under the shadow of a mortgage. It was time for Walt, now twelve years old, to think about

18

adding to the slender household purse. He had no ambition to be a lawyer, but he was ready enough to take a job in Lawyer Clarke's office on Fulton Street. Walt, who looked taller and older than his years, felt quite the man at the desk by the corner window. Mr. Clarke was not too busy to help him with his handwriting. He did better than that. He gave Walt a subscription to a circulating library.

Walt plunged into the "Arabian Nights" with the same zest with which he had plunged into the surf at Paumanok. He took ship with Sindbad, he explored the cave of the Forty Thieves, he rubbed Aladdin's lamp, he listened entranced to the soft voice of Scheherazade, there was no end to his adventures. Then he got hold of Scott's poems, a stout volume with drums and pipes on every page. Especially Walt loved the swing and drama of the Border Ballads: the wreck of good Sir Patrick Spens, the terrors of fire and flood, the wild flights, the bloody feuds. And when he had had his fill of these excitements, there were Scott's own rousing rhymes.

> Breathes there a man with soul so dead,
> Who never to himself hath said,
> "This is my own, my native land!"

No man that this young American could imagine or believe in. Paumanok had been the native heath of his people for something like two centuries. In revolutionary days during the Battle of Brooklyn the blood of his kinsmen had soaked into the soil of the town he lived in now.

> Sound, sound the clarion, fill the fife!
> To all the sensual world proclaim

19

One crowded hour of glorious life
Is worth an age without a name.

One crowded hour of glorious life? Why, there were
a thousand. Scott's poems were followed by Scott's ro-
mances: "Ivanhoe," "Kenilworth," "The Heart of Mid-
lothian." This last Walt read through a dozen times.
Oh, it was rich. The hours in Mr. Clarke's office taught
him little about the law, but he never forgot the treasures
of the circulating library to which the old man gave him
the key.

The Scottish ballads opened wider doors to Walt. He
began to scribble verses of his own. They were as good
imitations as he could make of the folk balladry that was
his passion, sentimental stanzas on love and death and the
vanity of ambition. Walt itched to see his verses on "the
bubble, fame" in print. Ever since the Whitmans had
come to Brooklyn, the carpenter had spent his evenings
over a copy of *The Long Island Patriot.* Perhaps Walt
could have his work published there. He offered some of
his pieces to the newspaper. They were accepted and
printed. Walt grew bolder. He sent a contribution to the
famous New York *Mirror.* He tried to keep down his
excitement when he saw the fat ruddy slow-moving old
carrier come down the street. But his fingers trembled
as he took the paper and turned the leaves. There was
his own piece in clear type on the white sheet. His heart
drummed as never before.

But delicious as it was to be a poet, he must think of
earning money. He left Mr. Clarke to become errand-boy
to a doctor. Medicine meant no more to Walt than the

law. As his simple candor rejected the intricacies of the one, so his healthy organism veered from the appeal of the other. Neither could hold the interest of this black-maned broad-chested fellow of fourteen.

Meanwhile things went ill at home. The carpenter had too many mouths to feed, what with himself and his wife and their two daughters and five sons—Edward, the sixth, a defective who was a burden all his life, had not yet come into the world. Whether he liked it or not, Walt had to set about earning his living in good earnest.

The Long Island Patriot was published by the post-master, S. E. Clements, whose tall lean figure in the long-tailed blue coat with the gilt buttons was familiar to his subscribers, for he drove about in his sulky, pulled by a fast horse, delivering his papers himself. It was Walt's good luck to become an apprentice on the *"Pat."* He boarded, like the other apprentices, with the publisher's granddaughter, and on Sundays was shepherded through the fields to the fortresslike Old Dutch Reformed Church on Joralemon Street by the faithful Mr. Clements.

Walt's particular friend was the old stationer, William Hartshorne, who ran the print-shop in the basement. A slight, fragile, sedate old man, who kept a quid of tobacco in his cheek, and flourished a cane when he went walking, he filled his pupil's ears with stories of the Revolution, and described General Washington and Thomas Jefferson as he had seen them face to face. The very building in which they worked, with its old brick walls and narrow doors and windows, dated from Revolutionary times.

When Walt first came to the *Patriot* he was scarcely tall enough, for all his inches, to reach the upper-case letters. Old Hartshorne piled up boxes of type for him to stand on, showed him how to hold the composing-stick and helped him laboriously to form the first line. The space-box was at Walt's breast, the box for quads off in the right-hand corner, the lower-case letters within easy reach. Walt noted the big "e" box particularly. In his excitement he pressed his thumb down too hard, the line burst, and the letters made the scrambled mass that printers call "pi." But Walt was on his way. He was a printer. He was a journalist. Were letters from God still dropped punctually in the street? Walt would find them, and print them, the short cruel ones along with the grandest, for every Long Islander, for every patriot to read.

3. A FONT OF TYPE

W ALT?" SAID Mr. Spooner, scornfully pushing out his lower lip. "Walt's an idler."
The boy had left *The Patriot* for *The
Long Island Star*, but the publisher of that paper was not
so fatherly as Mr. Clements nor so patient as old Hartshorne. That the idler was busy gathering and storing

23

impressions that were to fill a book, and a life, too, Mr. Spooner never guessed, and Walt did not trouble to tell him.

Perhaps because he could not satisfy his new employer, probably because he wanted more leisure for loafing and inviting his soul, he gave himself a recess from journalism and when the family moved back to Long Island returned with them to the Paumanok hinterland. Here he took a job as a schoolmaster.

The pay was nothing to boast of, fifty dollars every three months at most, but Walt did not care about money. He boarded round with the parents of his pupils: local farmers, those with rich acres and full stables, those battling hopelessly against poverty, the pious and the worldly, the good-hearted women who looked out for their young boarder and the others whom he studied without liking. People of all sorts and conditions fascinated him, and he was glad to get closer to the Long Island yeomanry. Besides, he had his own odd notions about how to conduct classes, and he wanted to try them out.

Most of the seventy-odd boys and girls crowded together in the unpainted room were scarcely younger than Walt. The studies were simple: seldom more than the three "Rs," a smattering of geography, and—this Walt specially relished—"speaking." He was keen on debates. He loved reciting poetry. It was not enough to have the youngsters "speak" their pieces. He would gather them around him and regale them with the Scottish ballads and sometimes with his own "yawp," which was neither so barbaric nor so grand as it became later, but which they liked to hear well enough.

He joined their games in the yard with a freedom and jollity they did not meet with in the would-be ministers and lawyers who commonly interlarded their serious studies with a spell of school-teaching. But when Walt crossed the worn threshold and stepped up to the desk on the platform, there was something about the tall broad black-maned youth with the heavy-lidded grey-blue eyes that hushed the giggling and whispering, and steadied the roughs on the back seats. He was big and sturdy enough to make them feel that he was not to be fooled with. Yet—this to them was the strangest thing about him —he never used the rod. After he had left the schoolroom behind him, he wrote a story, sub-titled "A Fact," about a master who literally frightened a boy to death and then, thinking him asleep, flogged his dead body. The writing was of the crudest, a piece of absurd melodrama of which Walt grew to be ashamed, but he was never ashamed of the feeling which prompted it. He had no patience with corporal punishment. He knew a trick worth two of that.

One day he noticed that the glib answers of young Charles Roe were coming, not out of his head, but from a half-hidden slip of paper which the boy held under his palm. Walt said nothing. He did not even throw a look at Charley. But before school was out he said he had a story to tell.

"There was a boy once," he began, carefully keeping his eyes off Charley, "who wanted to show how smart he could be."

25

The boy didn't care, Walt went on, whether or not he knew his lesson: he just wanted to have all the answers right, no matter how. So he copied them off—it was a list of famous names—on a slip of paper, and held it in his hand, and when he thought the teacher didn't see him, he sneaked a glance at it. Well, Walt didn't think much of that way of getting things right. He'd be sorry to have any of his scholars act so. He wondered how they felt about it. They needn't tell him. They should just think it over, each one for himself. Walt guessed they'd come to a grown-up view of it. Just think about it, said Walt.

"That's all. School dismissed."

There was a slam of books on desks, a shuffle of feet, a chatter and scramble to get out. Charley's face was flushed and hot and he didn't want to meet anyone's eyes, certainly not Walt's. He was as ashamed as if he'd been whipped. And yet Walt hadn't even mentioned his name. None of the others knew what he'd done. He'd never do it again, though. You could bet your boots he'd never.

A moment came, however, when even Walt saw the uses of a whipping. Out fishing one day he was so pestered by a teasing boy that he lashed out at him with his fishing-rod. The boy's father had Walt arrested. He was his own lawyer, and while he pled guilty to the thrashing, he said he had been defending the vested rights of fishermen. The jury conferred briefly and returned to their places.

"Have you arrived at a verdict?" asked the judge.

"We 'ave, your Honor," said the foreman, a farmer who hailed from Yorkshire.

"What is the verdict?"

" 'E didn't 'it 'im 'arf 'ard enough."

26

The judge protested, but the foreman persisted. Walt won his case.

In Brooklyn Walt had felt the pull of Paumanok. Now off in the farming country, he felt the call of the city. He turned his back on the school-house and the fish-pond and went to New York to follow his trade as a compositor. And then, with the smell of printers' ink strong in his nostrils, he got his younger brother George to help him start his own weekly paper at Huntington.

He bought a press and type in New York, and a good horse, so that he could ride round, like Mr. Clements, serving his papers himself. It took a day and a night to travel over to Babylon on the south side, and across the south road to Smithtown and Comac and then home again. Walt liked it all: the reporting, the editing, even the jobs of compositor and pressman, for in spite of George's interest in *The Long Islander,* and a little hired help, the bulk of the work fell to Walt. He liked the journeys on horseback, with the scent of the sea coming over the brush, the halts by the hay-fields to chat with the farmers about crops and politics, the social evenings in the print-shop. The young people, some of them his own pupils, were always dropping in, chiefly to talk about the books that Walt had lying about, or have a game of toss with the metal ring that swung from the ceiling. The trick was to toss it onto a hook in the wall, the winner to be rewarded with a quarter or, better still, a mince pie fetched by George.

Poetry and ring-toss, going off for a swim in hot weather or a long tramp of a crisp autumn day, interrupted work on *The Long Islander.* The weekly was apt

27

to come out once a fortnight and sometimes once a month. The editor was a good deal of a vagrant. Not unnaturally, he lost the interest of his backers, and gave up his own paper to work as compositor and contributor for *The Long Island Democrat*. He boarded at the home of the editor, James Brenton, thoroughly annoying Mrs. Brenton by his habit of loafing in the apple orchard as though there were nothing more important than noting the way the sunlight fell through the sweet-smelling boughs.

> Under the greenwood tree
> Who loves to lie with me,
> And tune his merry note
> Unto the sweet bird's throat,
> Come hither, come hither, come hither.
> Here shall he see
> No enemy
> But winter and rough weather.

Walt did not mind even such enemies as he strode along the lonely beach, shouting to the surf.

> Lord, Lord! methought, what pain it is to drown!
> What dreadful noise of waters in mine ears!
> What ugly sights of death within mine eyes!
> Methought I saw a thousand fearful wrecks;
> Ten thousand men that fishes gnawed upon;
> Wedges of gold, great anchors, heaps of pearl,
> Inestimable stones, unvalued jewels,
> All scattered in the bottom of the sea.

He did not need to drown to suffer a sea-change, from the busy pressman to the passive observer of the water-front. And good American though he was, no Revolutionary War could deprive him of one part of his English heritage. On these excursions Shakespeare was a familiar companion. Walt was the banished Duke in the forest. He was false Clarence, troubled by bad dreams. He was Lear on the heath, half mad with misery, wild with defiance of the elements and of human cruelty.

> Blow, winds, and crack your cheeks! rage! blow!
> You cataracts and hurricanoes, spout
> Till you have drenched our steeples, drowned the cocks!
> . . . . And thou, all-shaking thunder,
> Smite flat the thick rotundity o' the world!
> Crack nature's molds, all germins spill at once
> That make ingrateful man!

The sea was a good test of poetry, none better. Walt felt a heart, vast as a planet's, beating in that swell and surge. There was an element that could respond to those mighty lines, that huge expanse, that challenger of how many stubborn adventurers: the Vikings, the seekers of the Indies, the Hollanders and Britons who had been his own forebears—that savage wrecker and prover of men.

On the seashore the printing-room seemed a mean and narrow place. It was hard to go back. He would bask awhile longer in the salt sunshine, tasting the brine on his lips, watching the tireless combers, listening to that vague deep troubling murmur.

Was Walt himself "ingrateful"? Ah, but Shakespeare had the answer to that too: "To thine own self be true, and it must follow as the night, the day, thou canst not then be false to any man." True to himself, careless of

29

times and places and responsibilities, he threw up his chance to become a notable editor and went off to Manhattan, making occasional trips back to his native island, to take any job that came to his hand: printer, laborer, journalist, gardener.

Walt had left school at the age of twelve. He never went back. Now at twenty-two, when more fortunate and scholarly young men were completing their formal studies in college or training for one of the professions, he was an idler, a rover, a foot-loose journeyman. He was one of the crowds on the pavements of million-footed Manhattan. Mannahatta, the Indians called it, "the place encircled by many swift tides and sparkling waters." It was there he got half of his education. He missed nothing and forgot nothing.

He watched the Broadway pageant, and made part of it too, a tall big-boned figure with black hair blowing in the wind, his grey-blue eyes taking in the mixed show of the streets: the young mechanics with their bundles, the women in plumes and ruffles, the hurrying merchants and brokers, the swarthy sailors; James Fenimore Cooper in the court-room where this hot Democrat was conducting a libel suit against the Whig press; old John Jacob Astor, muffled in rich furs, being lifted into his sleigh (Walt admired the horses more than the millionaire). He took in the carriages and the heavy drays, the shipping at the Battery, the stage-coaches rumbling up and down Broadway and Fifth Avenue and across Twenty-third Street.

At night you would be likely to find him in the Park Theatre, waiting for the curtain to rise on old Booth

30

or the great Macready or superb Fanny Kemble, applauding the scene till his palms tingled. He listened spellbound to the Italian opera, delighting in every part of it, from the hawkers outside shouting: "Book of the opera! English and Italian!" and the tuning-up of the orchestra to the last note of "Il Trovatore" or the magic sextet from "Lucia." He never missed a performance by Mme. Alboni. And then there was Mario, the tenor, and the exquisite Grisi, and a dozen more. The melodies enchanted him, the audience stirred him almost equally. Was the music fine? Ah, but the play was the thing! Walt joined a company of amateurs and strutted the boards in high feather. But he needed no footlights. The city was his theatre.

He had a passion for riding in the omnibuses, mounted aloft beside the drivers, big-waisted ruddy fellows, in thick great-coats, their caps pulled down about their ears, their eyes covering the traffic, their hands tugging hard on the reins. Walt waited for their yarns, the rich brogue, the rough voices were as good as anything on the stage. Up there swaying on the seat beside them, the rush and roar of the city was as grand as the roar and rush of the surf. As he had shouted to the solitary sea, so now Walt declaimed to the busy streets the speech of Antony over dead Caesar's body, or some passionate outbursts from Richard III. Or he might cry out gaily: "A horse, a horse, my kingdom for a horse!"

He had his cronies among the pilots too. He never tired of crossing Brooklyn Ferry. Any evening you could find him leaning on the rail, to watch the crowding masts and funnels, steam-tugs, hay-boats, lighters, the circling gulls, the scallop-edged waves in the sunset. He liked best to be

31

up in the pilot-houses, matching stories of the sea's deviltry.

He had his own tale of the wreck of the good ship "Mexico," at night, with a wind that cut like a razor, and the wreck-guns sounding. In a lull, the moon broke through the clouds, and you could see the ship heading on, helpless in the toss of the tall waves. You heard the crash as she struck, the howl of the victims, no less fearful as they grew fainter, swallowed up by the noise of the sea. There was nothing a man could do. You ran down to the edge of the surf, drenched and frozen. You panted over the bodies flung ashore. Not one was washed up alive. The bitter night lightened slowly. In the dawn you helped pick up the dead and lay them down in the barn that was their burial-parlor.

One of Walt's pilot friends had a luckier yarn. It was the season for bad weather, and a steamer had lost her rudder in a gale. She was drifting helplessly, her passengers crowded on her decks. The skipper of another vessel, seeing the disaster, made through the storm for the stricken ship, and chalked on a board in huge letters for all to see at the first clear minute: "BE OF GOOD CHEER. WE'LL NOT DESERT YOU." Hour after hour, day and night, he worked toward them, following, tacking with them, refusing to give up. At last he came close. It was an unforgettable sight, the eyes of the women, chased by death for three days, as they got into the rescue boat, the infants with their little old faces, the tight-lipped unshaven men. Walt swallowed the story savoringly. It tasted good, it was his own now. He was

32

one of those men, he suffered with them, he was saved with them, every moment of it he was there.

The storms were not all on the sea. There was dirty weather ahead for the Ship of State too. Walt, who at intervals made a livelihood of news-gathering, had an ear for the threatening rumble.

The Revolutionary War, which had united men of different economic backgrounds and political faiths against a common enemy, was scarcely over when the country was divided into the two factions that had been at loggerheads ever since. On the one hand was the party of Hamilton, the New York lawyer, a party composed of bankers and businessmen, upholders of a strong federal government, demanding that power be kept in the hands of the well-born and the wealthy. On the other hand was the party of Jefferson, the Virginia planter, a party made up of agriculturalists, who emphasized the need for respecting States' rights, who wanted above all to save the common man from being taxed and exploited in the interests of the capitalists and industrialists. Walt had a young brother named Thomas Jefferson Whitman.

He had another brother named Andrew Jackson Whitman. The carpenter and his wife, like thousands of other simple Americans, had seen in Old Hickory the man who was carrying on Jefferson's battle for the rights of the common people. Walt grew up in the reign of Andrew Jackson, and that rough frontiersman, whatever his faults and errors, remained for him a "noble . . . simple-souled old man." *The Long Island Patriot* had strongly supported Jackson in his fight against the United States Bank,

33

a fight against the money-changers in the temple of democracy. This the young reporter who had started out as printer's devil for Mr. Clements was not likely to forget.

In 1840, when Van Buren was up for re-election to the presidency, Walt was ready to cast his first vote. But he was not content merely to have his say at the polls. He took the stump for his candidate. A lover of shows and crowds and lights and band-music, he was in his element during the fever of election-time. The wild shouting of "Tippecanoe and Tyler too," the cider-casks to be tapped on every street corner, the log cabins on the floats in the torchlight processions at night could not make him believe that a Whig candidate was more a man of the people than a Jacksonian Democrat. And to call a candidate a Democrat in 1840 was as inflammatory as to call him a Red in 1940. In fact, the Whigs didn't call their opponents by so kindly a name. Walt and his friends were dubbed Locofocos. Van Buren lost. But Harrison, the Eagle of Tippecanoe, died a month after his inauguration, and Vice-President Tyler took office.

This did not put an end to Walt's career as a politician. Tyler had been head of the Government some three months when a mass meeting of roused Locofocos was held in City Hall Park. The Whigs had introduced into the Senate a bill designed to uphold the power of the bankers at the expense of the plain people. The mechanics, farmers, and small shopkeepers who made up the bulk of the Democratic Party were "ag'in" it and were saying so in no uncertain terms.

Walt, standing above the crowd, inflamed with the

popular feeling, did not confine his speech to the Bank
Bill.

"Already there is talk of the candidate who is to lead
us in our next campaign. Fellow citizens," he said, "let
that be an after-thought. Our Party isn't struggling to
raise one man or another to power. We Democrats, we
Locofocos if you like, have a nobler aim than that. We're
not fighting for a man, but for a great principle, for a
mighty glorious truth. I was brought up to be a good
Democrat." Was he thinking of Andy—Andrew Jackson
Whitman—and of his young brother Jeff—Thomas Jefferson Whitman?

"I've done my bit for the Party, as some of you know.
But I tell you," he looked down at the flushed frowning
faces, the lit eyes of the crowd, "I tell you I'd scorn to do
the little I can to help elect the best Democratic candidate
that ever was nominated, for his own sake alone. It is our
principles, our beliefs, the democratic idea,—not any
man, or set of men, that we have to uphold. Our job now
is to consider policies and measures. Let the future decide
what man is to carry them out. The greatest candidate we
can elect is only the agent of the Party. My friends, I am
convinced that if we make our policy clear, if we understand what our great cause really means, that candidate
will be carried into power on an overwhelming tide. The
good genius that has watched over us since the days of
Thomas Jefferson will not desert us now. I feel as though
I could pierce the darkness that shrouds the future and
see that guardian spirit smiling on us. She will guide us
through the fight. She will lead us to victory in 1844, just

35

as she did in 1828, and '32 and '36. But we must hold to the sober second thought of the people. Then we are bound to win. It will be a real triumph for the Democratic idea."

When President Tyler vetoed the Bank Bill and showed that he had the interests of the commoners at heart, Walt turned about and worked for this Democrat in Whig's clothing. He started a paper in support of Tyler, and made himself warmly hated by respectable citizens.

Respectability was not Walt's long suit in any case. Some of his best friends—William Cullen Bryant among them—were respectable citizens. But his chief care was to be a good democrat, not only politically, but in the deepest sense of the word. Already his roving eyes were looking toward farther democratic vistas.

4. A POPULOUS CITY

W
ALT WAS a young man of twenty-seven when
his labors for the Party were rewarded by the
editorship of *The Brooklyn Eagle*. It was one
of the pleasantest "sits," as he put it, that he ever held. He
liked the owner, Isaac Van Anden. The pay was good,
the work was easy, and the hours, as Walt observed, "con-

venient." As editor of an urban daily he took life much as he had when he had managed his own rural weekly. He was boarding near Myrtle Street, about an hour's walk to the *Eagle* building on Fulton Street, and he would stroll from his home to his office of a morning, turning up there any time between eleven o'clock and noon. After spending the necessary time at his desk, he gave an hour or so to reading the newspapers, went for a walk, returning in time to read proof, and then traveled to the Battery to enjoy the sun and the water-front and pick up acquaintance with whom he might find.

There were evenings at the theatre and the opera. There were jaunts to the beaches, one especially fine, arranged by the contractors for the new City Hall, with sixty good fellows making off in stage-coaches, each drawn by six horses, for a clam-bake on Coney Island. Walt relished the clams, baked Indian style in a nest of brush-wood and chips, above the rest of the feast. There was a swim before dinner and champagne after, and then, not the least pleasure, the ride home in the starlight, with Walt perched up beside one of the drivers.

He roamed hither and yon in his familiar fashion, visiting the wharves and the foundries, the poorhouses, the prisons and the hospitals, stopping to listen to a bawling auctioneer and dropping in at a revivalist meeting, browsing in libraries and museums, and pausing for refreshment, chiefly of a conversational sort, in the taverns. One of the novelettes that he published about this time was a mawkish temperance tract called "Franklin Evans or The Inebriate." Walt said that he had dashed it off in a saloon under the inspiration of whiskey cocktails, with the printer's boy at his elbow waiting for the next batch of copy. The writing is quite bad enough to make this story credible, but perhaps Walt was joking. For all his indolence and irregularity, he was a temperate fellow, as full of health as an egg is of meat. His great body tingled with vitality, his skin was clear as a child's.

He was a tireless walker, perhaps because he was a slow one, in all places, seasons and weathers. One rainy Fourth of July, Walt, whose enthusiasm for the great day nothing could dampen—besides, he had written an ode for the occasion—splashed through the muddy streets along the line of march, calling out to every friend he met: "Fine day! Fine day!" When he was not down at the shore, he took his daily swim at Carey's Salt Walter Baths. Public baths, and hygiene generally, made the subject of more than one editorial in the *Eagle*.

Was Walt a reformer? Nothing so holier-than-thou-ish as that. No man with a grain of smugness in his make-up could scrape acquaintance with coachmen and car conductors, grocers and politicians, mechanics and seamen, and hold the friends he found so informally. But he had his own notions of good and evil, and he expressed them with a grand defiance of whether they tallied with general opinion. Not for nothing had he gone Sunday after Sunday to the old Tammany Hall in New York to hear Frances Wright speak for the rights of women and the rights of labor. She kindled him with her charm and courage as no other woman could. She was bound by no traditions, she held herself open to every new light. That was the very spirit of modern science. It put him in a glow only to think of her fine freedom.

39

The evils of capital punishment and of sweat-shop labor, the rights of the oppressed, whether they were factory-hands or servant girls or women unprotected by the law, were no thin abstractions to him. "People and servants," he said sardonically, "are two sorts of folks." It was the custom for department store clerks to work until nine or later in the evening, and there was no limit to the hours on Saturday nights. One winter the Brooklyn shops agreed to close at eight o'clock. Walt was glad of it. "It is sometimes suggested," he said, "that by letting the clerks of stores have their evenings, they may spend them badly. Similar logic would suggest that by letting a man have the use of his legs he might run off the dock, and get drowned."

He wrote more than one urgent editorial on the subject of wage-cuts and poor pay. There were hundreds of girls and women who were earning as little as two dollars to fifty cents a week making overcoats. Walt had no remedy for the miserable system. But he knew that the first thing was to "make the public aware that it is an evil—and that it sows a public crop of other evils."

He liked to repeat the story of the shipwrecked sailor, tossed on an unknown shore, who, wandering inland, caught sight of a gallows from which hung the body of a murderer. "Thank God!" cried the sailor, seeing this evidence of civilized justice, "I am in a Christian land!" One of Walt's angriest outbursts against capital punishment was called "Hurrah for Hanging!" It dealt with the case of a negro, ironically named Freeman, who had murdered five people and was to swing for it. Walt suggested

40

that the good citizens who acquiesced in this punishment examine the murderer's history. Freeman was a man of twenty-four, only a little younger than Walt himself. At nineteen he had been condemned to a term of five years in the State Prison for a crime of which he claimed to be innocent.

"For five long and weary years," Walt reminded the *Eagle's* readers, "he is shut up in prison, and left to brood over his wrongs. He can make no distinction between the inevitable mistakes of the law and human testimony, and what he imagines is a determination to crush him. He thinks only of his laborious imprisonment day after day, month after month, till it has taken possession of all his thoughts; and the purpose of revenge, which to him is justice, has become to him the very breath of life."

If society had made some effort to reach Freeman and reason with him during this dreadful period, if his story had been heard and considered, if the plain teachings of Christianity had been offered him, he might have been saved, and his five victims might still be alive. But the wretched negro had been left friendless and hopeless, with nothing to look forward to but vengeance. He had worked himself up to such a passion that when he was free to strike, he had killed not only the man whom he held responsible for his fate, but four people he had never seen before, who had never harmed him, against whom he could not possibly have cherished a bloody hatred.

"This very horror of the butchery shows how thoroughly diseased and confused the whole moral being of the murderer had become," declared Walt.

41

"What remains then? *Hang him*. In the work of death, let the law keep up with the murderer, and see who will get the victory at the last."

It was not because Freeman was a negro that Walt came hotly to his defense. Except for his childhood companion, old Mose, Walt had no friends among the colored people. Slavery as an existing institution did not rouse his spleen. He had been accustomed to see contented slaves on the farm at home. He may have been influenced by the ideas of his former employer, Mr. Clements, who hailed from the South. At all events, Walt felt that the negroes were better off in the hands of benevolent owners than were many free white men and women who worked twelve and fourteen hours a day in barracklike factories for a handful of coppers.

He went often to the New York Tabernacle, to hear the abolitionists speak and be heckled and hissed and applauded by the thousands who filled the great turtle-shaped hall. He revelled in the display of oratory, in the response of the stamping shouting crowd. William Cullen Bryant, the anti-slavery editor of the *Evening Post,* was Walt's good friend, and he came to know Henry Ward Beecher, the abolitionist minister, and may have heard Emerson's eloquent protests against the slave system. But their savage opposition to it Walt could not share. There was nothing of the fanatic about him.

What roused him to indignant outbursts was not the existence of slavery, but the attempt to extend the evil to new States entering the Union. The thought of an expanding America was wonderful to Walt, and he championed the war against Mexico with purblind fervor. But

42

when peace was declared and the Wilmot Proviso, excluding slavery from the newly acquired territory, was introduced into the House, Walt spoke for it in one fiery editorial after another.

"Is *this* the country," he cried, "is *this* the age, when we are told that slavery must be propped up and extended?" Will the exclusion of slavery from new territories shut out from them the majority of free Southerners who hold no human property, but who with axe and plough could open up the virgin soil? The carpenter's son could not cry out loudly and clearly enough that *"Labor must not be degraded."* Slavery meant the bondage not only of the negro who was bought and sold, but of the poor freeman who must compete with slave labor. It threatened the livelihood of the hardworking carter and millwright and machinist, above all, of the farmers, the workers of the land. There could be no halfway solution of this problem. In the new territories slavery for one group meant slavery for all.

Mr. Van Anden, as a prominent old-line Democrat, strong for States' rights, and aware that the slave-owning Southern planters made up the backbone of his party, was far from friendly to the views of his radical young editor. He made a point of publishing fat extracts from the letter of General Cass which helped to defeat the Proviso. Walt held stubbornly to his principles.

He had been with the *Eagle* for two years. That was a long time for him to stick to one job. His disagreement with Van Anden was sore as a boil and swelling. He was not sorry when it burst wide open. The Democratic Party was splitting in two: the Old Hunkers, or slave-soil fac-

43

tion, to which Isaac Van Anden belonged, and the free-soilers or Barnburners. They got their name from the legendary Dutch farmer who had burned down his barn to rid it of rats. Were the Barnburners prepared to destroy the Democratic Party to get rid of slavery? Walt was with them then. He could be as stubborn as any Dutchman; he was a sprout of the family tree that had borne Revolutionary soldiers. His blood was up. The story goes that the quarrel with Van Anden came to a head when Walt kicked a too vociferous Old Hunker downstairs.

It was a day in early spring when the publisher parted with his editor, the season, as the poets remind us, when folk long to go on pilgrimages and when young men's fancies turn to thoughts of love. Walt was not in love, except perhaps with living, and with this growing, changing, glorious America. But he was restless.

One night on a visit to the theatre he stepped out into the lobby between the acts, and with his usual knack for getting into talk, struck up acquaintance with a wealthy Southerner. His new-found friend had come to New York to find an editor for a newspaper that he was starting in New Orleans. Mr. McClure liked Walt. Walt liked him. They had a drink together, and within a few minutes the impulsive publisher had engaged Walt to come South and edit *The Crescent,* offering him two hundred dollars to clinch the arrangement and pay traveling expenses. Walt was to start work the first day of March.

The bargain was struck on a Wednesday. On Friday Walt was on his way to Baltimore, and on Saturday he had changed trains for the trip of nearly two hundred miles to Cumberland. Walt's jolly young brother Jeff was

44

on the seat beside him. Jeff, gun in hand, had often companioned Walt on jaunts to Peconic Bay or Shelter Island. The two were fast chums in spite of the difference in years and tastes, for Walt did not like hunting. Jeff had lately learned something of the printer's trade, and he could help the editor of *The Crescent* in more ways than one.

It would be hard to say whether the fifteen-year-old boy or the bearded, greying man nearing the mature age of thirty was more excited by the journey. When the train stopped at Harper's Ferry, not yet an historic name, there was a riot of bells and yells and a dozen men flung themselves at the travelers at once. They were agents from the rival hotels of the town, clamoring for patronage. Walt and Jeff took a chance on the most urgent fellow of the lot, and got a good dinner for two bits apiece. Then they boarded the train again for Cumberland.

This was the depot for western drovers and for the huge canvas-topped Pennsylvania wagons, each pulled by a team of four to six horses, that carried goods to and from the railroad. The horses were loosed at sunset, when they arrived, and the droves of cattle and hogs herded near the great white wagons reminded Walt of a Tartar caravan.

Here the two left the train for the drive through the mountains in a lumbering coach run by The National Road and Good Intent Stage Company. The ground was covered with snow, and there was a stop every ten miles to change horses. Walt stamped up and down before the fire at the posting-stations, and stared his fill at the rough-clad drovers lounging on the benches of the smoky shad-

45

owy room, with the vague grandeur of the mountains in the moonlight glimpsed through the doorway. He thought there was stuff for a real American painter in such a scene.

It was morning when they reached the western side of the Alleghenies, and after more wearisome coaching, boarded the small steamer "St. Cloud" bound for New Orleans. The "St. Cloud" carried other passengers, including live hogs, and coops of turkeys, geese and fowl that provided a barnyard concert all the way. The steamer would stop at a hail from the shore to take on a Kentucky farmer, or a load of freight in the shape of a hundred barrels of pork, lard or flour. Every moment of the trip was grist to Walt's mill. There was a rough passage shooting the rapids below Louisville, but the rest of the voyage was uneventful. He felt sorry for the ladies, who neither read nor smoked nor even talked, and alone seemed to have a dull time of it.

For all his easy ways, Walt was his mother's son and a stickler for cleanliness, and when the brothers reached New Orleans they had some difficulty finding a lodging that was both cheap and decent. But once they were settled, what a show the city offered! Following his old habit, Walt would spend the midday hours wandering about the streets, tramping for choice on the levees, heaped with bales of cotton, and barrels of sugar and molasses, crowded with negroes and their mule-drawn carts, and there make friends with the stevedores and the boatmen. The roomy barrooms delighted him, and the author of "The Inebriate" savored the old French brandies, and the cobblers in huge tumblers topped with strawberries and snow.

Everything interested him: the bare-legged sailors scouring the decks; the longshoremen in blue pantaloons, sleeping off a spree; a big red-faced customs officer hurrying to his vessel; the old woman with a basket of live crabs at her feet; the cat-fish man crying his wares; the flower-girl with lovely eyes and teeth who drove a thriving business on pleasant evenings. On Sundays Walt would visit the Cathedral and make a lazy tour of the old French Market, observing the hucksters, negroes and squaws, and splendid Indian types of all ages. There was one immense Creole woman—Walt judged she tipped the scales at 230 pounds—from whom he would buy a large cup of coffee ladled out from her shining copper kettle. With a biscuit, it made a delicious Sunday breakfast.

And then there were the New Orleans characters, better than anything out of Dickens. Walt never tired of the cry of Timothy Goujon, the French oysterman, which seemed to mix the notes of the French horn and the bassoon:

"Ah-h-h-h-h-h-h-h-h-h-h à bon marché—so cheap as nevair vas—toutes fraîches—var fresh—a veritable collection—jentlemens and plack folks. Ah-h-h-h come and puy de veritable poisson de mer—de bonnes huîtres—Ah-h-h-h-h-h-h-h!"

It must have been from Tim, among other vendors at the French Market, that Walt picked up the foreign phrases with which he liked to sprinkle his later poems. Tim told him that a year ago he had rented a corner shop, and advertised his wares by a triangular lantern covered with red worsted and inscribed: "Always Oysters, fryd, rost & in the shel." But it had not been a success, and he

47

had sold his stock, red worsted and all, and come down to the levee, where he kept his oysters in the boat beside him, and sold them fresh from the sea.

There were the auction rooms, where Peter Funk, as the mock bidder was commonly known, worked for "the man wot sells the watches." Walt would stop in the doorway, listening to the inveigling shout:

"Fivenaff, five-n-aff—only going at twenty-five dollars and-n-aff for this elegant gold watch and chain in prime running order, just sent in by a *gentleman leaving town,* and only five-n-aff! Did I hear you say six, sir?"

Walt hadn't said six, and he was careful not to so much as look at Peter Funk, for a look could be mistaken for a wink, and a wink for a nod, and a nod for a purchase by these gentry.

And then there was the Carolinian to whom Walt gave the title of "the hon. Daggerdraw Bowieknife," and who walked about with a shooting-iron in each trouser pocket, and a bowie knife weighing about a pound and a half thrust in his vest. He was one of those "damned, high-minded, honorable, clever fellows" who would rather shoot his creditor than pay him, and who was on his way from New Orleans to Texas, followed by the ghosts of half a dozen hearty men his pistols had shot daylight through.

Nor must pock-marked Pat the drayman be forgotten. He had come from "the swate Isle" to taste the dearer "swates" of independence—he had his own horse and cart—in the land of opportunity. The energy and ambition of Mrs. Pat had helped him to earn enough to "ate and dhrink" for himself and their brood, and he was full of hope and good-humor. Of a Sunday he would put on his best clothes and go for a walk on the levee. And when the lively Bridget "got her Irish up," Pat quietly took himself out of her way until she had stopped flourishing her broom and her tongue.

Walt attended the theatre too, and was rewarded with something not on the bill: a sight of Gen. Zachary Taylor, the hero of Buena Vista, with his officers, in the dress circle. And one fine Saturday night Walt went to a fancy dress ball. He even squeezed his big hands into white kid gloves for the gala occasion. He had bought sevens instead of nines, and, bound to wear them or burst them, he did both. But though his hands looked like cracked dumplings and he did not know where to put his hat, he marched through the crowded ballroom in high feather, scanning the ladies, especially those who went unmasked, for a glimpse of the fair one of his dreams. They were all lovely, but she was not among them. He went off to refresh himself with a glass of lemonade, and returning, found a cotillion in full swing.

Suddenly he saw a lady in fancy dress who seemed to send all the others into a mist. He watched her like a man enchanted. When she turned to smile at her partner, Walt was dazzled. He must meet her. At last he won an introduction. She was not only charming, she was intelligent. She knew her Dryden as well as the latest British novelist. She loved music as Walt did. She was quite willing to enter the cotillion with him, but alas, he had never learned to dance. She said she would rather talk. Walt asked nothing better.

Just as he was glorying in his good luck, a gentleman came up to them, and asked:

"Wife, ain't it time to go home?"

"Yes, dear," said the lovely lady.

Walt's *affaire du coeur* was over as quickly as it had begun. He confided it to the readers of *The Crescent* the next day in a humorous vein. But the incident must have left a sore spot in his heart.

The romantic old city, with its fantastic streets, its crowded colorful levees, its strange men and gay Southern belles and dusty Creole beauties, left its mark on Walt. Years later he was to publish a poem which refers to those half-sweet, half-melancholy days:

Once I passed through a populous city imprinting my brain for future use with its shows, architecture, customs, traditions.
Yet now of all that city I remember only a woman I casually met there who detained me for love of me . . .

It must have been easy to fall in love with this tall sturdy young man, whose early greying hair and beard set off the clear freshness of his complexion, whose heavy-lidded grey-blue eyes looked out on the world with such candid curiosity and affection. The mystery of Walt's beloved has never been solved. Rumor has it that there was a secret marriage, that there were children of the union. But all that is really known is that they loved and parted, and that the parting must have gone hard with both.

And Mr. McClure, and his partner, Mr. Hayes, publishers of *The Crescent,* what of their relations with their young Northern editor? There was no trouble with him on the slavery question. He was still a furious free-soiler,

50

and it is notable that during his editorship *The Crescent* did not defend slavery, though it did print advertisements of slave auctions. But he could see the other side too, and he did not hesitate to publish the story of a runaway slave woman who had returned to her master's plantation near New Orleans, preferring life there as a slave to the kind of liberty she had found in her two years in Ohio. When Walt saw a negro teamster shying a stone at his balky mule, Walt said he wished he owned not the animal, but the negro: he wouldn't treat him as he had treated his mule, he'd just present him with a cowhide to whip himself with.

When Walt had been a month on *The Crescent,* he got news that his mother was ill, and he thought of throwing up his job to go to her. But he wanted to save a thousand dollars, in the hope of buying a small farm back home so that the family could settle there and resume the good life of the old days. He stayed on. But gradually a coolness grew up between him and his employers. Did he spend too much time on the streets and the levees? Was his luckless love affair occupying him too deeply and interfering with his work? Or was he getting restless again and a little homesick?

One day he sent down to the counting-room for a small sum and instead of getting it, was given a statement that Mr. McClure could not make any further advances. Walt replied proudly that he was not in debt to the paper, and asked to be relieved of his duties. Within two days he and Jeff were on their way home.

5.   FULL OF LIFE NOW

I F THE trip back was not the adventure that the
journey South had been, it had its moments. Walt
could not have liked sleeping on the floor of the
crowded steamer that carried them up the Illinois River.
But he enjoyed stretching his legs and looking over the
towns at which they stopped. The rich ample farmlands

of Wisconsin delighted him, and he was not the man to forget that this was the most progressive State in the Union. He decided on the spot that if the Whitmans ever moved from Long Island, the proper place for them to come to would be Wisconsin. He was struck by the rare lively color of Lake Michigan, and looked forward to his first glimpse of the Falls of Niagara. When at last he stood before that huge rush of tumbling waters, Walt had no words. He could only breathe: "Great God! What a sight!"

The landscape on either side of the lordly Hudson was fine. And to come home at last, and find his mother well again was fine too. All in all, Walt was not sorry to be back.

There had been a Democratic convention in session at Albany when Walt reached there, but it was made up of Old Hunkers, and he had not troubled himself to look in on it. He was a hotter Barnburner than ever. While he was still editing the *Eagle,* there had been some talk of running his own paper, but he had not been able to get a backer. He had not been in Brooklyn a week when Henry Lees, whose journal was in savage opposition to the *Eagle,* met the tanned traveler on Fulton Street. The next morning Lees publicly predicted one thing as "a dead certainty: if our Barnburning friend does not put forth a daily here in Brooklyn, there'll be no fun." And he went on to declare that no bull-dog had ever more stubbornly clutched a cow's tender muzzle, no cat ever more thoroughly worried a mouse "than our amiable Locofoco friend, the ex-editor of the *Eagle,* will be likely to clutch and worry Old Hunkerism in Kings County."

53

In less than six months the prediction came true. The money was put up by Judge Johnson, a man hated by the planters for his assistance to the underground railroads that were rescuing runaway slaves; and by the early autumn of 1848 Walt was editing a free-soil weekly appropriately called *The Freeman*. He was a delegate to the convention that nominated Van Buren for president on a free-soil platform, and came home from Buffalo eager to take up the cudgels for his candidate.

He was in love with his work, passionately devoted to the idea of keeping slavery out of the newly acquired territories. But the course of true love did not run smooth. The very night that the first issue of *The Freeman* came off the press, a fire broke out in the neighborhood of the plant. The volunteer firemen of Brooklyn, fighting the blaze with hand-pumps, were almost helpless, and together with many more, the building which housed *The Freeman* was burnt to ashes. There was no insurance to cover the loss. It was a heavy blow.

Two months later the paper came alive again, bright as a phoenix. The editor was determined to go ahead. "Smiles or frowns," he asserted, "thick or thin, we shall establish a Radical Newspaper in Kings County."

By the spring of the year the weekly had done so well that Walt turned it into a daily. The Whitmans were prospering as never before. The carpenter's son built a two-story house for the family, using the ground floor for his printing-office and a small book shop.

But the good days did not last long. The Old Hunkers got control of his paper. Walt was ousted. And on September 11, just one year after *The Freeman's* first appearance, he offered a challenging farewell to his readers:

"After the present date, I withdraw entirely from *The Brooklyn Daily Freeman.* To those who have been my friends, I take occasion to proffer the warmest thanks of a grateful heart. My enemies—and Old Hunkers generally—I disdain and defy the same as ever."

Walt was footloose again, free to obey the call of the open road. Whether to revisit once more those glimpses of the moon which had shone upon so much happiness, to bid a final farewell to the woman he loved, or merely to cure his wanderlust, he shouldered his duds and set out once more. He explored the Mammoth Cave in Virginia. He lingered along the banks of the Ohio. He stopped at a farm on Blennerhasset Island, where Aaron Burr had hatched his conspiracy against the Republic.

It was on this historic spot that Walt wrote the poem called "Isle of la Belle Rivière," beginning: "Bride of the swart Ohio," his first experiment in the free unrhymed lines that characterize his mature work. It must have been this journey that furnished him too with the substance of a poem that was to take shape ten years later: "O Magnet-South." Recalling with fresh delight the slow-moving rivers, the lakes and forests, the lemon and orange groves, live-oak and bay-tree, spreading fields of cotton and sugar-cane, the mysterious swamps, the mocking-bird singing in the moonlight, Walt felt himself a part of it all, a very native of that marvellous land. "O magnet-South!" he cried, "O glistening perfumed South! My South! . . . I will go back to Tennessee and never wander more!"

But however passionately he loved it, Walt could not

55

stay. Within a few weeks he was home again, free still. Had he ever been bound? He was always one to come and go as he pleased, careless of the hours for meals, the deadline for his copy, needing, beyond anything else, to satisfy his endless curiosity about people, his lively sense of comradeship with them. He was free now to mix with the crowd, striding along with a slow rolling gait, a tall figure in workingman's clothes, his shirt open at the neck so that his throat was as sunburnt as his bearded cheeks, his broad-brimmed felt tipped back, his eyes looking eagerly into the faces of those about him, lighting up at the sight of every friend, whether it was the spare figure of William Cullen Bryant, the gentlemanly editor of *The New York Evening Post,* or one of the Baulsir boys, the ferry pilots, or Christmas Johnny, the stage-coach driver.

Walt never lost his passion for the stages, with their picturesque names, the Yellow Birds, the Knickerbocker, the Red Birds, their sides painted in gay colors, and two to four horses stamping in harness. He would swing up beside the driver's box lightly and quietly as a swooping hawk, and drive up and down Fifth Avenue or Broadway mounted beside some burly ruddy-faced pal. He knew them well, the few slouches and the many good fellows. He drew their histories out of them. He loved listening to their yarns as much as ever. He had his stories to tell too, or he would shout some grand passage from Richard III or Julius Caesar against the rumble and roar of the street.

Came a day when Walt got the chance to ply the reins himself. One of these cronies fell ill—was it Broadway Jack or Old Elephant, Harlem Charley, Yellow Joe, Long Boston or Pretty Ike? For more than a fortnight Walt

56

kept his job for him by driving the stage until his friend could get up on the box again. Walt loved horses, the more mettlesome the better. It was good to feel the lunge of these muscular animals, to tug at the reins in the surge of traffic.

He spent days and nights on the ferries, chumming with the pilots and deck-hands. Everything about the boats fascinated him, from the knotted end of the bucket-rope to the intricacies of the engine.

"Tell me all about it, boys," he would urge them. "These are the real things I can't get out of books."

But he would have a book with him all the same, and read the best bits to his companions.

"No, no," he would say, when his ranting got the better of him, "that's the way a bad actor would do it." And he would start over again in a quieter, more telling way. He had a wonderfully rich voice. He knew how to use it.

Sometimes he thrust the volume on his listener to read later for himself. You might see a boy swabbing the deck with Walt's Homer crammed into the pocket of his monkey-jacket. Walt found these men easier to talk to than the passengers. The travelers were puzzled by this tall sunburnt man, whose splendid head contrasted oddly with his rough clothes. "Who is he?" they would ask, mistaking him in turn for an actor, a slaver, a clergyman, a smuggler, and a retired sea-captain.

Once a pilot friend—perhaps Johnny Baulsir, whom he had nursed through typhoid fever—gave him the wheel, and he nearly ran into another vessel. It was Walt's first and last attempt. A ferry was not so easy to manage as a team of horses.

He took the train to the heart of Long Island, his ears cocked for all the rough music at the station, the shouts of the newsboys, the rich brogue of the Irishwomen peddling peaches, the noise of the panting engine, the bell ringing the signal for "All aboard." There were picnics, with impromptu dinners or old-fashioned clam-bakes between a swim and a sail. Often there were long solitary rambles, companioned only by the sound of the surf and the vague voice of childhood memories, the stirrings, deep and powerful and full of mystery as the sea itself, of Walt's great secret dream: to be the poet of his America.

He would have a box of lunch with him, a towel, and a book. More often he would pull out of his pocket the crushed pages of some article on architecture or chemistry or astronomy, ripped out of an old magazine. "Hurrah for positive science!" cried Walt lustily: "Long live exact demonstration!" And he would have his small leather-bound notebook, with a pencil thrust between its loops, for jotting down the strange thoughts that came to him as he wandered there, thoughts tested and proven by the light of sky and sea.

"Be simple and clear"—those are the first words Walt pencilled in his notebook. And then he set down his notion of what the American character was like at its best. At a time when the country was expanding rapidly, being drawn together by railways and telegraph, being split apart over the slavery question, when steamships were replacing sailing vessels and Europe seemed closer than before, when revolutions were boiling and bubbling over in France and Italy, in Hungary and Prussia, at such a time a young man with the blood of rebels in his veins and democratic visions in his head might well consider what it meant to be an American.

It was a good deal nobler, to Walt's way of thinking, than to be an aristocratic gentleman, or the sort of person you read about in novels, or those who lived uneasily under the monarchs of Europe and in slavish Asiatic countries. "It is to accept nothing except what is equally free and eligible to everybody else," Walt scribbled in his notebook. "It is to be poor, rather than rich—but to prefer death sooner than any mean dependence."

Walt wanted to be a poet. But he did not want to write sugared verses on old stale themes. He had been slow to find his own style and his proper matter. No one who read his early newspaper verse, the sentimental ballads and patriotic odes that celebrated the soaring of "our red-eyed eagle," could have imagined that the author would ever achieve the poems that were stirring in him now. His first step was to shed rhyme and write in blank verse. Only when he reached the age of thirty did he begin to experiment with the loose unrhymed cadences which are all his own. He knew now that he must break down the barriers between verse and prose. He was glad to be writing in English, "the powerful language of resistance . . . the dialect of commonsense." He wasn't going to try for elegance or originality, for a style that would hang between him and his readers like curtains.

To be a poet was to be himself, to express himself frankly and fully and clearly, and so the America that was fibre of his fibre. It meant being able to greet the President in the midst of his cabinet as a friend and the negro hoeing the sugar field as a brother, and have both

59

understand him and feel that his speech was right.

Never had Walt been so sure of himself, so deeply alive and aware. He was not afraid of evil, though he knew pain and fear intimately enough, and had seen death close. A favorite story of his was that of the village boys who set about scaring a simple old woman. One boy dressed up in hooded black, with improvised horns and a tail, and ran after her howling. "Who are you?" asked the old woman. "The devil!" yelled the boy. "Ah, poor critter!" said the old woman. Walt felt much the same way. Marching up and down beside the sea, listening and looking and pondering, pausing to jot a few words in the pages of his worn little book, he lit upon a truth that was to become increasingly plain to later generations of men: "Wickedness," he scribbled, "is most likely the absence of freedom and health in the soul."

There was a frightening lack of spiritual health and freedom in American life just then, and Walt knew it. He saw men walking with dimes on their eyes like the dead, the many sweating and ploughing and threshing to get nothing but chaff in the end, the few idle owners continually claiming the wheat. The money power was growing, and the slave power with it. He was sick at the thought that fellow-countrymen of his were trying to make it a crime to help or harbor a runaway slave.

In 1850 the Fugitive Slave Law became a fact. It was rigid and terrible in its provisions. Special commissioners were appointed to enforce it. Runaway slaves were not allowed to testify on their own behalf, nor to have the benefit of trial by jury. There were penalties in wait for officers who refused to enforce the law or who allowed a

60

fugitive to escape, penalties for everyone who helped the runaways in their flight for freedom. If a question came up as to the rights of the case, the commissioner received a fee of ten dollars when his decision favored the owner and only five dollars if it favored the slave.

Walt had seen slave auctions in New Orleans. It had shamed him to the core of his being to watch men and women being handled like cattle, being bought and sold like senseless things. He had known fugitives who had escaped by the hazardous underground railroad, seen them slumping weakly on a wood-pile outside the door, their eyes rolling fearfully, their bodies sweaty and bruised, wincing at the kindest touch. The men who put a price on the head of a runaway slave were no better to Walt than a pack of Judases. He said as much in a bitter poem called "Blood Money." It was not a good poem, but it had a strange new form that Walt was to perfect with time, and Bryant, as an abolitionist, was glad to publish those angry lines in his paper.

Walt had no trouble finding a place for the political verses that sputtered from his pen, or the occasional articles. He had good friends among the newspaper confraternity. As the urge to write himself down grew stronger, he came more and more to associate with those who felt a similar itch.

One day he was invited to talk before the Brooklyn Art Union, a group of young men who were boldly painting pictures of American subjects, with no backward glances toward Florence or Paris. Walt was writing barrels of lectures, which he got no opportunity to deliver. He enjoyed standing before these young fellows, who had his

61

own view of what native painting should be. He talked to them freely. He could tell them—because he felt that they already knew it—that there was something of an artist in every hero, every man or woman who showed moral beauty. He spoke of the rebels of the hour, the Hungarian patriot Kossuth in prison, the Italian republican Mazzini in exile. He quoted his own poem addressed to the European revolutionaries, outlawed, tortured, imprisoned, hanged for their devotion to the idea that Walt felt was the vital principle of the American Union of States.

Not a grave of the murdered for freedom but grows seed for
    freedom . . .
Liberty, let others despair of you—I never despair of you.
Is the house shut? is the master away?
Nevertheless, be ready, be not weary of watching,
He will soon return, his messengers come anon.

Walt thought much and deeply about slavery. He knew it was not only of the body, but of the mind. One of the books that he liked to thumb through had been composed by a slave. It was the Discourses of Epictetus, who had been in the service of one of Nero's courtiers. He managed to buy his freedom, but scarcely bettered his fortunes. Banished from Rome as a philosopher, he led a mean life in the city of his exile. He was a cripple, and poor, owning no furniture beyond a bed, a cooking-pot, and an earthen lamp. Walt's room at home was furnished almost as simply. It had only a cot-bed, a wash-stand and a pinewood writing-table. He felt a great sympathy for this old Stoic, who had said that the only real bondage

62

was slavery to foolish wishes, was being possessed by possessions. Emerson had hold of the same truth when he wrote:

Things are in the saddle,
And ride mankind.

Emerson too would insist that a man's property is not what he owns, but what he is. The only freedom lay in being true to your convictions. If you must die for them, you died a free man.

Walt was completely independent in his opinions and in his work. He earned his living partly by writing for editors who held his own views, largely by helping his father in his house-building projects. Walt was not ashamed of manual labor. He much preferred the rough flannel shirt of a journeyman carpenter to the frock coat he had felt it necessary to wear when he started out as a journalist in the great city of New York.

His father's health was failing, and the old man needed all the help that Walt and his brothers could give him. Jesse, the oldest, was an incompetent. Young Jeff had a job on the city waterworks. Edward, the last-born child, then in his middle 'teens, with a mind that never grew up, was always to be one of Walt's responsibilities. The situation was saved for the Whitmans by a building boom in Brooklyn. The able men of the family would erect a house, they would all go to live in it for a year, sell it at a profit, and move to the next house they had built.

But though Walt was ready enough to take up his tools with the dinner-pail his mother filled for him, he was equally ready to lay them down when he felt a call to loaf.

A man had to earn enough to be independent, but prosperity had no great appeal for Walt. George, who was never to take any account of his brother's chief interest, could not understand what was wrong with him. Here was a golden opportunity for money-making, and this incorrigible idler cared nothing for it. When George pressed him, he would say simply: "We won't talk about that."

It would be easy, Walt scribbled in his notebook, to be rich owning a dozen banks, but to be rich— He did not finish the sentence. To be rich in his fashion, he later made plain, was to own not a dozen banks, but a dozen books, and those not on the shelves but in your own mind, part of your thinking and doing and being. The only wealth worth having was the kind no thief could break in and steal. For himself he wanted no more than "the independence of a little sum laid aside for burial-money, and a few clapboards and shingles overhead on a lot of American soil owned, and the easy dollars that supply the year's plain clothing and meals." He despised "the toss and pallor of years of money-making . . . with their stifling deceits and underhand dodgings . . . or shameless stuffing while others starve."

When George thought he was idling, he was occupied with the pages he had read at lunch hour. One day it was a kindling volume by Emerson. Or he was busy with the thoughts that were to crowd the preface to his own book, which he had been mulling over, on and off, for nearly ten years. There was a piece of paper tacked over his writing-table on which he had pencilled in huge letters: "MAKE THE WORK." But his writing hours were not

64

spent at his desk. He could scribble anywhere when the mood took him: on top of a stage-coach, in his gallery seat at the opera, leaning against a door-jamb in the street. When he seemed most to be drifting, he was hard at it, "making the work," clarifying his ideas not only about what it meant to be an American poet, but about the needs, first and last, of men and women living in a democratic society.

"This," he came to the conclusion, "is what you shall do: Love the earth and sun and the animals, despise riches, give alms to everyone that asks, stand up for the stupid and crazy" (was he thinking of his stupid brother Jesse and his crazy brother Eddie?); "devote your income and labor to others, hate tyrants, argue not concerning God, have patience and indulgence toward the people, take off your hat to nothing known or unknown" (there spoke Quaker independence), "or to any man or number of men—go freely with powerful uneducated persons" (like stage-drivers and pilots, farmers and fishermen), "and with the young, and with the mothers of families" (his own mother, little as she understood his poetry, was his pattern of womanly wisdom); "—re-examine all you have been told in school or church or in any book, and dismiss whatever insults your own soul." So Walt dismissed the chance for becoming a rich man.

One mild day he took his father down to Huntington with him to revisit the land where he was born and bred, and the restoring sea. It was old Walter Whitman's last sight of these home scenes. In July, 1855 he was dead.

By a kind of poetic justice, in July, 1855, Walt held in his hands the book that meant for him the beginning of

65

a new life. It was a large thin volume bound in green leather, with a decoration of dangling roots in gold foil on the fanciful cover, containing the twelve poems that he liked well enough to put into the first edition of his "Leaves of Grass." He had set the type himself in a small print-shop belonging to two friends of his, Tom and James Rome. The author's name, which occurred in one of the poems, did not appear on the title-page, but his signature was in every line of the verse and the prose preface, and there was a photograph of him, a grey-haired, bearded young man of thirty-six, in his shirt-sleeves, with his hat tipped back, and the easy bearing of a workingman. He had printed eight hundred copies, and he sent some of them to the papers for review and to those celebrated men whom he most respected. Whittier threw his copy into the fire. Emerson sat down and wrote to the author: "I give you joy of your free and brave thought."

Proudly Walt showed the family his great letter from America's great man. His mother was glad for him. His brother George, who did not think Walt's book worth reading, took no account of it. But George's shrug meant as little as Whittier's gesture of angry scorn. Walt had not said these things for a dollar, or to fill up the time while he waited for a boat. The roughs and the children would understand him, and those who went up to the hills or down to the sea.

His book broke all the rules. For one thing, his lines did not rhyme. They were almost as formless as prose. While the established American poets were writing pretty verses fit for the albums on parlor tables, Walt was sending his barbaric yawp over the roofs of the world. They might write of nature, but it was a tame, domesticated nature, filled with the babble of brooks rather than the roar of his savage mysterious ocean. And then he allowed himself to talk freely of things that polite society was content to ignore.

But Walt had no wish to astonish, any more than the daylight astonishes. His thoughts were not original with him, they were the thoughts of all men in all ages and places. "If they are not yours as much as mine," he said, "they are nothing, or next to nothing." More than thirty years later Walt was to receive a visit from a Southern admirer, a farmer named Johnson, who had read and re-read "Leaves of Grass" because it told him what he knew, spoke the thoughts he had been thinking. Down home Johnson went gunning for 'possums, and when he found traces of one he would say to himself: "The old varmint's been here as well as I." So when he read Walt's book and came upon a familiar thought, he would say: "The old varmint's been here." He came to the conclusion that there was no place Walt hadn't been.

It was true enough. As his legs never tired of walking, so his imagination never tired of roaming. All the objects in the universe were letters to Walt, he must get what the writing meant. Whether he came into his own today or in a thousand years didn't matter: he could take it now cheerfully, with equal cheerfulness he could wait.

6. STRONGER LESSONS

WALT WAS not as patient as he believed himself to be. Nobody was buying his book, and the reviewers had not Emerson's keen responsive eye. Even those who made an attempt to understand him could not satisfy a man with Walt's passionate concern to reach his public. He would mend that, if he had to review the book himself. And so he did, publishing unsigned notices in several friendly papers, in which he advertised his purpose and his achievement in no uncertain terms.

Emerson had said in his letter that he liked "Leaves of Grass" so well that he thought of striking his tasks and visiting New York to pay his respects to the author. He did not obey the impulse at once, but he suggested to Moncure Conway, an alert young Southern minister with strong abolitionist sympathies, that he visit this startling new American poet. Conway was glad to go.

It was a hot September day when he reached the small frame house on the outskirts of Brooklyn to which the Whitmans had recently moved. He found Walt lying on the grass in an open meadow near by, careless of the sun, his workingman's shirt, open at the neck, almost the color of his greying hair, and of the burnt turf on which he lay. The heat was too much even for a native Virginian, if not for Walt, so the pair went off to Staten Island for a dip. There was only one other place where you could get to know Walt as well, and that was in the heart of the city.

A few days later Conway picked him up in the print-shop where he was setting type for an article on his book, and the two made a day's jaunt of it. Every so often Walt was met by a hail or a hand-clasp. What struck his companion was that most of those who greeted him were workmen. Conway made an opportunity to ask a fellow in corduroys if he knew the grey-bearded sunburnt giant.

"That be Walt Whitman," said the workman.

"Have you known him long?"

"Many a year."

"What sort of man is he?"

"A fustrate man is Walt. Nobody knows Walt but likes him. Nearly everybody knows him, and—and *loves* him," answered the nameless one in corduroys, with a curious look, as though he had astonished himself by saying just what he felt.

"He's written a book, hasn't he?" pursued Conway.

"Not as I hearn on."

Among the odd places to which Walt took the stranger was the Tombs prison. He had friends there too, eager for a word with him, sure he would right their grievances if any man could. One prisoner, held on some petty charge, was confined to a filthy cell. Walt went promptly to ask for his transfer to a decent one. "In my opinion it's a damned shame," he said to the warden. Surprised to be addressed in such free language by a man in clothes as rough as those of an inmate, that gentleman looked Walt coolly up and down. Walt's clear grey-blue eyes looked straight into the warden's. For a moment the two stood there confronting each other without a word. Then abruptly the warden turned and gave the order for the transfer.

Conway went home with the sense that he had met a man as big and strange and remarkable as his book. The man *was* his book. But, with the grand exception of the philosopher at Concord, no one seemed to care for it. The reading public, like his laboring friends, "hadn't hearn on it." The reviews rankled. Must Walt give it all up as a bad job, as a will-o'-the-wisp? George was pressing him to stick to business and get on with their house-building

70

projects. Walt didn't say, "We won't talk about that," but he wanted time to consider, to decide whether he was really on the wrong track.

He packed his carpet-bag, waved farewell to his mother, and made for the shore. There, in the region of Peconic Bay and Shelter Island, he would think it all out.

He felt that the United States were essentially the greatest poem, that here at last was something in the doings of man that corresponded with the broadcast doings of the day and night. He must look at his own work, which he wanted to make expressive of America, in the light of the biggest thing nature could offer. Alone with the autumnal sea, in the fresh salt air, studying without interruption the broadcast doings of the day and night, he would learn whether he should obey that deep instinct of his.

Two profound emotional experiences seem to have helped him to discover himself as a poet. One was the tragedy of separation from the woman he loved. The other was the exaltation he felt in the presence of nature, his religious delight in the physical world.

> Stop this day and night with me and you shall possess
>   the origin of all poems,
> You shall possess the good of the earth and sun . . .
>
> I am he that walks with the tender and growing night,
> I call to the earth and sea half-held by the night . . .
>
> I believe a leaf of grass is no less than the journey-
>   work of the stars . . .
> And the running blackberry would adorn the parlors
>   of heaven,

71

> And the narrowest hinge in my hand puts to scorn all
> machinery.

What Walt guessed when he loafed on the grass and again when he walked the beach under the paling stars of dawn became the faith he clung to all his life. If you would understand him, he said, you must go to the heights or the water-shore. You, as he, pocketless of a dime, might purchase the pick of the earth. He did not need to understand God, he heard and beheld God in every object. Creation was the friend whose embracing awakened him.

Those hermit weeks, living with the ocean, the sunlight and the stars, thinking things out, equally glad of the animal health of his body and the freedom of his mind, were the happiest of his life. He might be laughed at, denounced, rejected, but rejection was not in his nature. Life was too full.

Why, he said, who makes much of a miracle? He knew nothing but miracles, whether he walked the streets of the city or thrust his bare foot in the surf, whether he sat at dinner with the rest, or looked at strangers riding opposite him in the street-car, or at animals, feeding in the fields, or at the sky by sunset and moonlight, or the airy dance of insects. Every hour, every inch of space, outdoors and in, was alive with the miraculous. And most of all the sea: the fish swimming in its depths, the rocks lifting their heads above it, the ceaseless motion and music of the waves, the ships full of men like himself,— what stranger miracles were there?

He remembered all his crossing and re-crossings on Brooklyn Ferry, looking back at mast-hemmed Manhattan,

72

River and sunset and scallop-edged waves of the flood-tide,
The sea-gulls oscillating their bodies, the hay-boat in the
    twilight, and the belated lighter.

He saw again the faces of those leaning on the rail, the ships coming up from the lower bay, the foundry-chimneys casting ruddy lights and black shadows over the house-tops.

He would write down what he had seen and smelt and tasted and heard and known. He was buoyed up by the great Idea, "the idea of perfect and free individuals," and he hoped the look of him was something to cheer up slaves and horrify foreign despots.

There was much to remind him of these gentry. It was a time of tyrannies and revolt against tyranny. He considered the work of the prison and the scaffold. He thought of the great speakers and writers in exile, lying sick in far countries, of strong throats choked with their own blood, and of young men who dropped their eyes when they met. But liberty and the idea of liberty would not pass away until there was not a living man with the memory of heroes and martyrs. "Whoever degrades another," said Walt, "degrades me."

There were moments when he nourished active rebellion. Who went with him, he warned, went with spare diet, poverty, angry enemies, desertions. Who went with him must fight the slave power wherever it reared its ugly head. There were trembling hands spread to shelter that old evil, but there was stern opposition to it too, which would not cease till slavery itself ceased.

Walt thought of the populous cities of America. The great city was not a place of wharves and factories, rich

73

buildings and shops, not the place of the best schools and libraries, and millions of inhabitants. It was where the men and women were equal, where there were healthy fathers and mothers, and self-dependent children, where the governors of the people were the paid agents of the people. The great city was that which had the greatest men and women. He was looking for them, he was finding them. He built for America, because America was building for mankind.

"I see now," said Walt, "that this America is only you and me." Its roughs and its proud men, its prairies and rivers and towns, its seasons of war and of peace, the manners and speech of its young men, its inventions and science, and the perpetually arriving immigrants, all these, he repeated, "are you and me."

Those solitary autumn weeks at the shore confirmed him in his purpose. Henceforth nothing would shake him, not failure, not success. He went home determined to bring out a new edition of his book, better, ampler, truer than the first.

In November Emerson sent him another envoy in the person of Henry David Thoreau. The two men did not find it easy to talk. Walt might play the hermit when the need came, but unlike the naturalist of Walden Pond, he had no scorn for his neighbor. He could not understand Thoreau's distrust of the average man.

"Whitman," said the Concord solitary, "do you have any idea that you are rather bigger and outside the average?"

Walt did not answer. It was not this, he felt, that might make him immensely significant.

74

When Thoreau said that Walt's poems reminded him of the writings of the Oriental sages, Walt had to confess that he had never read them. So much the better. He would read them now, and discover far-off kindred.

Thoreau was not charmed as Conway had been, but he felt the sincerity and the power of the man. He decided that Walt might turn out "the least braggart of all, having a better right to be confident."

And then one fine day there was a low knock on the door of the little house and Walt heard a slow sweet male voice say to his mother:

"I came to see Mr. Whitman."

"He's here," she answered, letting the stranger in. A tall lean figure of a man, with keen clear eyes in a strong-featured face, greeting his host with a simple,

"How are you, Mr. Whitman?"

It was Emerson himself.

As unembarrassed as his distinguished visitor, Walt had an hour's talk with him, and when Emerson went away, felt that he had left behind "the taste of lovableness." There was a genuineness, a simplicity and sweetness about him that Walt found in no other man. The time would come when Walt was to say that Emerson's writing was like good butter and good sugar, yet that to be eating nothing but butter and sugar all the time might prove too much of a good thing. Now he felt only that he understood why the dour Scotch writer, Carlyle, had said that having Emerson in the house was like the apparition of an angel.

Walt could not have known what Emerson had said of him when he sent that savage Scotsman a copy of

75

"Leaves of Grass." It was a book, he wrote his friend across the water, "with terrible eyes and buffalo strength," adding that if, after looking into it, Carlyle thought it only "an auctioneer's inventory of a warehouse," he could light his pipe with it.

There were to be more talks later on, and strenuous disagreements. Emerson was to find Walt half song-thrush, half alligator. But this time there was only a heart-ening interchange.

Walt, as Thoreau had discovered, was rich in self-con-fidence, and as easy in his approach to the great as to the simple. Among the other visitors his strange book brought him was the Londoner, Monckton Miles, later Lord Houghton. Walt made no bones of asking him to share his supper, though it was only roast apples.

For himself, he liked plain fare, but he was ready enough to join a good companion at a feast. He liked to foregather with the crowd in Pfaff's rathskeller on Broad-way near Bleecker Street. There he could rub elbows with men of letters and young doctors from Bellevue Hospital; listen eagerly to the actress, Ada Claire, a pale elegant tragic figure with a keen mind as well as a lovely face; drink lager in the gas-lit vault that rang with good talk and laughter, while the crowd passed and re-passed on the pavement overhead. He was the only member of that bohemian crew who was never tipsy and never broke.

He went sometimes to a less frequented place on upper Broadway to visit the Egyptian Museum. It was a queer thing to step out of the stir and clamor of the street into the room filled with relics of life thousands of miles, thousands of years away. Walt spent hours chatting with

Dr. Abbott, the curator, an English physician who had assembled these foreign treasures during his quarter of a century in Cairo. One day the doctor entertained his visitor by appearing in full Oriental costume to give him his private lecture on the exhibit.

Often Walt dropped into the Phrenological Cabinet run by Fowler and Wells. On one occasion he had Mr. Fowler examine and analyze every bump on his head. Walt was quite ready to believe that phrenology was a science. Hadn't Mr. Fowler found that his bumps of amativeness and adhesiveness were most prominent, and that he had also big bumps of caution, intuition, firmness, self-esteem, benevolence, destructiveness, and good living? There was evidence of all these characteristics in his poems, both those in the book he had published and the twenty new ones that he planned to add to a second edition.

He persuaded Fowler and Wells to issue it for him. But they were afraid to attach their imprint to the book. Walt had the frankness of a terrible child, and they understood very well that the new volume was bound to raise a bigger outcry than the first.

Walt was afraid of nobody. This time his name appeared on the cover, and the contents included all that had been written about the first edition, good and bad.

The public was already acquainted with Emerson's glowing tribute. Walt had shown it round to his literary friends, and Richard Henry Dana, Jr., the managing editor of the *Tribune,* had convinced him that it would be a good thing to publish it. When Emerson was told that his letter had appeared in the columns of the *Tribune,* he was chilled by his young friend's boldness. If he had known that Walt was going to print this impulsive private comment, he would have added a big "but" to all his praise. Walt did not know that he had offended the great man. He published Emerson's letter along with the reviews at the back of the second edition, and printed one fine sentence from it, with Emerson's signature, in gold letters on the back cover: "I greet you at the beginning of a great career."

Emerson could not have liked this bit of advertising any better, especially as he had not seen the brutally honest poems that swelled the second edition. As for Fowler and Wells, they were heartily glad that they had not publicly acknowledged their hand in the venture. There were some who would have liked to indict Walt for his too free speech, and who were stopped only because they feared they could not get a jury to convict him. If the literary world had been startled by the first edition of "Leaves of Grass," it was outraged by the second. The author was a rowdy. He knew as much about art as a hog does of mathematics. His poems were "muck." He had "the soul of a sentimental donkey that had died of disappointed love."

Readers accustomed to the conventional prettinesses and formal style of current verse were appalled by the liberties he took. His language was too plain, his large loose rhythms too strange to be acceptable. He had no manners. They did not appreciate that he had a manner, all his own, fit for his liberal thought. They resented too the fact that Walt, to whom whatever was natural was beautiful, did not hesitate to speak of things not men-

78

tioned in the poetry of the day, or indeed, in the prose
either.

Had Walt failed? He knew that there could be no
success that did not produce the necessity for a greater
struggle. Thinking it all over years later, he was to ask
if you learn lessons only from those who admire you and
are tender with you. Don't you learn stronger lessons from
those who reject you, who brace themselves against you
and treat you with contempt? He knew at the start that
he did not want to repeat the words of other men, to
import or imitate anything, however fine. Poems distilled
from other poems were useless. His affair was bigger than
that. It concerned every boy and girl, every man and
woman in this great, growing, changing country, "the
Union, always swarming with blatherers and always sure
and impregnable."

Walt was sure and impregnable. His reviled book had
no sale. But he did not now want to go back to house-
building. He had a message to deliver and he was not to
be stopped. He dug into his barrel of lectures. Perhaps on
the platform he could put across the ideas he could not
sell in print. He drafted talks on democracy and religion
and art. Democracy was his religion and the poet his
priest.

He didn't care about the money. At most he would
charge ten dollars a lecture, or fifteen cents for individual
admissions. But perhaps he knew that he was not cut out
for the rostrum. He was too slow and quiet. He could
make his points best in a room with a few intimates, or
reading to a companion from the open book of nature.

He was not a speaker. He was a journalist. *The Brook-*

lyn Daily Times needed an editor. Walt needed a job. He accepted this one. For two years he was again in harness, but with enough leisure to roam the streets as before. Many of his editorials had to do with what he saw there.

He studied the worst quarters of the city at night, and wrote about them with the frankness of a man who knew that there was no health in hiding evil things. He sketched the characters he saw in the court-rooms: battered rowdies, flashy young counterfeiters, unkempt old women, ragged boys getting their education for the prison and the gallows. He described sympathetically the poor devil of a scribbler who was hounded from one cheap rooming-house to another and lived on four-cent pies. He renewed his attacks on capital punishment. He dealt with matters of immediate concern to the citizens of Brooklyn, making repeated pleas for a decent water-system. Bad milk and cheap rum were doing their work to injure his fellow-townsmen, but to Walt's thinking foul city pump-water was nastier than either. He spoke up for his free-soil convictions.

He was ready to grant that the negroes might be better off on an American plantation than in the wilds of Africa, but he could have no traffic with the men responsible for the horrors of the slave-trade. Where liberty did not draw out the blood of slavery, there slavery drew out the blood of liberty. Further than Emerson from the fanatical abolitionists, Walt insisted that America was "not the land for slaves, on any grounds." Everything was against the system: the geography of the country, the interests of its farmers and mechanics, its expanding industry, and the just designs of the Founding Fathers. Walt was still a Jeffersonian Democrat.

He might not have called himself that. Party politics at this time disgusted him thoroughly, and with reason. "Are parties to forever usurp the government?" cried Walt, in a furious piece that did not get into print. "Are lawyers, dough-faces, and the three hundred and fifty thousand owners of slaves, to sponge the mastership of thirty millions? Where is the real America? Where are the laboring persons, ploughmen, men with axes, spades, scythes, flails? Where are the carpenters, masons, machinists, drivers of horses, workmen in factories? Where is the spirit of manliness and common sense of these States?"

He was attacking Buchanan and Fillmore, two men running for the presidency on different tickets, but both looking to Walt like the same old foul breed of party politicians. He could not find language strong enough to describe the men who were pushing such as these toward the seats of power, "crawling, serpentine men, the lousy combings and born freedom-sellers of the earth." He was not to be satisfied with the campaign orators' big beautiful words. "A parcel of windy northern liars are bawling in your ears the easily-spoken words Democracy and the democratic party," wrote Walt. "Others are making a great to-do with the word Americanism, a solemn and great word. What the so-called democracy are now sworn to perform would eat the faces off the succeeding generations of common people worse than the most horrible disease." And those who clamored about Americanism were no better.

Walt had his own idea of the sort of candidate he

81

wanted. He would be "some heroic, shrewd, fully-informed, healthy-bodied, middle-aged, beard-faced American blacksmith or boatman come down from the West across the Alleghanies." Walt wanted to see such a man, dressed in clean working-clothes, with tanned face and chest and arms, walk into the presidency.

He said this in 1856, the year that the anti-slavery Republican party was coming to the polls for the first time. It was defeated. Walt said nothing of the man who ran for vice-president on the new ticket. But he was to hear of him again, and to be noticed by him too, in war-time Washington. His name was Abraham Lincoln.

7. DRUM-TAPS

WALT LOST his job on the *Brooklyn Daily Times* as he had lost it on the *Eagle,* for speaking his mind too freely. Walt was never one to keep his mouth shut when he wanted to speak out.

His dismissal worried him. He needed money, not so much for himself, as for those he was helping as well as he could. He jotted down in his notebook that he must stir himself to provide for "M." He may have meant his mother, or more probably the initial was that of one of the many stranded friends for whom he dug into his pocket. He tried his hand at stories again, with small success. But there was hope ahead. He was going on with "Leaves of Grass," the book that was his life-long work. In a few months he had a third edition ready, and in spite of everything, he had a publisher. Possibly he had found the firm of Thayer and Eldridge through Emerson's kind offices, for they were located in Boston. Accordingly, in the spring of 1860 Walt went to the centre of the American literary world.

Six years earlier, when the great old city had failed to oppose the Fugitive Slave law, he had written an indignant piece called "A Boston Ballad," in which he imagined the ghosts of the American Revolutionaries, in mothy cocked hats and crutches made of mist, aiming those crutches like guns at the marshals who were hand-cuffing runaway slaves and sending them back into bondage. Those Bostonians were no better than the British tyrants their forefathers had defied. But it was another city to which he came now. It was a roused city, full of convinced abolitionists, prepared to fight for their principles every foot of the way.

One of the first men Walt met in his publishers' offices was William Douglas O'Connor, a young man who had just finished writing an anti-slavery novel. The fiery young novelist and the middle-aging poet became fast friends at once.

It was probably O'Connor who took Walt to the court-room where a Bostonian abolitionist, Frank Sanborn, was on trial on the charge of having had a hand in the raid on Harper's Ferry. Walt had not been stirred up over John Brown's crusade against slavery to the same extent as his friend Emerson. He did not believe in the old Kansan's bloody way of righting the wrong. But as he thought back on the story, he was overcome with a deep sense of what that fight had meant. The year of 1859 had been a year of meteors, and John Brown, whose body was now mouldering in the grave, had been one of the brightest. Walt could see him, an old man, tall, with white hair, mounting the scaffold in Virginia. He forgot that he had eaten his supper as comfortably as any the night the old man was hanged. It seemed to him now that he had been there.

I was at hand, silent I stood with teeth shut close, I watched,
I stood very near you old man when cool and indifferent, but
　　trembling with age and your half-healed wounds, you
　　mounted the scaffold.

Sanborn had not taken part in the raid. He had merely been one of several sympathizers who furnished Brown with funds, ignorant of how he was going to use them. He could not have been over-anxious about being turned over to the Federal authorities. There was a group of citizens ready to risk hazards for his defense. Yet it was no trifle to be held on such a charge.

He noticed Walt in the court-room. It was impossible to fail to notice him, a tall, ruddy, bearded man, who might have been a laborer, except that his rough clothes were spotless, and that there was something striking about

85

his face, for all the mildness of the blue eyes under the drooping lids. Who was he? What was he doing there? He was Walt Whitman, and he had come to see that justice was done.

Justice, yes, but he had no wish to sit on the magistrate's bench. He had said that the poet judged "not as the judges, but as the sun falling round a helpless thing." One night, roaming the streets of Boston, Walt ran into a battered youth whose face, dreadful as it was under the gas-lamp, he recognized as one he had known in child-hood. Walt was not daunted by that strange, terrible look. He stopped the wretch and drew out his story. He had just fled from New York, where he had been in a bloody fight. A man had been killed. Maybe he had killed him. Maybe. Walt listened quietly. He put his hand in his purse and gave the poor devil some money. His heart ached as he looked into the ugly, bruised, terrified face of his old companion. Then he leaned over, put his arm about the neck that might yet know the noose, held him a moment, and kissed the supposed murderer on the cheek. The outcast turned silently and ran off. He was crying. And Walt? He had embraced him and judged him, like the sun falling round a helpless thing.

There were happier encounters for him in Boston. One bright crisp morning in February Walt returned Emerson's visit.

"In Boston," said his friend, "when one wants to talk he goes to the Common."

So the pair wandered out to the historic park. For two hours they walked up and down under the old elms, talking about Walt's new book. It was Emerson who talked and Walt who listened. Emerson was afraid of the startling things that Walt wanted to put into this new edition. He spoke too openly about matters that most people agreed not to mention. It was not only that he wrote a queer blend of verse and prose. His subject-matter was unusual. His language was uncommonly strong. His readers would be sure to misunderstand him. The argument had all the soundness of Emerson's careful thinking, the force of his emotional conviction. It seemd to Walt as though the words moved like an army corps, reconnoitering, reviewing, attacking, pressing home all that could be said against those terribly candid poems.

Emerson did not have Walt's full healthy responsiveness to all that his senses gave him. He regretted this. He felt that to care more for the things of the mind than for the physical world was a defect in him, and said so. Walt, to whom the body was not more than the soul, nor the soul more than the body, felt so too. Compared with his own heartiness, there was something thin and airy about the Concord sage. And yet, though Emerson was not perfect—what human being is?—it seemed as though he were somehow beyond defect. Was it not a book of Emerson's, carried to work with him and read with mounting excitement over his open lunch-box at the noon hour, that had clarified his own thinking? He had been simmering, simmering, simmering, and Emerson had brought him to a boil.

The stern sweet New Englander was no prude. He was not shocked by Walt's poems. He could stand straight talk. He liked it. But he was sure that Walt's fearless honesty would offend a public used to polite evasions.

People would hate and despise a book that had important things to say to them. Walt did not need his readers as much as they needed him.

"Understand, Mr. Whitman, that my idea is not that there is evil in your book. My idea is that by leaving some things out of it, you will help to remove some of the evil that is in people."

For once, the Concord philosopher was taking the view of the world, and putting it into words that carried immense weight. Each statement he made was unanswerable. No judge's charge could have been more complete and convincing. Walt knew he would never hear the points put better. Yet deep within him he felt that he must disobey his mentor, that, come what would, he must go his own road.

Emerson had talked himself out. He paused a moment.

"What have you to say to such things?" he asked.

"Only that while I can't answer them at all," said Walt, "I feel more settled than ever that I must stick to my own theory, and act on it."

So the two, as unshaken in their respect and fondness for one another as in their opposed convictions, let the argument drop, and went off to the American House for a good New England dinner.

Walt had had his private preachment. Boston also afforded him a public one. On a quiet Sunday morning he went down to the church where he could hear the famous Father Taylor. This preacher had been a sailor and a whaleman, and his congregation was made up chiefly of those who went down to the sea in ships. The church itself, low-ceilinged, dusky, with polished timbers and a not unpleasant smell of old wood, had the look of a ship's cabin, and over the pulpit hung an oil-painting of an old-fashioned sailing vessel driving through the gale on a dark and stormy sea.

Curious as the church was, and deeply as its weather-beaten occupants fascinated Walt, he soon forgot everything but the voice and presence of the sailor-preacher. Strikingly Father Taylor mixed the grandest phrases of Scripture with homely references to the seaman's life that the simplest old salt could understand.

Perhaps Walt heard him preach the sermon on Jonah that was set down in "Moby Dick," the great whaling-story that Herman Melville had published some ten years earlier. If he did, there were passages that must have struck home to Walt with special force.

Jonah, fleeing from his duty and his God, was flung thousands of fathoms deep, where the sea-weed wrapped about his head and the cold black caverns of the ocean roared around him. But when he cried aloud, repenting of his sin, God heard and answered. Jonah was spewed forth from the belly of the whale onto the warm and sunny land, to hear once more the word of the Lord.

"And Jonah, bruised and beaten—his ears, like the two sea-shells, still multitudinously murmuring of the ocean— Jonah did the Almighty's bidding. And what was that, shipmates? To preach the Truth to the face of Falsehood! That was it."

This, cried Father Taylor, was one of the chief lessons of Jonah, "and woe to that pilot of the living God who slights it. . . . Delight is to him—a far, far upward and inward delight—who against the proud gods and commodores of this earth, ever stands forth his own inexorable self. . . . Delight is to him, who gives no quarter in the truth, and kills, burns, and destroys all sin though he pluck it out from under the robes of Senators and Judges. Delight,—topgallant delight is to him, who acknowledges no law or lord, but the Lord his God, and is only a patriot to heaven."

To stand forth against the proud commodores of this earth, ever his own self, to give no quarter in the truth, to be only a patriot to heaven—what else was Walt's own mission, his own message?

Luckily for him, to be a patriot to heaven was to be an American patriot too. To oust slavery, to protect the Union, that was the immediate business of the day. So, his affairs with his publishers settled, Walt left Boston and went home, more sure of himself than before, to do his work as poet and citizen.

The campaign for the presidency was on, one of the hottest in American history. Walt must have been part of the torchlight processions of the "wide-awake" clubs, zig-zagging through the streets at night in "rail-fence" marches, shouting for the rail-splitter who headed the Republican ticket. When election time came, Walt cast his vote for the man who, like himself, put the saving of the Union above every other consideration. And when he heard that his triumphant candidate was to pass through New York on his way to Washington, Walt was agog to catch a glimpse of him.

It was not the first time he had stood with the crowd to welcome a famous man. There had been the unforgettable occasion of Lafayette's visit to Brooklyn on the

Fourth of July. Nearly a decade later, when Walt was fourteen, he had seen Old Hickory bowing from his open barouche, his white hair brushed up stiffly, his eyes darting sharp glances at the citizens lined up on either side of the street to welcome their President. As a young man Walt had shared in the wildly enthusiastic reception of the Hungarian exile, Kossuth, and had caught a glimpse of the visiting English novelist, Charles Dickens. After Perry had opened up Japan to American commerce, he had witnessed the novel spectacle of the Japanese envoys, bare-headed, saffron-cheeked, each with his two swords, riding up Broadway between rows of curious Americans. A year earlier he had stood at the pier to watch the shapely black steamship, the "Great Eastern," move up the bay, surrounded by small craft, carrying Edward, the young Prince of Wales. How the crowd had roared then, shouting like joyous thunder!

But this was different. There was ominous quiet as the thousands of onlookers gathered about the Astor House, where Lincoln was to stop. His enemies outnumbered his friends in New York. It was understood that neither faction would make a demonstration. But there were knives and pistols in many pockets, if a riot began. Each side was ready for a move on the part of the other.

Walt climbed up onto the box of a stage-coach beside the driver to watch. Presently several shabby hacks made their way through the crowd and drew up before the entrance to the Astor House. From one of the barouches stepped a tall uncouth black-clad man, his stove-pipe hat pushed back from his bushy black hair, his face swarthy, seamed and canny. He craned his long neck to observe

91

the façade of the old hotel, stretched his arms and legs, and then, his hands clasped behind his back, turned slowly to look with good-humored curiosity at that thousand-headed monster. The crowd looked back at him, curious too, and silent as before. He stretched himself again, and then moved slowly up the steps, and without a word was swallowed up by the doors of the Astor House.

It was a sullen dangerous time. Not the president alone was threatened. The integrity of the nation was threatened. By the time Lincoln was inaugurated, seven States had withdrawn from the Union.

On the night of April 13, 1861, Walt went to the opera. The performance was over near midnight and he was walking down Broadway on his way home when he heard the yells of newsboys. They came tearing through the street, wildly shouting, "Extry! Extry!" Walt bought a paper and stepped across to where he could catch the light blazing from the Metropolitan Hotel. In a moment there was a knot of men poring over their papers. Off at the side one read aloud to those who had none. Fort Sumter had been attacked. The Confederates had fired on the flag. For perhaps two minutes the crowd of some forty people stood there, absorbing the fact. Not a word was spoken. Slowly, silently, they moved off. The Civil War had begun.

8. THE WOUND DRESSER

THE FEELING in the North was a mixture of anger
and contempt. Nobody could quite believe in the
reality of the war. It was said on high authority
that it would all blow over in a couple of months. Why
not? Walt saw two companies of the Brooklyn 13th march
out, each man with a piece of rope tied to his musket in-

tended for a prisoner to be brought back with a noose round his rebel neck.

But one July morning Walt opened his paper to read of the defeat at Bull Run. As he visualized the ragged grimly silent troops pouring into Washington in the rain, men crowding around the soup-kettles on the sidewalk, men dropping in doorways and areaways from exhaustion, he was sick at heart. The old assurance was smothered in rage and shame and stupefaction. But the cause was not lost. They had only begun to fight.

His brother George had enlisted as a private in the 51st New York Volunteers. Walt seems to have felt that his pen was mightier than his sword-arm. He began writing poems that were as urgent as recruiting-posters. If there was too much of the Quaker in him for him to follow in George's footsteps, there was no doubt as to how he felt about those who were trying to disrupt the Union.

One evening in Pfaff's rathskeller he found himself in a mixed company of Unionists and Copperheads, as Southern sympathizers were scornfully called. One man lifted his glass with the toast, "Success to Southern arms!" Walt burst out indignantly. There was a savage argument which stopped just short of a fight. Walt got up and left the place. It was to be twenty years before he returned.

He found room for his patriotism in his poetry. Most of his journalistic work at this time was mere pot-boiling. His brother Andrew had a family of his own to care for. Jeff too was married and living at home with his wife and small daughter. The ninety dollars a month that he earned as assistant to the engineer on the city waterworks was the chief support of the household. George was with his

94

regiment and his wife had to be looked out for. There was nothing but bad news from Walt's married sister Hannah in far-off Vermont. Jesse, the eldest brother, was an incompetent, and Ed, the youngest, was helpless. Rheumatism and years of household cares were robbing Walt's mother of her old spryness. It was well that he could put something in the family purse.

So the months went by, not very differently from before, except for the strange exciting gloomy tone that the war cast over everything. Whatever the news, the Whitmans sighed with relief when they read the casualty lists and found one name missing. Then, on December 15, 1862, George Whitman's name appeared in the list of wounded at Fredericksburg. There was no knowing how serious the injury might be. Walt packed his carpet-bag and went off at once to find his brother if he could. He had to change trains at Philadelphia, and had his pocket picked in the crush, so that he landed in Washington without a dime. He ran into William O'Connor, who had a job in the Treasury Department and who insisted on Walt's coming home with him. But there was small joy in the meeting. Walt had never suffered such agonizing suspense in his life. For two days he tramped from hospital to hospital, searching the wards, a heart-sickening business, ran about from office to office trying to get information, and finally made his way to the camp at Fredericksburg.

There was George, alive and well. The relief was enormous. But the camp itself, crowded with men who for months had known nothing but stiff marching and tough fighting, men horribly familiar with wounds and

95

danger and sickness and death, impressed the fact of war on him in a fresh way. One of the first sights he saw was a heap of amputated legs and arms piled up at the foot of a tree in front of a brick mansion that had been converted into a hospital. In the dooryard near the bank of the Rappahannock were new-made graves with the names of the dead marked on fragments of barrel staves or broken boards.

Walt went through the dismal house, relieving the wounded as well as he could. The brigade hospitals were even worse. These were no more than tents in which the sick men lay on the ground, lucky if they had a mattress of pine-boughs under their blankets. What could Walt do for them? He was no doctor. But these boys were his own sort, farmers' sons, young fellows from the eastern factories and the western prairies. He could talk their language. He seemed a piece of home to them. They begged him to stay with them. The bad cases clung to him convulsively. At night Walt went out and sat around the camp-fires. Sometimes he did picket duty. It was all strange and terrible and absorbing. Suffering, horror and grit were the stuff of life here. They were the stuff of poetry too.

In January Walt journeyed back to Washington with a boatload of sick soldiers. He had his hands full all the way. One man died on board. When they reached the capital Walt was determined to get some job, any job that would keep him going, and spend every spare moment in the hospitals.

It was painful work, going from bed to bed, trying to

96

nerve these hurt homesick fellows, few of them more than twenty years old, some mere boys of fifteen. He could write letters home to the worried mothers and lonely girls they had left behind them. He could cheer the wards with small gifts of oranges and jellies and ginger-snaps or the pipe and tobacco that the men longed for and that no one else would supply. He learned to dress the ugliest wound. Often he would sit through the long dreary hours of the night, his big gentle hand in the feverish hand of the dying. The camp at Fredericksburg had taught him how to do such things. He knew the lesson by heart, in more senses than one.

There were hundreds of men, sometimes up to a thousand, in each of the hospitals. These were long whitewashed one-story wooden barracks, about which were clustered tents and special buildings for the contagious cases, the surgeons' quarters, the sutlers' stores, and the guard-houses. The emergency was so great that beds were set up temporarily in the Patent Office. There was something almost theatrical about the place at night, with the gas-lights flaring down over the gallery filled with beds, and below, the glass cases exhibiting curious machines and gadgets, the sick and dying placed in rows between them.

The soldiers had to bear more than their wounds. Many were suffering from exposure: often they had lain for days on the field before they were picked up. They had been living on a diet of pork and hard biscuit, with bad water or none to wash it down. Even in one of the hospitals, Sunday dinner was generally nothing but rice and

97

molasses. There was a want of the most necessary supplies and medicines. The surgeons did heroic work, but they had barely enough help.

What angered Walt most were the troops of officious subordinates who insisted on military discipline among the sick, the rascally attendants who would steal a soldier's pay from under his pillow, the visitors who came to gape—sometimes to faint—at hospital sights, the ladies who picked out the handsome soldiers to flirt with over the bandaging. What was needed was women like his mother, wise and strong and tender, women who had sons of their own and knew how to deal with the boy masked by a bearded face, and the manliness of children. The nurse Walt liked best was a red-faced old Irishwoman who could not read or write, but who knew just how gently to lift a sore body.

Walt did the work no one else could do. He had the right word for the teamsters and the negro soldiers. He was not afraid of catching typhoid fever or smallpox. If there were times when the task seemed too heavy, he reminded himself of the darky's philosophy at Charleston when the boat ran on a flat to the rattling bullets of the Rebel sharp-shooters: "Somebody mus' jump in de water an' shove de boat off." So Walt shoved.

Once as he was leaning over to tend a strange patient, the man looked up at him and murmured,

"I reckon you don't know who I am. I'm a Rebel soldier."

Walt smiled at that. You couldn't think of the pale figure on the bed as an enemy, he was just a wounded boy, lying sick among strangers.

If he had any favorites among these helpless hundreds it was the Southern Unionists. They were the real thing. There was John Barker, for instance, of the Tennessee Volunteers. He could have had anything he wanted if he had joined the Confederacy. He refused even to take an oath not to fight for either side. His wife and young child were turned out of doors, his small property ruined. He was held in the Secesh prisons for nearly a year. Three times he was hung up by the heels to make him give up his Unionism. Once he was cut down for dead. He stuck it out. Finally, worn out with torture and sick with scurvy, he was exchanged for a Rebel prisoner and sent up to Washington. A large, slow, shrewd, silent fellow, he reminded Walt of his father.

One day Walt asked him why he hadn't taken the Southern oath to get his freedom. The fire in Barker's eyes at that question would have singed him if he had meant it. The boy was sterling stuff. He had had no education, but he understood the issue as well as any man. If anything, he was firmer than his Northern friend. War seen so close horrified and disgusted Walt. The country seemed a vast slaughter-house filled with devils butchering one another. He knew it was impossible to withdraw until the Union was safe. But the horrors were almost unbearable.

He fed the men who had no arms with which to lift a spoon. He stilled the wild look in the eyes of those who knew their lives were running out. He cleaned wounds that smelled as foully as they looked. It was all part of the day's work. He set it down plainly, every cruel detail, in "The Wound Dresser."

99

I am faithful, I do not give out,
The fractured thigh, the knee, the wound in the abdomen,
These and more I dress with impassive hand (yet deep in my
    breast a fire, a burning flame).

He could be quiet and cool enough going through the wards. But hours later, alone, he would find his throat choked with tears and his knees shaking. Some day he would have bad dreams. There was no dreaming now. He was glad of what sleep he could snatch.

He had got a copying job in the paymasters' offices that took a couple of hours a day, and he did some hack work for the newspapers. This kept him going and left something over for small presents to the soldiers. Those who knew of his work sent further contributions for the hospitals. For himself, he needed little enough. At first he lived with the O'Connors, who refused any payment for boarding him. But dependence on his friends irked him, and he moved to a lodging-house, where he got his own meagre breakfast. Toward the middle of the day he went to a restaurant for a dinner of meat and plenty of potatoes which cost him a quarter.

Walt grudged every cent he spent on himself now. His high boots wore two great round holes through his faded old trousers just above the knee, and he admitted to his mother that even without this he produced a sufficient sensation. His shirts came back from the wash a bundle of rags held together with starch. He finally bought himself a new suit, but he was grateful for the shirts and old coats sent from home. The cake that came with them he wanted to put under his pillow so that he could wake up in the night and eat some. Instead he carried a big chunk of it to a young fellow in the hospital and sat by his bed watching him relish it, and had a mouthful himself, and finished the feast by a swallow of tea from the soldier's cup.

Several times Walt made an effort to get a better job, but nothing came of it. When he saw Preston King in the parlor of the Senate, that stout worthy shook his jowled head.

"Why, how can I do anything for you? How do I know you're not a Secessionist?" he asked Walt. "You look for all the world like an old Southern planter—a regular Carolina or Virginia planter!"

And so he did, with his huge build, his booted legs and broad-brimmed hat. He thought to himself that his untrimmed beard made him look more like a wild buffalo.

After another interview, King gave Walt a couple of letters to help him in his office-hunting. He had letters from Emerson as well, one to Charles Sumner, another to Secretary Chase, but he hesitated to present them.

One day O'Connor introduced him to John Trowbridge, who was a guest of the Secretary of the Treasury, and so Walt's neighbor. Chase's mansion was diagonally opposite the tenement where Walt had a bare back room on the third floor, and Trowbridge had only to cross the street to visit him.

On the morning he did so there was a fresh wind blowing, and Walt's window was open, so the visitor kept on his overcoat. The furniture consisted of a bed, a cheap pine table, a small sheet-iron stove where a tin kettle was hissing, and a couple of chairs, littered, like the table, with newspapers. Walt was making breakfast,

101

toasting bread on a jack-knife over the few live coals in the stove, and buttering it out of a brown paper bag. Another paper bag held the sugar for his tea. His larder was an up-ended pine box.

When he had eaten and drunk and put his butter-dish in the fire, Walt brought out his new poems for Trowbridge to see. He had nearly a bookful, which he was eager to publish under the title of "Drum-Taps." They were no ordinary poems, as he said in the lines called "Eighteen Sixty-One":

Armed year—year of the struggle,
No dainty rhymes or sentimental love verses for you terrible
  year,
Not you as some pale poetling seated at a desk lisping cadenzas
  piano,
But as a strong man erect, clothed in blue clothes, advancing,
  carrying a rifle on your shoulder,
With well-gristled body and sunburnt face and hands, with a
  knife in the belt at your side . . .

As a matter of fact, it was Walt's first book which stood in his way with Chase. When Trowbridge presented Emerson's letter to the Secretary, the answer was that he could do no favors for the author of "Leaves of Grass": the man was a rough. Trowbridge told Walt about it.

"He's right," said Walt, "to preserve his saints from contamination from a man like me."

" 'I cock my hat as I please, indoors and out,' " quoted Trowbridge slyly.

"I don't blame him," Walt smiled. "It's what I expected." But he was as much disgusted as amused when

102

he heard that Chase had kept the letter for the sake of Emerson's autograph.

Walt had never had much patience with big-wigs. The war lessened it. He was seeing the horror at first hand, not only in the Washington hospitals but on the torch-lit wharf in the rain where the bloody batches of wounded from the battle of Charlottesville were being carried off the boat, and down at the front, where the field hospitals were a collection of tents on the bare ground, heated by a fire kindled at one end of a tunnel covered with old railroad iron and earth. When Walt turned from these scenes to wander through the Capitol, with its marble columns, its rosy frescoes, its heavy chandeliers and rich bronze and gilt, the grandeur seemed sickeningly out of place.

In these grim days just to live, to have one fair meal a day, seemed bounty enough for any man. Walt dreamed of going home and getting what he called a "ranch" for the family, really a small subsistence farm. He would build the house himself. An Irish shanty would suit him best, but he wanted his mother to be comfortable. Writing home, he begged her not to worry about the grocery bills, but to make sure that she got a good beefsteak once in a while, and in the next breath he repeated his strong feeling that the war had taught him to be content with the meanest shelter and one meal a day.

Perhaps Walt could comfort the soldiers, who came from every State in the Union, because he knew so well what it meant to be homesick. He fretted endlessly about his mother, he was never done missing her; about poor Han in Vermont; about Andrew, who was dying, though

103

Walt refused to let his mother think so, of a disease of the throat; about Jeff, whose salary was cut and who might be drafted and leave the family stranded; about the youngsters—there was a new baby whom Walt had not even seen. He longed to go back, if only for a day. He missed the good times, too, the opera most of all, though once he was home again, he wasn't going to gallivant in the old way. He remembered with gusto one stormy night when they had had front seats and topped off the glorious music with an oyster supper at the Fulton Street market. He could still hear the waiter sing out: "Pewter them ales!"

Life was not beer and skittles now, but bitter medicine and farewells. More than once the boys asked Walt to play the priest. There was one young soldier who begged him to read aloud some chapters from the New Testament, and when he had done, asked him,

"Do you enjoy religion?"

"Perhaps not, my dear, in the way you mean," answered Walt honestly, "and yet maybe it is the same thing."

There was another lad who felt himself going and begged Walt to give him his blessing.

"I am no scholar," said the soldier, "and you are."

"I hope from the bottom of my heart that God will bless you," the "scholar" said, swallowing the lump in his throat, "and make you well yet."

He was cheered enormously when one of the boys would take him aside, as happened more than once, and insist that Walt had saved his life. The soldiers knew that he would get them what they wanted most, whether it

104

was a clergyman of their own faith to help them out of the world, or a pipe of tobacco, or a surgeon's promise not to amputate. Once it was a toothpick. He had special treats for them, buckets of oyster-soup, and one day ten gallons of ice-cream—some of the Westerners had never tasted it before.

Walt made a point of looking as fresh as possible on his hospital visits. His worn clothes were immaculate, his smile as jolly as he could manage. These battered boys drew a kind of strength from the sight of his vigorous sturdy figure.

One day as he was going past the White House, Lincoln happened to be standing at the window. The bearded giant in the broad-brimmed felt, striding along with his hands in his overcoat pockets and his head up, took the President's eye.

"Who is that?" he asked his companion.

"Walt Whitman."

"Well," drawled Lincoln, *"he* looks like a MAN."

But the strain told on Walt, and after treating scores of gangrened wounds with impunity, he caught an infection. In the autumn of 1863 he was forced to take a brief holiday and he went home. Even there he could not escape from hospital sights and smells and sounds. Andrew was desperately ill.

And there was another deep disappointment. He had taken with him the manuscripts of two books, his war poems: "Drum-Taps," and a kind of diary called "Memoranda of a Year," which gave an account of what he had witnessed and endured. "The real war," he said, "will never get into the books." It got into his book, as

105

honestly and terribly as he could put it there. But the publishers would have none of it. He had to carry both manuscripts back with him to Washington. A few days after his arrival, he got word that Andrew was dead.

There was only one comfort at this dreary time, and this was the sense that the back of Secession was breaking. For another six months Walt carried on his work, but with failing strength. He had to go home again to recuperate. There were war hospitals in Brooklyn too, and as soon as he could, he took up his task there.

But Walt was as restless as ever. His heart was in Washington, where he had done the better part of his work, where the need was greatest. He lived in dread that George would be wounded again, and he would not be there to nurse him if he were sent up from the front. George was not wounded, but he was taken prisoner, and held at Petersburg, Virginia. Walt knew what some Confederate prisons were like. He had seen the soldiers who returned from them, mere bags of bones, so starved that they could barely close their fleshless lips over their teeth. He had heard stories of Rebels firing on trains of wounded, plundering, torturing and murdering the Northern prisoners. Thinking of these things, he felt as though there were live coals where his heart should have been. He tried to get through the lines to his brother, but in vain. Finally, the Whitmans got word that George had been exchanged.

As for Walt, as soon as he was able, he returned to the capital. He had not given up hope of finding a regular post there in a Government office, and indeed, in January, 1865 he was finally granted a clerkship in the Indian Bureau.

One of the rewarding things about living in the capital was that Walt could watch the troops parading through the city. The finest moment, of course, was when General Burnside's regiment passed through the streets and Walt, after three impatient hours, caught sight of his brother George and fell into line beside him. He kept him talking so fast that when they marched past the balcony where the President stood, George failed to salute. He found it hard to forgive Walt that.

The lean figure in black, with the dark seamed face, and the sadness always lurking behind his smile, was a familiar sight to Walt. He never forgot the President's appearance at the reception after the second inauguration, all in black except for his white kid gloves, shaking hands dutifully and looking as though he would give anything to be somewhere else. Lincoln got to know Walt's face so well that the two men would salute each other in passing, although they had never met. It seemed to Walt that here was the very type of American character at its best, gentle, plain, shrewd, resolute, and just. No human man could have done a better job.

That job was almost done. On Sunday, April 9, 1865, Lee surrendered to Grant at Appomattox. The war was over. Six days later Abraham Lincoln was dead.

9. QUICKSAND YEARS

W ALT WAS on a visit home when the news came that the President had been shot. That Saturday dragged out endlessly. He bought every extra, hoping against hope for a miracle. The Ship of State had weathered the storm. The fearful trip was done. But what were the wreaths of victory worth, what the shouts of the crowd and the exulting bells, if the Captain himself were lost? Mrs. Whitman prepared the meals as usual, but they stood on the table untouched. Toward evening Walt went for a walk in the woods. As he tramped through the dusk, carrying his load of sorrow, hearing, as in a dream, the notes of the hermit-thrush, with the scent of the cedars in his nostrils and the remembered smell of blossoming lilac, all he had witnessed through those cruel bloody years passed before him again. The song of the little grey-brown bird and the mournful evening star mingled with the thought of death. Until at last heartbreak eased itself in an echoing song of his own:

Comrades mine and I in the midst, and their memory ever to
    keep, for the dead I loved so well,
For the sweetest, wisest soul of all my days and lands—and this
    for his dear sake,
Lilac and star and bird twined with the chant of my soul,
There in the fragrant pines and the cedars dusk and dim.

A few months before, Walt had given the public his "Drum-Taps," printing the book at his own expense, since no publisher would chance it. Now he felt that there was yet another word that must be said, if his war poems were to be complete. He stopped the sale of the book, and reissued it with two more poems at the end. One of them was "Captain, My Captain," a more formal piece than was usual with Walt, and one that he himself did not like as well as the rest, perhaps because it erred on the side of sentimentality. The other was the haunting elegy, "When Lilacs Last in the Dooryard Bloomed." Ever after, when spring came, with the fresh smell of lilacs in the dooryard, and the song of the hermit-thrush rising, as though the evening star had found a voice, it would take Walt back to the dark hour when he learned that Lincoln was dead.

But though much was over and ended, his work was not done. The hospitals were not yet emptied of the wounded. Walt had been promoted to a clerkship of the second class in the Department of the Interior, and must be at his desk. In the drawer of that desk lay a copy of the Boston edition of "Leaves of Grass" in which he was pencilling changes and new verses for the book that was, in more senses than one, his life.

Walt's superior was James Harlan, a former Methodist preacher, whose political ambitions had carried him to the Senate, and led him to dream of the vice-presidency. Lincoln had refused to run on the same ticket with him. When Harlan's Methodist friends urged that he be appointed Secretary of the Interior, Lincoln had hesitated, preferring someone else. But at the meeting that was to decide the matter, Harlan's sponsors outnumbered those of his rival, and Lincoln, on the grounds that the Methodists were a good and great body, and had stood by the Government, gave the post to the ex-preacher.

Walt had held his clerkship only a month when Harlan announced to him that he was dismissed. He gave no reason. Walt could not understand what was wrong. He asked his friend Hubley Ashton, the Assistant Attorney-General, to find out.

To Ashton's query Harlan answered that this Whitman was an unprincipled fellow, the author of a scandalous book. What book? "Leaves of Grass." Hadn't the Secretary known of it when Whitman was appointed? No, he

110

had only just got hold of it. But it was out of print. Rumor had it that Harlan had stolen Walt's copy from his desk drawer and read it after office hours. With all the misplaced zeal of a fanatical prude he determined that he would oust the author from his Department. Harlan told Ashton that the President himself couldn't get him to reinstate Whitman; he would rather resign.

The story soon came to William Douglas O'Connor. At once his Irish blood was up. The passion of a man whose friend's honor has been challenged, the weight of all the classical scholarship he could command, O'Connor poured into a pamphlet defending Walt. He called it "The Good Gray Poet." The name stuck permanently. O'Connor's arguments were those of every spokesman for free speech and a free press. He cited examples of enduring literature, from Walt's own favorites: the Bible and the plays of Shakespeare, on down, demanding whether, because they contained matter that might offend squeamish minds, such books should be burned to make a Methodist's holiday. He argued with Milton that one might as well almost kill a man as kill a good book; that the liberty to know, and to speak freely according to conscience, was above all other liberties. Yes, Walt had written frankly about things that polite people preferred to hide and ignore. What of it? He spoke the truth that was in him, without dodging or evasion. He was as honest as the daylight, and as clean. As for Harlan, Walt's defender could hardly find words stinging enough in which to characterize the snooping bigot.

Harlan did not try to defend his position. He gave that job to his assistant, Lanman, who hinted that Walt was

111

a drunken incompetent. O'Connor, outraged by these boldfaced lies, demanded that Lanman state his charges directly. This Lanman was afraid to do, and when Harlan was forced to give his reasons in writing for the abrupt dismissal, his lame excuse was that it was dictated by post-war economy.

How did Walt feel about it? It must have been in a moment of half-amused disgust with just such as Harlan that he wrote that passage in "Song of Myself" where he says,

I think I could turn and live with animals, they are so placid and
    self-contain'd,
I stand and look at them long and long.
They do not sweat and whine about their condition,
They do not lie awake in the dark and weep for their sins,
They do not make me sick discussing their duty to God,
Not one is dissatisfied, not one is demented with the mania of
    owning things,
Not one kneels to another, nor to his kind that lived thousands
    of years ago,
Not one is respectable or unhappy over the whole earth.

Walt recognized that Harlan had only a dim light in his noddle and had to steer by that. "His heart said, 'Throw Walt Whitman out,' so out I went." The man had at least the courage of his convictions, and Walt had a sneaking admiration for his act because of this.

He knew that he was bound to be misunderstood. It was not the people in parlors who would know what he meant, and in libraries he lay "as one dumb, a gawk, or unborn, or dead." What he had failed to put in his book was as important as what got into it. Those who thrust it into

112

their pockets and strode off to the hills or the sea knew him more intimately perhaps than those who studied each syllable. His poems would not do good only: he remembered Emerson's warning, though he could not heed it. But, after all, what was the main drift of them? It was the distinctiveness of each single, separate man and woman.

In each person he looked for that bright particular quality that he discovered in certain faces. In Lincoln's face, with all its homeliness, as in the faces of old farmers and sea-captains, Walt found something as impossible to show in a portrait as the taste of a wild fruit or the passionate tone of the living voice, yet as distinct and remarkable. He admired that individual flavor and character. He wanted the sort of world that would bring it out in everyone. Walt's poems had a religious purpose, but one that the average pious church-goer would find it hard to grasp. His was the religion of democracy, the ideal of the States. Perhaps it puzzled people because it was so profoundly simple.

He heard that it was charged against him that he sought to destroy institutions. But really, he was neither for nor against institutions. He said so plainly.

Only I will establish in the Mannahatta and in every city of
    these States inland and seaboard,
And in the fields and woods, and above every keel little and
    large that dents the water,
Without edifices or rules or trustees or any argument,
The institution of the dear love of comrades.

It was as simple as all that.

O'Connor's violent pamphlet counted for nothing with a man like Harlan. But though Walt was not reinstated,

113

Hubley Ashton soon managed to get him another clerkship in his own Department. So Walt continued to live in Washington, dividing his time as always between his desk and the city streets, less colorful than those of New York, but still fascinating to him, writing new and stronger poems, making new and greater friends.

He must have missed the ferries and above all the New York stage-coaches. He had to make up for them by long trolley-rides in the Washington horse-cars, chumming, instead of with pilots and drivers, with the conductors.

One hot summer day toward sunset Walt was standing in the rear of a crowded trolley chatting with just such a uniformed friend. The platform was crowded. In the jammed doorway stood a workingwoman with one child crushed against her and a plump petulant baby a little more than a year old in her arms. The infant fretted without let-up, the passengers scowled and grumbled, the mother was red with heat and weariness and vexation. As the car lumbered up Capitol Hill the baby burst into a nerve-racking wail. At the top of the hill the car stopped to let off passengers, and Walt reached over and lifted the howling little creature out of its mother's arms to give it a breath of air. Abruptly the cries ceased, as the child pushed fat hands against Walt's chest and stared fearfully and curiously into the bearded face under the great white hat. The answering look must have satisfied it, for the baby snuggled into Walt's neck and within a few minutes had quietly dozed off. A block or two further on the conductor got off for his dinner, and Walt himself took charge, one eye on those inside the car, one hand free to

114

pull the bell to stop and go, all the while firmly clutching his fat sleepy armful, to the relief of the exhausted mother and the amusement of the passengers.

Walt made one friend among the Washington conductors whom he kept to the end of his life. Getting onto a trolley late one stormy night, he found himself the sole passenger. He had a blanket wrapped round his shoulders, and what with his stout figure and ruddy, grey-bearded face, he had the look of some old sea-captain. It was blowing a gale, a dark night and lonely. The conductor felt moved to go in and have a word with the singular passenger. The two struck up a friendship at once. Late and wild as the night was, Walt went to the end of the trip with him and then rode all the way back again.

The young fellow was an Irishman named Peter Doyle. He was a Confederate prisoner who had been paroled in Washington and got a job with the street-car company. It was an empty sort of life for him until he met Walt. Then everything was different. There were tramps to take when Pete was off duty, a new earth to explore, and a new heaven too, for Walt would tell him about the stars, sometimes to find that he was lecturing to deaf ears, for Pete, tired out with his day's work, would drowse off, his head dropped on Walt's shoulder like a chunk of wood. Though he was nearing fifty, Walt was still boy enough to buy a watermelon from a market-wagon and sit on the cellar-door of Bacon's grocery with Pete to relish it. If passers-by looked at the pair and laughed, Walt nudged Pete and said, "They can have the laugh. We've got the melon." When Pete got off the car at night they might go to a hotel for a glass of beer, and Pete falling asleep

115

over it, Walt would sit quietly by, and only tap him on the shoulder when it was time to go home. He watched over him like a father, lending him books and money, giving him the jolliest kind of education on their ten-mile tramps along the Potomac, trolling arias from the operas in a lusty voice or spouting passages from Shakespeare, comforting him when he was lonely.

Walt knew what it was to be lonely. Dearly as he loved Pete, who stood to him as a kind of son and brother, one man for all the hundreds who had filled his heart during the years of hospital service, there was something wanting in their comradeship. Pete was always ready to listen to his ideas about the new America and the new poetry that was to speak for it, but he was too ignorant to argue such questions, and often too weary to listen when Walt came to him full of excitement over his latest poem.

Walt had other friends, men like O'Connor and Ashton, and Charles Eldridge, his former publisher. There was too a clerk in the Treasury Department, John Burroughs, who knew more about birds than anyone Walt had ever met. The pair would often go to sit on the high stools at Harvey's for an oyster supper, and every Sunday morning Mrs. Burroughs kept the buckwheats and coffee hot until Walt tardily sauntered in. There were important people like Senator Garfield, who would come up behind Walt on the street and greet him gaily with a line of his own poetry, and then maybe walk up and down with him between the Capitol and the Treasury for a talk. But neither Pete's admiring affection, nor the give-and-take with men of wider interests, was quite enough.

Years earlier, in New Orleans, Walt had met a woman

116

whom, had circumstances permitted, he might have married. But something stood in the way of their union and it would appear that after a brief interchange, he never saw her again. Now, when he was old enough to have grown sons, he was still, among his host of friends, alone. Once more, this time in post-war Washington, he met a woman who seemed the perfect companion. She remains anonymous. Apparently she had fallen in love with Walt, or with his poetry and then with the poet, and he had responded warmly. But she too was married, and divorce was a more difficult and appalling affair in those days than it has become since. She may have had children. In any case there were circumstances which forbade the thought of a step so radical. Walt met her a few times. They exchanged letters. Then the husband stepped in and put an end to all communication between them.

Walt wrote a poem of tender farewell, of mournful resignation. He had lived so long with the sea that it had become for him the symbol of life and of fate. He returned to it again and again in his poetry. And so in this love lyric he used the same image. They were separated, he said, by the irresistible sea, but they were not so much divided from one another, after all. Each was a part of that cohering sea.

> . . . Know you, I salute the air, the ocean, and the land,
> Every day at sundown, for your dear sake, my love.

Just when his personal happiness was at ebb, the tide of his fame was rising, not only in his own America, but in foreign countries as well. When Walt was editing the *Brooklyn Daily Times,* a member of the staff had made

117

a vain attempt to translate some of his poems into German. Ten years later, in 1868, the German poet Freiligrath published his version of parts of "Leaves of Grass" in an Augsburg daily, with an essay on Walt. There were propagandists for his work in Dublin and Paris and Copenhagen too, but the greatest enthusiasm was among the English. Tennyson found in Walt "a vast something" for which he had no words, but which made him eager for a visit from this grand American barbarian. Swinburne, rebelling against the stodginess of his compatriots, was so delighted with what he saw of Walt's work that he addressed a poem of his own "To Walt Whitman in America."

Rossetti was all for publishing an English edition of "Leaves of Grass," although he was doubtful about presenting to the staid British public the poems that had shocked American readers. He wrote to Walt, asking him to cut out the cruder and more doubtful pieces. Walt could not agree to do this. There were things in "Leaves of Grass" that he might say differently now or not say at all. But they should stand, if only as proof of what formerly he had been and felt. He was willing, however, to let Rossetti make his own selection for British consumption, and in 1868 the volume appeared in England.

It fell into the hands of Mrs. Anne Gilchrist, the widow of an English man of letters and herself a gifted woman of advanced views. Walt's book acted on her like an enchantment. She read and re-read it. She wrote Rossetti an enthusiastic letter which he quoted to O'Connor, and of course the champion of the Good Gray Poet passed the word on to him. Walt was delighted. Such praise from

118

across the sea, especially coming from a woman, sensitive and mature, made him feel that he had indeed spoken truly. He sent his photograph to his admirer—he did not even know her name—enclosing it in a letter to Rossetti which he had permission to show her.

Mrs. Gilchrist, now thoroughly in love with Walt, re-worked her own laudatory letter to Rossetti into an essay: "A Woman's Estimate of Walt Whitman," for the *Boston Radical*. Walt was fairly bowled over by the article, but he did not communicate directly with the author. He could not know how steadily and intensely all her thoughts were bent on the man who had set himself down so frankly and splendidly, the great democrat, the true modern, the poet of comrades, of the woman no less than of the man, of the body equally with the soul.

When, after a year's silence, Mrs. Gilchrist finally wrote to Walt, it was with the passionate sincerity of a woman who felt that she was speaking to the one man in the world who could understand and value the emotion his work had aroused in her. She was ready to take her children and cross the Atlantic. She wanted to join her life to his. Walt did not reply to her letter. She had fallen in love with the image of him that she found in his book, but she did not know him. He must have believed that silence was the kindest answer.

After two months Mrs. Gilchrist wrote to him again. Had her letter miscarried? She must have some word from him. This time Walt did write to her, as gently and wisely as a man who had himself been disappointed in love could write to a stranger who loved him in vain.

He had been waiting, he said, for the right time and the

right mood, to answer her in the serious spirit in which she had written. He was grateful for her affection. He sent her his love. But with the next breath he made clear that for him there could be no personal meaning in the word. She must not be disappointed if he was brief. His book was his best letter, his response, the truest explanation of all. She understood this better than any, and he understood fully and clearly the loving letter it had called forth. "Enough that there surely exists so beautiful and delicate a relation, accepted by both of us with joy."

Poor Anne Gilchrist! She could not believe that Walt meant what he said. She had lived with her dream too long to be reconciled to his rejection. She continued to write to him, and he sent her letters now and then, friendly, interested, impersonally affectionate. The dear love of comrades that he celebrated was quite another thing from this passionate devotion that he did not quite know what to do with.

Mrs. Gilchrist had fallen in love with the poet of personality. Though all else slipped away in the quicksand years, Walt held fast to his belief in the strong, self-possessed human being. "When shows break up," he asked, "what but One's-Self is sure?" For him that theme was inextricably bound up with the theme of democracy.

Grim as was the aspect of post-war America, and he tried to look at his country with the eye of a physician diagnosing some deep disease, he was sure of its recuperative powers. The period following the Civil War was marked by shameless fraud and corruption in high places, by ruthless money-grabbing and hollow hypocrisy. Living in the capital, working as a clerk in a Government Depart-

120

ment, Walt knew the worst. That he could still hope for the best he made clear in a pamphlet which he published in 1870.

There, speaking plainly about the evils he saw on every side, he insisted on the greatness of America's "Democratic Vistas." Nature was superb in her shows of night and day, her seas and prairies and mountain-peaks. But as Walt listened to the roar of the streets, as he considered the wharves, the shops, the playhouse and the exchange, the streams of industry and commerce, the ingenious constructions on every hand, he felt that the works of man were no less wonderful. And topping all were the realities of a democratic way of life.

They were not political only. To be a voter was not so much, but to be truly a free man, able to develop your highest capacities, that was the main thing. For everybody to achieve this would be indeed to discover America, like another Columbus, and, more than that, to bring about eventually the brotherhood of the peoples of the earth. Democracy could not prove itself until it displaced the gilded feudalism of the European past, and made every man and every woman too equally independent. The building up of the masses by building up great individuals—that was the marrow of his book. He was not concerned with the American way as a new political scheme, but as a new mode of life, a new and vital faith. Walt had not lost his sense of the poet as prophet. In the face of one of the blackest views America had yet presented, he asserted his patriotism with all the force of religious conviction.

He said much the same things in his "Song of the Exposition," when he was invited to deliver a poem before the American Institute in New York. He was well pleased with the setting: a barnlike structure with timbered arches like the ribs of a skeleton ship, filled with hundreds of men and machines. He liked his mixed audience, and he had a congenial theme in labor and invention. But the poem was long-winded, prosy and somewhat forced, a fact which he did not admit either to himself or his public. With the childish braggadocio that he could not outgrow, he wrote up the occasion in an anonymous article for the Washington *Chronicle*.

A few months later he was in New Hampshire, delivering the Commencement Poem at Dartmouth. He had been invited at the instigation of some students who hoped he would shock the orthodox Congregationalists on the faculty. The oratorical strophes of his poem: "Thou Mother With Thy Equal Brood," for all its resplendent vision of America, does not seem to have startled anybody, but "this plain unsuspected old customer, dressed in gray and wearing no neck-tie," as Walt described himself in another anonymous piece, won his audience in spite of the rather windy character of his verses.

If no one else would speak for him, then Walt would speak for himself. He dared have no doubts. His vision was vast, his will was strong and his hope brave. He recognized evil, but he would not kowtow to its power. He was no revolutionary. He believed in making haste slowly. Though he insisted that men and communities should be free, he warned that the time came when they should not be too free. "Be cocky—be cocky, you young quarrelers," was his advice to radical youth, "but not too

122

damned cocky." Although he hated slavery and fought hotly to keep it from spreading, he had never been an abolitionist. When the Fifteenth Amendment came up, he was more than doubtful about the wisdom of giving the vote to the ignorant freedmen. He had a violent argument with O'Connor on the subject. The next day he met that fiery fellow on the street, and O'Connor ignored his friend's outstretched hand. The quarrel lasted more than ten years, though Walt was ready enough to bury the hatchet.

One of his poems about a ship gives the substance of his philosophy. Those few lines tell not only of his feeling about the sea-going craft he loved. They express Walt's attitude toward the Ship of State too, yes, and toward the whole universe:

> When, staunchly entering port,
> After long ventures, hauling up, worn and old,
> Battered by sea and wind, torn by many a fight,
> With the original sails all gone, replaced or mended,
> I only saw, at last, the beauty of the Ship.

Walt himself was more battered and worn than he knew. He had been forced to take several furloughs during his work in the hospitals. After the war was over he went home more than once for a badly needed rest.

Washington's Birthday, 1873, was ushered in with storm and sleet. Walt was in the Treasury building that February night, reading an English novel before a comfortable fire. He did not feel well and kept putting the book aside and taking it up again. At last he decided to go to his room, which was in a lodging-house just down the street. When he got to the door of the Treasury Walt

123

looked so ill that the guard wanted to see him home. Walt refused. The guard pleaded with him.

"No," said Walt, stubbornly, "I can go well enough."

So the man stood there with his lantern until he saw Walt arrive safely at his own door.

He went to bed and to sleep. At about three o'clock in the morning he awoke. He was surprised to find that he could not move his left arm or leg, but he was not frightened. He had no pain, and he was sure the trouble would pass off as it had come, so he went to sleep again.

But it did not pass off. When daylight came, Walt could not stir. His friends found him, several hours later, lying in bed, helpless. They called a doctor. He looked very grave. Walt had turned into an old man overnight. He was only fifty-four and he had a long span ahead of him. But the best years were over. He must learn more perfectly than before the word of which he had written in "Drum-Taps," as he thought of the sisters Death and Night, softly incessantly washing again and ever again this soiled world, the word: reconciliation.

10. AFTER THE DAZZLE

BEFORE HIS work with the wounded had begun to
take its heavy toll of his strength, Walt had
thought often of death. The sense of it was borne
in upon him in these later years. It held no terrors for
him. He recognized it as a part of life, he was not sure
but the most significant part. His poem, "Passage to

India," written to celebrate the joining of East and West by the finished Suez Canal and the transcontinental railway, was really a paean to man's greatest journey—the passage into the Unknown.

Cut the hawsers—haul out—shake out every sail!
Have we not stood here like trees in the ground long enough?
Have we not grovel'd here long enough, eating and drinking
    like mere brutes?
Have we not darken'd and dazed ourselves with books long
    enough?

Sail forth—steer for the deep waters only,
Reckless O soul, exploring, I with thee, and thou with me,
For we are bound where mariner has not yet dared to go,
And we will risk the ship, ourselves and all.

As Walt studied the noiseless patient spider, throwing filament after filament out of itself, he compared it to the soul, venturing its more delicate difficult bridges. When he watched the ploughman, or the sower following the furrows, or the harvester gathering in the crops, he saw something vaster than any of these. Life, he said, is the tillage, and death the harvest according.

Suddenly he was forced to meet death not as one of war's necessary evils, nor as a matter for meditation, but as brute fact in his personal life. Jeff's wife, Martha, was in the last stages of consumption. Walt ached for Jeff, in far-off St. Louis, with this trouble upon him. He himself loved Martha as deeply as if she were his own sister. Barely a month after he was stricken, word came that she was dead. But there was a deeper anxiety, a more enduring pain that Walt had to fight.

His mother, now nearing eighty, was seriously ill. She
126

had gone to live with George, who had a prosperous business in Camden, New Jersey. Walt dared not let her know how bad things were with him. Such letters as he managed to write her were full of courage and cheer. The wife of his friend, Hubley Ashton, had begged him to come to them to be luxuriously cared for. But Walt in health had never cared for "little extra fixings," they only annoyed him in sickness. Pete and his other good friends in Washington were looking out for him. His mother must be easy about him.

Toward spring he was able to get about a bit, and even go to the office for an hour or two. But the news from Camden was troubling. He was resolved to go home to see his mother in June. Before May was over he was summoned, to sit beside her sick-bed and watch the dearest life he knew go out.

She was the perfect mother, in Walt's eyes the generous image of the finest America could show in a woman. Of his poetry she knew little. She was one of those "powerful, uneducated persons" it celebrated. She could not even spell properly. But it needed no great intellect to grasp what Walt was after. There had always been a profound sympathy between them. She had the understanding heart that was his need, his rest and refreshment. There was no one like her. There could never be anyone to replace her.

He stayed on in Camden, living in her old room, dragging his battered hulk of a body about George's house, utterly lonely.

He was a man, familiar with suffering. His paralytic stroke, though he made a partial if temporary recovery, had turned him into an old man. Yet neither age nor pain

127

nor experience could teach him to accept this loss. Years passed, and his sorrow was still fresh.

He was not spared other troubles. The agents who handled his books cheated him of the small profits he made from them. For some time he held onto his clerkship in Washington by employing a substitute, but it became plain that he would never be strong enough to go back, and he was dismissed. In spite of George's generosity, the house of this prosperous man of business was not one in which Walt could feel at home. George cared more for pipe-lines than for poems. Walt had no real friends in Camden. He could not go on his old jaunts on the ferries and busses. He missed the comradeship of Peter Doyle, the good talks with John Burroughs. He was not even able to go down to the healing sea. His body was broken, his pockets empty, his heart sore. Yet he had immense reserves of energy. One good day was enough to make him write to Pete that he was feeling a lot better: "Guess I'll come out in the spring," he announced, "with the frogs and the lilacs."

Almost at the same time he wrote two strongly affirmative poems, the "Prayer of Columbus," in which he identified himself with the old admiral in his hour of despair, and the "Song of the Universal," which was read for him, since he was not able to make the trip, at Tufts College Commencement.

> A batter'd, wreck'd old man,
> Thrown on this savage shore, far, far from home,
> Pent by the sea and dark rebellious brows, twelve
>   dreary months,
> Sore, stiff with many toils, sicken'd and nigh to death,

128

> I take my way along the island's edge,
> Venting a heavy heart.

So the prayer opens, but though it goes on to recount all the disasters that came crowding round the adventurous old man, "in shackles, prisoned, in disgrace," it affirms courageously the faith, Walt's own faith, in newer better worlds.

> Let the old timbers part, I will not part,
> I will cling fast to Thee, O God, though
> the waves buffet me,
> Thee, Thee at least I know.

The worn sailor is racked, mocked, perplexed, yet as if some miracle, some divine Hand unsealed his eyes, he sees

> Shadowy vast shapes smile through the air and sky,
> And on the distant waves sail countless ships,
> And anthems in new tongues I hear saluting me.

In the "Song of the Universal" Walt sang even more cheerfully his hymn to the future.

> Come said the Muse,
> Sing me a song no poet yet has chanted,
> Sing me the universal.
>
> In this broad earth of ours,
> Amid the measureless grossness and the slag,
> Enclosed and safe within its central heart,
> Nestles the seed perfection.

Strongly he asserted his belief in universal good, in triumphant health and peace and joy. Walt did not deny

129

evil, he knew it in every form: guile and fraud, disease and sorrow. Yet the ideal, which would be realized, he was sure, in his own America, was immortal.

> Is it a dream?
> Nay but the lack of it the dream,
> And failing it life's lore and wealth a dream,
> And all the world a dream.

Walt was never to know sound solid health again. But joy he could find in a hundred curious places. The years that followed were treacherous years, sucking him down into a dark whirlpool, but through sickness and poverty and enmity Walt held fast to his faith in himself and in the future to which he felt that he belonged.

Tireless in his notations of what pleasured him, Walt in his sixties published a little book called "Specimen Days." From those diaries, from his poems, and the memoranda of his growing circle of friends, especially his devoted disciple, young Horace Traubel, it is possible to get brief glimpses of the vivid hours in the nineteen years granted him after his stroke put a period to his vigorous manhood.

It is summer, and Walt is boarding with a farmer in a little town near Camden. His favorite haunt is Timber Creek. Here, off in the woods, he can take a dip and have his sun-bath, far from curtained, carpeted rooms, where you sit on a stuffy sofa to read tiresome books or listen to tiresome small talk. When business and politics and even friendly interchange no longer satisfy, Walt asks himself, what remains? Nature remains. So he goes to nature.

He hobbles down the farm lane. He knows each patch of moss on the stones, each bunch of briers, each hole and splinter in the worn fence-rails, as he knows the lines on his own palm. He has an eye for the fowls picking and clucking in the yard and the pigs in their pen, for the field of sweet-smelling buckwheat and the crowding stalks of tasseled corn. He listens to the brassy drone of the locust, the far-off axe of the wood-cutter, the soft sough of the wind in the trees like the sound of surf. Flanked by a group of willows bubbles the brook.

Walt hangs his clothes on the fence-rail, takes out his brush and scrubs himself scarlet, bathes in the clear-running water, towels himself, and then gives himself to the grass and the sun. He rambles about, he moves his camp-chair from one tempting spot to another, every sense alert for the airs and odors, the flicker of light and leaf and wing, the twitter and call and hum, that fill this retreat for him with small delicious wonders.

Every hour, every day, every season has its special quality. May is the month for bees, the low loud swelling drone suggests a bumble-bee symphony. The meadows are blue with wild violets, the orchards rosy with apple-blossom. May—Walt's birth-month—offers fresh earth-smells and the sweet memorable scent of lilac. September is loud with the harsh cawing of the crows, the scream of a flock of guinea-hens. Now the fields are bright with russet corn-sheaves, orange pumpkins, the pearly green of cabbages, melons bulging under broad silver-streaked leaves.

Walt takes account of the trees, the shrubs, the vines, the sweet-gum, the sassafras, the black walnut, pine and

131

persimmon, laurel and holly. He waits through the night for the calls he recognizes when the birds migrate. He watches from dusk till long past midnight the march of the stars, silver Venus well up in the west, the moon a thin crescent, Arcturus bright overhead and nature almost a palpable presence as the night advances. The constellation of the Water-Serpent coils over more than half the heavens, the Swan spreads its wings down the Milky Way, Lyra and the Eagle hold their places in the vast blue-black dome, and as the evening star vanishes with the moon, alertness and peace couch calmly in the fluid shadows.

It is bright December weather and Walt is off for a holiday. He is well enough now for an hour's ride on the railroad—he wishes it were the one where Pete has found a job—and down to the shore. He has made a good break-fast, with some strong coffee, that tasted all the better for having been prepared by his sister Lou, and he enjoys every minute of the trip through the salt meadows. There is a drive over sand so hard the carriage-wheels scarcely dent it, and then dinner, and after that time enough for a long lonely walk. Walt reaches some deserted bath-houses, and makes himself at home on the verandah of the main building.

He has the whole expanse to himself, the clumps of sedge and Indian grass, the brownish-grey stretch of sand beyond, the rolling combers, the nearer brigs and schooners, and on the far horizon the barely visible smoke of a steamer. The air is cold and salt. The view is infinitely spacious. The waves perpetually rolling in, rustling as they break in lacy foam on the shore, the continual hoarse

132

murmur and low thump of the sea, fill his solitude with immensities.

Walt had haunted the shore as a child, as a boy, as a young man. The ocean fascinated this offspring of a sailor-breed. One of his companions said that you could smell the sea within ten yards of him. Almost as far back as he could remember he had wanted to put into words the meaning of this monotonous vast majesty. As an old man he would wake in the night and see it moving before him, hear its harsh, endlessly absorbing music. He rejoiced in the shout of the incoming flood. He watched in the ebb and flow the rhythm of death and birth. He imagined submitting his book to the judgment of the ocean. He tried to tally his work with what it inarticulately told him. What word would hold it? It took him seventy years to find the strange right phrase, "With husky-haughty lips, O sea!" Yet even then, he could not compass what he was after. For he must ask, and ask again, what central heart, of which the tides were the pulse, vivified the universe. Walt would have given up the chance of matching Homer and Shakespeare, if he could catch the undulating trick of one wave in his verse, or leave there the odor of one breath from the sea.

When all else goes, nature remains. And human nature. For Walt never tired of the crowds he met on the ferries when he was able to travel on them again, or the restless pageant of the streets. Broadway, New York's greatest thoroughfare, perhaps the world's greatest, and St. Charles Street in New Orleans, and Tremont Street in Boston, and the broad pavements of Pennsylvania Avenue in the capital, all had been his theatre. And now he takes

133

in with the same avid eye the narrower range of Chestnut Street in Philadelphia. The morning is foggy, but the day seems all the brighter when the cloud lifts. Soon after midday Walt is sauntering along, absorbing the show.

He guesses there are plenty of hard-up folk in the crowd, but it is made up mostly of women in gay spring costumes, and well-fed, flush-looking men. Walt picks out the more entertaining figures: a handsome young peddler of canary-bird whistles, the men selling canes, and toys, and toothpicks, the hawker calling out, "Sleeve-buttons—three for five cents," the old negress squatting on the pavement with a basket of matches, pins and tape, the young black beggar-woman with her coffee-colored twins in her lap, the gigantic policemen on the corners, the grey-uniformed postmen jostling each other in a one-horse post-office wagon.

He admires the rare orchids and snowy lilies in the conservatory of the Baldwin mansion, the show of plump poultry, fish and beef in the restaurant windows, the luscious tropical fruits, the delicate china and glass, the costly curios and books and pictures, and, queerest of all, two fine fat sheep, their tawny wool streaked with black, exhibited in a fragrant litter of clover and hay behind the plate-glass of a clothing-store, looking out at the crowd with thickfringed patient eyes.

It is the fall of the year, and now, in the autumn of his days, Walt is in for a great adventure. He is on his way West. There is the heart and trunk of America. He is hungry for knowledge of it. There is an old saying that is a favorite with him: Always, after supper, take a walk half a mile long, and if convenient let it be upon your

134

own land. It is after supper for Walt. He has turned sixty, and has had his fill of living. What other nation could afford him such a jaunt over his own land?

He crosses the prairie States, feeds his eye on a thousand miles of waving corn and wheat. He meets old friends too. There is an ex-soldier, married now and keeping a hotel in Kansas, who begs Walt to stay all winter.

At Topeka he stops off and joins a group of officials on a visit to some Indians in prison there. During his brief clerkship in the Indian Bureau Walt had seen something of these early Americans: Omahas, Winnebagoes, Navahos, Apaches. He never forgot the heroic character of those faces, daubed, most of them, with red paint, under thickly-woven colored braid or circlets of eagles' feathers or an empty horned buffalo skull. Notable were the chiefs in their bright blankets, blue or scarlet, a few black. He remarked particularly young Hole-In-The-Day, a tall calm handsome young chief, with yellow-painted cheeks under a richly feathered head-dress, buckskin leggings, and a shirt loose enough to show his splendid throat and chest. Walt had had no personal dealings with the aborigines, but in their few awkward interchanges through an interpreter they must have felt his admiring respect. Here in Topeka the Indians make no motion to greet the Government officials, but one of the chiefs, perhaps recognizing the stout ruddy grey-haired old fellow from Washington days, perhaps merely conscious of Walt's friendly interest, holds out his hand and says, "How." "How," says each of the others after him. Walt is set up to find that he isn't confounded with the big guns of officialdom.

At last his journey takes him within hail of the great

135

mountain ranges. Talk of Roman ruins, stately palaces, feudal castles—they can show nothing comparable to the beauty and terror and power of these peaks. Walt discovers in the Rockies the law of his own poems. He falls in love with Denver. At a Colorado mining-camp, the piles of silver bullion heaped in the open remind him of a confectioner's pyramid at a swell dinner in New York. The foreman tosses up a small wooden shovelful for him as you might toss beans.

He notes the ant-hills and the buffalo wallows of the cattle country. He would like to chum with the swarthy hawk-eyed cowpunchers, their raised arms swinging loosely as they lope in the saddle after the herd. He is eager to see Yellowstone, to travel the Sante Fé trail, but he must turn back. He cannot look long enough at the receding peaks, he grins delightedly when his locomotive friend tells him the Mile-shoe curve is "the boss railroad-curve of the universe."

He reaches the great waterway. He refuses to believe that the Nile or the Danube, the Yangtze Kiang or the Amazon can compare with the Mississippi. There is a visit to Jeff in St. Louis, and Walt falls ill and is laid up there for three months. But it is good to be with Jeff, the companion of his New Orleans venture long ago. And it is good to get well enough to go home.

Home again, but not to stay. While he can travel, he will. He has a new friend, Dr. Bucke, a Canadian alienist, now head of an asylum for the insane in London, Ontario. Walt goes to Canada for a visit with him. On the way north he has a glimpse of Niagara. A lucky five minutes, reminding him of rare thrilling moments far away and long ago: a wild storm witnessed one winter day off Fire Island; the stage at the Old Bowery with the elder Booth superb as Richard III; a night at the front, with the stars high over a Virginia battlefield.

He goes up to Quebec and near Tadousac steps into a queer little old French printing-office. It is even more primitive than the print-shop of his friend William Kurz on Federal Street in Camden. It takes him back to the time when an excited boy with inky fingers made pi for old Hartshorne.

There is much in this rugged region to remind him of home. The farmers, the lumbermen, the trappers, are his own sort. He sees a group of young boatmen eating their dinner: a loaf of bread as big as a bushel-measure from which they cut great chunks with their jack-knives. It would be feast enough for Walt. Canada is a fine place. He goes home convinced that it will yet form two or three great sister States, equal and independent, with the rest of the Union. The St. Lawrence and the Great Lakes were never meant to be a frontier, but a mid-channel.

"Chalk a big mark for today" was a saying of a sportsman friend of Walt's when he came back with a fine bag of birds. Walt chalks up a big mark for the day he goes into New York and lands in Pfaff's restaurant at Twenty-fourth Street. The stout host, taciturn but jolly, has not seen him for twenty years. He brings up a bottle of his best champagne for the occasion and the two sit at the table, saying little but remembering much, drinking bumpers to the old days on Bleecker Street before the war.

It is an Indian summer afternoon and Walt is sitting under the elms at the Sanborns', watching the haymakers

137

across the Concord river pitch the sweet-smelling crop into the wagons. The slow strong movements of the men, the waning sun, the fragrant air, the shrill chirp of a cricket, a boat gliding by under the stone bridge, it is all a feast of contentment.

But the evening, after dinner, is even better. For then the neighbors come, Bronson Alcott and his clever daughter Louisa, and Emerson, aged now, and silent through all the talk, but clear-eyed and alert. Walt is quiet too. He has, as the saying goes, his own pail to milk in.

And best of all, the day following, when he goes to have Sunday dinner with the Emersons in the house they have occupied for thirty-five full years. The furniture has a plain elegance, an old-fashioned simplicity that suits Walt's taste. Emerson does not say much, but when he puts in a word or two it is just right, and the smile lighting up the strong-featured face is right too.

Twenty-one years have passed since Walt went to Boston to see him and talk over "Leaves of Grass." On this trip he is again busy with his book. Among the casualties of the Civil War had been the firm of Thayer and Eldridge, the publishers of "Leaves of Grass." It went ill with the book after that. On the occasion of the centennial of the signing of the Declaration of Independence, Walt had issued two volumes of prose and poetry, which he jobbed and sold himself, and which brought handsome returns from the subscriptions of his English friends. Now the Boston house of J. R. Osgood came forward with an offer to back him and Walt saw a new edition of his book hopefully through the press, and felt vindicated when it sold two thousand copies. But there were still citizens of

Harlan's stripe who could not stomach Walt's candor.

At the instigation of the Society for the Suppression of Vice, the Boston District Attorney advised the publishers that "Leaves of Grass" was subject to prosecution. Osgood asked Walt, as Emerson had asked him twoscore years before, to strike out the offensive passages. Walt considered the matter, and agreed to cancel about ten lines and a dozen words. The District Attorney insisted that this was not enough. Eighty lines at least would have to go. Walt refused. Osgood did not dare continue the sale of the book, so he turned the plates over to Walt, instead of the $500 royalties he would otherwise have received, and Walt issued a small edition on his own. The matter was closed, and the book went on selling even better than before. O'Connor, outraged by this new attack on the Good Gray Poet, again came to his defense, and one happy effect of the trouble was the resumption of this old friendship.

The trip to Boston was Walt's last journey. But his solitude was broken now and again by visitors of sorts.

One afternoon about Eastertime his housekeeper shouts up the stairs,

"Walt, here's some carriage folk come to see you."

Walt limps downstairs to find a stately old Quaker, accompanied by a tall shy youth and a handsome girl. It is she who is Walt's admirer and who introduces the family. Their name is Smith. Mary Smith had read "Leaves of Grass" with enthusiasm and could not wait to pay her respects to the poet. She does not say that her father violently disapproved of the pilgrimage from their home in fashionable Germantown to this mean neighbor-

139

hood, to call on a man of such doubtful reputation. Walt takes to Mary Smith at once; she reminds him of the beautiful and daring Frances Wright.

He leads them upstairs to his own room for a talk. The parent's chilliness melts in that genial atmosphere, and when it is time to go he astonishes his children by suggesting that Walt drive back with them to spend the night.

"No, Mr. Smith, I think I won't come."

But when Walt looks out of the window at the fine carriage and pair, he changes his mind, packs his little bag, and hobbles downstairs for an overnight visit. He remained for a month.

He made several other visits to the mansion in Germantown, charmingly described by the son of the house, Logan Pearsall Smith, in his "Unforgotten Years." Particularly memorable was an evening on which there was to be a big dinner party. Walt had not even brought a jacket to wear over his knitted vest, so he showed his respect for the proprieties by appearing at dinner in his overcoat, although the night was warm. And there are those who say he had no sense of humor.

There were frequent drives through the Park, enlivened for Walt and Mr. Smith senior by following as closely as possible the pairs of lovers who also went buggy-riding there, and noting the "buggy-angle" of the enamored couple. When it leaned toward an embrace, the two old gentlemen felt that their excursion had been well rewarded.

But the time soon came when even such jaunts were forbidden. In the spring of his sixty-fourth year Walt

140

settled in the little house on Mickle Street, Camden, which was the nearest he ever came to the Irish shanty of his dreams. The years just behind him, for all the chalk-marked days, had had long dreary stretches. There had been dismal periods of helplessness and mean physical pain. And although his partisans had rallied round him staunchly, he had had to bear hostility and neglect. The few years ahead were to be grimmer and emptier.

Walt was old and poor, sick and alone. In the fulness of his strength he had cried exultantly: "To be at all—what is better than that? . . . I think I could lift the girder of the house away if it lay between me and whatever I wanted." He still savored the rare good hour, rolling it on his palate like a mouthful of sunned fruit. No, said Walt, not successful love, nor the triumphs of the market-place and the political arena, can bring the rich serenity of this mellower light, when the apple hangs really finished and indolent-ripe on the tree. Nothing that went before could equal those halcyon days. But they were few and far between, and haunted by the fear that the glooms and aches, the crankiness and lethargy of age might filter into his final songs. He kept them out. Painfully approaching his seventieth year, he could say in all honesty,

> After the dazzle of day is gone,
> Only the dark, dark night shows to my eyes the stars.

11. SO LONG!

I T IS a two-story frame house on a poor street. Through
the open windows come the hoots of the ferry-
whistles, the chugging and puffing of trains from
the railroad station, the jolting rattle of trolley-cars. The
air is ugly with odors from a near by guano factory. But
there is a lilac-bush blooming in the back yard, and Walt

can sit under his own grape-vine and pear tree. He eats in the kitchen. Mrs. Davis does for him, simple, generous, lonely Mrs. Davis. She had made a secret marriage with a sea-captain in her youth, and he had been drowned. Because of the secrecy of the marriage, she had no claim on his property, and had to make her way as best she might. She cooks and cleans and mends for Walt and gets in exchange free lodging and free storage: the little house is crammed with her furniture. Crammed, too, with piles of unsold copies of Walt's books.

His room upstairs is like a large ship's cabin, furnished with the mementoes of an old sailor. The floor is bare, the chairs uncushioned. There is a huge uncomfortable wooden bed, a sheet-iron stove, a gas lamp, pegs, hooks, shelves, boxes, and two big tables, one a century old, the other built by his father, both piled with books, old magazines, fresh proof-sheets, letters and clippings and scribblings, which overflow onto the floor and under the wash-stand, where Walt stirs them about with his cane, miraculously lighting on the paper he wants. One table holds his old stand-bys: the Bible, some volumes of Shakespeare, Homer and Burns, and among a few other favorites, the stout worn copy of Scott's poems that has been his companion for more than fifty years. A canary trills in his cage overhead. Off in a corner stands an ancient trunk with double iron bands and locks, and near the window a great broad-bottomed arm-chair with a grizzled wolf-skin flung over it, where Walt sits and hails the ferryman and the postman as they pass, and sometimes drops pennies for the youngsters playing below to scramble for.

One cruel thing about poverty is that you cannot make small presents. Walt is always fretting about how to provide for his helpless brother Eddie, and he keeps sending such sums as he can to his sister Hannah in Vermont.

He had had a chance to live with George in his fine new house in Burlington, but that did not suit him. He did not want, either, to accept George's offer of a cottage near by. He has his moments of rebellion against his dependence. It makes his gorge rise sometimes, and he speaks bitterly of bending his bearded throat and high-held forehead to the gutter. But as he looks back over the chances and changes, the losses and sorrows and vagaries of his life, his spirit reasserts itself. He feels like some old broken soldier, hobbling along in the twilight to answer company roll-call:

> *Here,* with vital voice,
> Reporting yet, saluting yet the Officer over all.

When his brother moved away from Camden, Walt took a room where he "batched it" meagrely enough. On fine days he would limp through the streets of Camden or Philadelphia with a basket of his books on his arm, peddling them as he could. He was desperately hard up. One cold winter morning neighborly Mrs. Davis gave him a much needed breakfast. She made Walt so welcome that he came often, and soon she was doing all manner of small services for him. When he finally found a publisher again, and realized a tidy sum on a new edition of "Leaves of Grass," he bought the Mickle Street house, and before long Mrs. Davis was established there with her household goods. Like Mrs. Gilchrist before her, she expected more

144

from Walt than he was able to give. For him the arrangement was a matter of mutual convenience, a fact which his housekeeper seems to have secretly resented, though she looked after him devotedly, with some professional help, to the end.

It was a dismal life for Walt, though he would not admit it, even to himself. Most of the time he was marooned with his memories in his upstairs room. Here he read and meditated and scrawled his loose jottings. Here he received the few friends who braved the scorn of the town and the indifference of the polite literary world to come to his mean hermitage. He made no distinction between the local expressman and the frock-coated pilgrim from abroad.

Walt, like Robert Frost after him, had at first been more widely acclaimed in England than in his own country. Although a few compatriots, Emerson foremost among them, recognized the power and nobility of his best work, at home he was largely ignored or abused. It was only toward the close of his life that his work won its place in American letters.

Even then he was not a popular poet. The things he said and his way of saying them were too different from what the average man, whom he so wanted to reach, had learned to think of as poetry. His long unrhymed lines and prosy phrases were not easy to hold in the memory.

There was much in his work to distress even the friendly critic. Some passages, as Emerson said, appear to be no more than an auctioneer's catalogue. Occasionally his free cadences are nearer prose than verse. Not seldom he indulged in rather windy oratory. But his finest poems

145

are like the high peaks and the ocean whose natural grandeur was his own test for poetry. Visitors from abroad came to see him as they came to see Niagara.

But Walt himself went nowhere. Perhaps the heaviest burden of these years was his inability to get about. No more mixing with the crowd in the streets, nor wandering off to the woods, nor tramping along the shore. Confinement irked him as sorely as the illness that compelled it. Mrs. Davis bestirred herself to mend matters, and at her suggestion a group of Walt's friends clubbed together to buy him a horse and buggy. Among the subscribers were his comrade of the Washington days, O'Connor, and Mark Twain, whose "Adventures of Huckleberry Finn" had only recently been published, and Edwin Booth, the actor, whom Walt had applauded so heartily in his great parts long years ago. The Quaker poet who had thrown his complimentary copy of "Leaves of Grass" into the fire, when approached for a contribution, wrote gently:

Dear Friend:

I am sorry to hear of the physical disabilities of the man who tenderly nursed the wounded Union soldiers, and as tenderly sung the dirge of their great captain. I have no doubt, in his lameness, that a kind, sober-paced roadster would be more serviceable to him than the untamed, rough-jolting Pegasus he has been accustomed to ride—without check or snaffle. I inclose my mite for the object named in thy note, with all good wishes.

I need not say perhaps that I have been pained by some portions of W. W.'s writings, which for his own sake, and that of his readers, I wish could be omitted.

Thy Friend

John G. Whittier.

Walt relished the buggy-rides. And on three different occasions, for all his infirmity, he found it possible to leave Camden and appear on the public platform to deliver an anniversary address on Abraham Lincoln. Walt recalled his first glimpse of the President that February day in 1861 when the gaunt black-coated figure stood silently surveying the silent crowd before the Astor House in New York. He went on to speak of the war days, terribly present to him still: "the long marches in summer—the hot sweat, and many a sunstroke, as on the rush to Gettysburg in '63—the night battles in the woods, as under Hooker at Chancellorsville—the camps in winter—the military prisons—the hospitals (alas! alas! the hospitals)."

He quoted the advertisement spread all over the Washington *Evening Star* on April 14, 1865: "The President and his Lady will be at the Theatre this evening." He remembered having thought how funny it was that Lincoln, the leading actor in the stormiest drama known to history, should sit there and be absorbed in the trifling comedy. He rehearsed the scene at the theatre as vividly as if he had witnessed it; Peter Doyle had been there and told him all: the festive audience, the quiet figure in the box, the pause as the actors made an exit, the pistol shot. Pete had been one of the last lingerers and a soldier furious with rage and grief had shouted to him to get out: "We're going to burn this damned building to the ground!" It was a climax-moment on the stage of Time, with the historic Muse at one entrance, and the tragic Muse at the other, suddenly ringing down the curtain. Not any of the great deaths, Walt affirmed solemnly, not Caesar stabbed

147

before the Roman senate house, nor Napoleon dying that stormy night on St. Helena, nor calm old Socrates drinking the hemlock, outvied that end of the secession war, that seal of the emancipation of three million slaves, that rebirth of a really free Republic, a genuine Union.

The murder of the greatest American he had known remained for Walt not only a national tragedy but a personal sorrow. But now he must reckon with more intimate griefs. Mrs. Gilchrist, in spite of Walt's warnings that she must not construct an imaginary figure and call it Walt Whitman and give it her full devotion, in spite of his attempts to dissuade her from an adventure promising disappointment, had belatedly come to America to see her beloved poet face to face. With the aged and ailing man the only possible relation was one of quiet friendship, and this the two enjoyed heartily during her stay in the States. She took a house in Philadelphia which was always filled with interesting people. Walt, though he found most intellectuals too stiff and bookish for a free old hawk like him, was completely at home there. He was delighted with her talented son Herbert and with charming "Giddy," as they called her daughter Grace. Above all, this middle-aged woman, rosy and brown-haired still, offered him an intelligent sympathy in which he basked. Mrs. Gilchrist stayed two years in America, and then went home to England, sustaining their intercourse by many warm letters. Walt, though he had never responded to her romantic attachment, felt a deep affection for her. When the news came to him that she was ill with cancer, his heart ached for this great good friend. And now she was dead, and all that remained was a memory, "none more

148

beautiful," he wrote sadly to her son. And to O'Connor, "I am not sure but she had the finest and perfectest nature I ever met."

Walt tried to disregard the feebleness of his own health. As often as possible he had his attendant, Warry, wheel him down to the Camden wharf. Warry, Mrs. Davis's foster-son, a black-haired, black-eyed young sailor who had three times sailed round the world, was a comfort in more ways than one. He knew all about ships and could help Walt out with the right word when he wrote, as he often did, about seafaring.

But the wharf itself was not an unmixed joy. Walt liked watching the boys fish there as he used to do on Long Island. But that miserable wretch, the Mayor of Camden, had forbidden them to bathe in the river. He objected to their stripping for a swim. Walt was furious. Given a chance, these lads would grow up to be fine fellows. But like the prudish mayor, their parents were too intent on having them "genteel." Walt didn't hold much with gentility. When he thought back over the good old days at Pfaffs, he regretted especially the end of William Winter. Willie hadn't died of hard drinking or got shot in the war—but he became respectable. It seemed to Walt a pitiful fate.

One summer afternoon, after a visit from Dr. Bucke, he drove his friend to the ferry and then, neglecting the time, as he had ever done, drove north to Pea Shore. Toward sundown he came to the river-bank. The evening was fine and the sunset magnificent. Walt urged his horse into the water, and lingered there, watching the splendor die out of the sky, and the dusk creep up, careless of the

149

evening damp, looking, reflecting, remembering. Remembering everything but his years—he was approaching seventy—and the enemy that had struck him down in his prime. The stroke that followed this adventure left him motionless and without the power of speech. He was as close to death as a man can come and yet survive. Walt survived.

There were still festive hours ahead. Two years later he was able to travel to Philadelphia to deliver his talk on Lincoln. He had to be helped at every step, but he must pay his tribute while he had breath. And then came a glorious birthday celebration at Reisser's restaurant. Robert Ingersoll, the famous lawyer and lecturer, made the train-trip from New York especially to honor the author of "Leaves of Grass." When he rose to speak, he stood facing Walt, and after each passage of powerful praise he repeated: "I thank you for that." Walt had never felt so proud.

And yet—and yet Ingersoll, in all his glowing comment, had omitted to touch on one thing, the central faith that animated Walt's book. Ingersoll was a materialist and an atheist. Walt, none more than he, loved the physical universe, but if he said that the soul was not more than the body, he asserted too that the body was not more than the soul. He could not help reminding Ingersoll of this. As for immortality, he declared roundly, "Well, Robert, I don't know—for anybody else but *myself*. But for *myself*—I am as certain of it as that we're all here!"

Walt would have liked to hear the comment that one of his old scholars, Sandford Davis, made about this time to an English friend of his. Davis had never read "Leaves of Grass," but he knew its reputation.

"There's some that say his book has bad things in it," he ventured, "but they don't understand his meaning. Walt would write nothin' but what he believed was good, proper and true."

When the Englishman observed that Walt would have to be buried a hundred years before he was appreciated, Davis looked at him sharply.

"Bury Walt Whitman, did you say? No sir-r," he cried. "They'll never bury Walt Whitman! Walt Whitman'll never die!"

One good friend was missing from the company at Reisser's, the faithful William O'Connor. When the news of his death had come to Walt, he took it silently, only saying after a moment in a deep voice, "And *such* a friend!" It was hard to feel the old ties break like this. Whatever hopes he might have for the immortal soul, the evening was desperately lonely.

Disagreement had not finally estranged Walt from O'Connor. It could not estrange him from Robert Ingersoll. That valiant speaker championed Walt again before an audience of two thousand people at a lecture given for the old man's benefit. When it was over, Walt, with whom personal give-and-take counted for much, rose from his chair, a grand figure of a man still, however broken by age and illness, with his great frame and white-maned, white-bearded, benignant head. He wanted to thank his friends with his living voice for coming and Robert Ingersoll for speaking. Did he feel in his old bones that it was the last time that he would meet his readers face to face? Briefly, serenely, he bade them "hail and farewell."

There were not a few, close and dear to him, whom Walt would never see again. Word came from St. Louis that his brother Jeff had died of a heart attack. Walt wrote an obituary notice of him for the *Engineering Record*. He was proud of him as "a theoretical and practical mechanic of a superior order." He spoke of his achievements in his chosen field. But he lingered more on his memories of the "handsome, healthy, affectionate smart child" with whom he had gone boating and tramping around and across Long Island, the man he loved for being "very good-natured, very plain, very friendly."

The year that held this great sorrow held also a great joy. On Walt's seventy-second birthday, when he was too frail to think of going to Philadelphia for a public banquet, his friends arranged a celebration at 328 Mickle Street. About five o'clock in the afternoon Walt had a bad spell, but he came to himself within an hour and Warry got him dressed and down the stairs in time for the feast —Walt was sorry for Warry: it was like carrying down a great log. The faithful Traubel had a goblet of iced champagne ready for him, and he swigged it off, determined that if he was to go down, it would not be without a desperate struggle.

Some forty people, men and women, were crowded into the little frame house. The caterers had provided a capital dinner of chicken soup, salmon, roast lamb, and other good things, and Walt kept himself up with plenty of champagne. There were speeches and cables and letters. Walt felt that he must say a few words honoring his

152

fellow-poets, Emerson, Bryant, Longfellow, the great good dead, and old Whittier too, and Tennyson, whose congratulations had come with the mail from England, and whom Walt called "the boss of us all." His speech lasted perhaps four minutes, but after that there were three full hours of talk, and toasts, and more talk, fond and absurd and jolly. Walt rejoiced in the tributes of all these good friends. Finally he turned to the painter, Thomas Eakins, who had done his portrait some two years earlier, and asked him if he had something to say to the company.

"I am not a speaker," said Eakins diffidently.

"So much the better," retorted Walt, "you're more likely to say something."

And so he did, to the effect that when he had started Walt's portrait, he had begun in the usual way, but had soon found that the ordinary methods wouldn't do.

"Before all else," said the painter, "Mr. Whitman had to be treated as a *man,* whatever became of the principles of art."

Toward the end of the dinner the talk turned on free trade. Walt recalled his differences with a protectionist who had argued that the main thing in America was for Americans to look out for themselves. Walt couldn't hold with that.

"We're all embarked together," he said, recurring to the sea imagery that pleased him best, "we are all embarked together like fellows in a ship, bound for good or bad. What wrecks one wrecks all. What reaches port for one reaches port for all."

Walt had reached haven at last. An old man, he

153

thought of old farmers, travelers, workmen, no matter how old and bent, old sailors, old soldiers. For them to have survived the trials and struggles, the dangerous voyages, the campaigns, the wounds, was victory enough. He was as unflinching as any. Nay, more, he was full of thanks, for the health he had enjoyed, for the sun at midday and the fresh air, for mere life. He told over his blessings, the long memories, the days of peace and of war as well, grateful for shelter, wine and meat, for deeds and thoughts, books and friends, for hardy men, the captains of the soul. For all, at the end of the long road, the battle over, he uttered a traveler's, a soldier's thanks.

Almost with his final breath he sang the commonplace, with delight forever renewed. In the midst of his worst sufferings he found voice to cry, "How cheap is health! how cheap nobility!" to insist that the main lesson was to be learned not from books and less from the schools, but from the common day and night, the common earth and waters, by each man from his farm, his trade, his work whatever it might be, to acclaim "the democratic wisdom underneath, like solid ground for all."

It was the war that practically killed him. Even his superb physique, as his physicians recognized, could not stand the emotional strain of his years in the hospitals. Yet it was largely the war that confirmed his faith in the democratic idea. He played that theme with his "Drum-Taps." He envisioned it in his "Democratic Vistas." He returned to it again and again. Years after the war was over he chanted his paean to the faith of free men that was for Walt the real triumph, that cemented the Union

154

of the States and would yet mean the fraternity of the peoples of the earth:

> To thee old cause!
> Thou peerless, passionate, good cause,
> Thou stern, remorseless, sweet idea.

It could not be realized in his time, Walt knew well enough. He had seen close up the shames of the reconstruction period. He had moments of grave doubt and cold despair. And if he was sick of what his country showed him, he was sometimes thoroughly sick of himself, wondering whether any other man had ever known such discouragement and distraction, whether any had been so puzzled and conscience-stricken. Yet he held stubbornly to the promise of his manhood, and of these States. When he wrote "One Song, America, Before I Go," it was not to sing of past failures or present fears, but to hail the future. This was no abstraction to Walt. It was as real and solid as the young men and women whose children were to show forth what he had only suggested. Nor did he care about the means of achieving a truly democratic society. He liked the proverb of the Old Dutch flourmiller: "I never bother myself what road the folks come—I only want good wheat and rye."

Even before the war Walt had envisaged his POEM OF THE NEW WORLD—he could not publish his great thought in letters big enough—a poem announcing and compelling an ampler, richer, freer way of life for every man and every woman in America, and in the new world abroad that would take pattern by America. Whether he

155

should ever make that poem, whether he should be justified in the vision at which he hinted, did not depend, he insisted, upon him. It depends, says Walt, upon you, whoever you are now filling the presidency, upon you, governor, mayor, congressman, but not on the people's chosen agents and representatives only. It depends upon you, contemporary America. That is the marrow of Walt's message: it depends upon you.

When he was somewhat recovered from his first attack, he went one day to attend the dedication of a new public school in Camden. He was filled with an old man's thoughts of school, thoughts tinged with a nostalgia and warmed by a hope that youth could not know. Only a lot of boys and girls? asked Walt. Only the tiresome spelling, writing, ciphering classes? Only a public school? He laughed at that. He recalled the cry of George Fox, the stubborn Quaker: "Is it this pile of brick and mortar, these dead floors, windows, rails, you call the church? Why, this is not the church at all—the church is living souls." And you, America? Walt queried. When you cast up the reckoning, when you consider the lights and shadows of the time to come, for good or evil, look for your school to the live teachers, the living boys and girls.

But now, for Walt, school was out. He was dismissed. He might have learned other lessons, but there was no time. He managed to assemble a small sheaf of poems of farewell, and, with the tireless help of Horace Traubel, to put together a final edition of "Leaves of Grass," his chief book, that had taken thirty years "a-borning." December found him desperately ill with pneumonia, aggravated by serious complications. It seemed impossible

156

that he should live to see the book published. But the printer—Walt, who had an old affection for printers, must have loved this one—rushed the binding of a few copies, and early in the year they were ready for Walt to send as parting gifts to his closest friends.

One of his last poems recalled a talk he had had after supper with two old miners in Nevada. "Believe it or not," one of them said, "it is all true, and my mate there could tell you the same, we've often confabbed about it; sometimes in spring, oftener in autumn, just after sunrise or at sundown, perfectly clear weather, aloft to the right on the skyline or plainly there to the left on the hill-tops, I can see a church wedding, or a funeral, or the folks at Thanksgiving dinner, or maybe the wharves, or the shop-fronts in the city, or the farm, and the dooryard at home with the lilac in the corner; people and scenes, plain and distinct as I see you." Was it the same for Walt, chained faster to his bed during those fatiguing, painful, difficult months than the miners to their shaft? Were there mirages beckoning at the window, of the camps at the front, and the hospitals, of the populous streets of Manhattan, and the husky-haughty ocean, of the little old print-shop in Brooklyn, or his mother setting the supper table on the farm at home, and the dooryard with the blossoming lilac?

It was impossible for him to move, his wasted body had to be shifted continually on the bed. It choked him to lie on his right side, and when he lay on his left, the pain was unbearable. His friends wanted to get him another bed, he slipped away from them so in this one. "One of these fine mornings," retorted Walt, "I'll be slipping away from

157

you forever." It was hard even to breathe. "Well," he would ask the doctors, "what is the verdict today?" It would be a satisfaction, he told them, to know which way the cat was going to jump. He could be humorous, he could be patient. He was willing to die, but his body stubbornly refused to let go its hold on life. What he had written a quarter of a century earlier was being proven truer than ever for him now.

> At the last, tenderly,
> From the walls of the powerful fortressed house,
> From the clasp of the knitted locks, from the
>   keep of the well-closed doors,
> Let me be wafted.
>
> Let me glide noiselessly forth;
> With the key of softness unlock the locks—with
>   a whisper,
> Set ope the doors, O soul.
>
> Tenderly—be not impatient,
> (Strong is your hold O mortal flesh,
> Strong is your hold O love).

Strong, indeed, was their hold, for though his pain was intolerable, and no amount of shifting could make him easy on his bed, Walt could not let go. On March 26, 1892, a little after six o'clock, he breathed: "Shift, Warry." With that breath, the struggle ended. Long and long ago he had heard a surgeon describe the gentle death of an old sailor with the words: "He went out with the tide and the sunset." So, with the tide and the sunset, Walt himself went on his last journey.

158

But the ebbing tide flows back; though the sun must set, yet it rises. Walt but advanced a moment to hurry back in the darkness. Yet he did not doubt the sunrise.

Not today is to justify me or answer what I am for,
But you, a new brood, native, athletic, continental, greater than
      before known,
Arouse! for you must justify me . . .
I am a man who, sauntering along without fully stopping, turns
      a casual look upon you and then averts his face,
Leaving it to you to prove and define it,
Expecting the main things from you.

A SELECTION FROM THE POEMS OF WALT WHITMAN

ARRANGED SO AS TO PRESENT HIS OWN LIFE-STORY

for classroom reading

THERE WAS A CHILD WENT FORTH

There was a child went forth every day,
And the first object he look'd upon, that object he became,
And that object became part of him for the day or a certain part of the
    day,
Or for many years or stretching cycles of years.

The early lilacs became part of this child,
And grass and white and red morning-glories, and white and red clover,
    and the song of the phœbe-bird,
And the Third-month lambs and the sow's pink-faint litter,
    and the mare's foal and the cow's calf,
And the noisy brood of the barnyard or by the mire of the pond-side,
And the fish suspending themselves so curiously below there,
    and the beautiful curious liquid,
And the water-plants with their graceful flat heads, all became part of
    him.

The field-sprouts of Fourth-month and Fifth-month became part of him,
Winter-grain sprouts and those of the light-yellow corn,
    and the esculent roots of the garden,
And the apple-trees cover'd with blossoms and the fruit afterward,
    and wood-berries, and the commonest weeds by the road,
And the old drunkard staggering home from the outhouse of the tavern
    whence he had lately risen,
And the schoolmistress that pass'd on her way to the school,
And the friendly boys that pass'd, and the quarrelsome boys,
And the tidy and fresh-cheek'd girls, and the barefoot negro boy and
    girl,
And all the changes of city and country wherever he went. . . .

The mother at home quietly placing the dishes on the supper-table,
The mother with mild words, clean her cap and gown,
    a wholesome odor falling off her person and clothes as she walks by,
The father, strong, self-sufficient, manly, mean, anger'd, unjust,
The blow, the quick loud word, the tight bargain, the crafty lure,
The family usages, the language, the company, the furniture,
    the yearning and swelling heart,
Affection that will not be gainsay'd, the sense of what is real,
    the thought if after all it should prove unreal,

The doubts of day-time and the doubts of night-time,
        the curious whether and how,
Whether that which appears so is so, or is it all flashes and specks?
Men and women crowding fast in the streets,
        if they are not flashes and specks what are they?
The streets themselves and the façades of houses, and goods in the
        windows,
Vehicles, teams, the heavy-plank'd wharves, the huge crossing at the
        ferries,
The village on the highland seen from afar at sunset, the river between,
Shadows, aureola and mist, the light falling on roofs and gables
        of white or brown two miles off,
The schooner near by sleepily dropping down the tide,
        the little boat slack-tow'd astern,
The hurrying tumbling waves, quick-broken crests, slapping,
The strata of color'd clouds, the long bar of maroon-tint away solitary
        by itself, the spread of purity it lies motionless in,
The horizon's edge, the flying sea-crow, the fragrance of salt marsh and
        shore mud,
These became part of that child who went forth every day,
        and who now goes, and will always go forth every day.

IN CABIN'D SHIPS AT SEA

In cabin'd ships at sea,
The boundless blue on every side expanding,
With whistling winds and music of the waves, the large imperious
        waves,
Or some lone bark buoy'd on the dense marine,
Where joyous full of faith, spreading white sails,
She cleaves the ether mid the sparkle and the foam of dav,
        or under many a star at night,
By sailors young and old haply will I, a reminiscence of the land, be
        read,
In full rapport at last.

Here are our thoughts, voyagers' thoughts,
Here not the land, firm land, alone appears, may then by them be said,
The sky o'erarches here, we feel the undulating deck beneath our feet,
We feel the long pulsation, ebb and flow of endless motion,

166

The tones of unseen mystery, the vague and vast suggestions
  of the briny world, the liquid-flowing syllables,
The perfume, the faint creaking of the cordage, the melancholy rhythm,
The boundless vista and the horizon far and dim are all here,
And this is ocean's poem.

Then falter not O book, fulfil your destiny,
You not a reminiscence of the land alone,
You too as a lone bark cleaving the ether, purpos'd I know not whither,
  yet ever full of faith,
Consort to every ship that sails, sail you!
Bear forth to them folded my love, (dear mariners, for you I fold it
  here in every leaf;)
Speed on my book! spread your white sails my little bark
  athwart the imperious waves,
Chant on, sail on, bear o'er the boundless blue from me to every sea,
This song for mariners and all their ships.

CROSSING BROOKLYN FERRY

1. Flood-tide below me! I see you face to face!
    Clouds of the west—sun there half an hour high—I see you also
      face to face.

    Crowds of men and women attired in the usual costumes,
        how curious you are to me!
    On the ferry-boats the hundreds and hundreds that cross, returning
        home, are more curious to me than you suppose,
    And you that shall cross from shore to shore years hence are more to
        me, and more in my meditations, than you might suppose.

2. The impalpable sustenance of me from all things at all hours of the
        day,
    The simple, compact, well-join'd scheme, myself disintegrated,
        every one disintegrated yet part of the scheme,
    The similitudes of the past and those of the future,
    The glories strung like beads on my smallest sights and hearings,
        on the walk in the street and the passage over the river,
    The current rushing so swiftly and swimming with me far away,
    The others that are to follow me, the ties between me and them,

167

The certainty of others, the life, love, sight, hearing of others.
Others will enter the gates of the ferry and cross from shore to
shore,
Others will watch the run of the flood-tide,
Others will see the shipping of Manhattan north and west,
and the heights of Brooklyn to the south and east,
Others will see the islands large and small;
Fifty years hence, others will see them as they cross, the sun half an
hour high,
A hundred years hence, or ever so many hundred years hence,
others will see them,
Will enjoy the sunset, the pouring-in of the flood-tide,
the falling-back to the sea of the ebb-tide.

3. It avails not, time nor place—distance avails not,
I am with you, you men and women of a generation,
or ever so many generations hence,
Just as you feel when you look on the river and sky, so I felt,
Just as any of you is one of a living crowd, I was one of a crowd,
Just as you are refresh'd by the gladness of the river and the bright
flow, I was refresh'd,
Just as you stand and lean on the rail, yet hurry with the swift cur-
rent, I stood yet was hurried,
Just as you look on the numberless masts of ships
and the thick-stemm'd pipes of steamboats, I look'd.

I too many and many a time cross'd the river of old,
Watched the Twelfth-month sea-gulls, saw them high in the air
floating with motionless wings, oscillating their bodies,
Saw how the glistening yellow lit up parts of their bodies
and left the rest in strong shadow,
Saw the slow-wheeling circles and the gradual edging toward the
south,
Saw the reflection of the summer sky in the water,
Had my eyes dazzled by the shimmering track of beams,
Look'd at the fine centrifugal spokes of light round the shape of my
head in the sunlit water,
Look'd on the haze on the hills southward and south-westward,
Look'd on the vapor as it flew in fleeces tinged with violet,
Look'd toward the lower bay to notice the vessels arriving,
Saw their approach, saw aboard those that were near me,
Saw the white sails of schooners and sloops, saw the ships at anchor,

168

The sailors at work in the rigging or out astride the spars,
The round masts, the swinging motion of the hulls,
    the slender serpentine pennants,
The large and small steamers in motion, the pilots in their pilot-
    houses,
The white wake left by the passage, the quick tremulous whirl of
    the wheels,
The flags of all nations, the falling of them at sunset,
The scallop-edged waves in the twilight, the ladled cups,
    the frolicsome crests and glistening,
The stretch afar growing dimmer and dimmer,
    the gray walls of the granite storehouses by the docks,
On the river the shadowy group, the big steam-tug closely flank'd
    on each side by the barges, the hay-boat, the belated lighter,
On the neighboring shore the fires from the foundry chimneys
    burning high and glaringly into the night,
Casting their flicker of black contrasted with wild red and yellow
    light over the tops of houses, and down into the clefts of
    streets.

4. These and all else were to me the same as they are to you,
I loved well those cities, loved well the stately and rapid river,
The men and women I saw were all near to me,
Others the same—others who look back on me
    because I look'd forward to them,
(The time will come, though I stop here to-day and to-night.)

5. What is it then between us?
What is the count of the scores or hundreds of years between us?

Whatever it is, it avails not—distance avails not, and place avails
    not,
I too lived, Brooklyn of ample hills was mine,
I too walk'd the streets of Manhattan island,
    and bathed in the waters around it,
I too felt the curious abrupt questionings stir within me,
In the day among crowds of people sometimes they came upon me,
In my walks home late at night or as I lay in my bed they came upon
    me,
I too had been struck from the float forever held in solution,
I too had receiv'd identity by my body,

169

That I was I knew was of my body, and what I should be
    I knew I should be of my body.

6. It is not upon you alone the dark patches fall,
    The dark threw its patches down upon me also,
    The best I had done seem'd to me blank and suspicious,
    My great thoughts as I supposed them, were they not in reality
        meagre?
    Nor is it you alone who know what it is to be evil,
    I am he who knew what it was to be evil,
    I too knitted the old knot of contrariety,
    Blabb'd, blush'd, resented, lied, stole, grudg'd,
    Had guile, anger, lust, hot wishes I dared not speak,
    Was wayward, vain, greedy, shallow, sly, cowardly, malignant,
    The wolf, the snake, the hog, not wanting in me. . . .

7. Closer yet I approach you,
    What thought you have of me now, I had as much of you—
        I laid in my stores in advance,
    I consider'd long and seriously of you before you were born.
    Who was to know what should come home to me?
    Who knows but I am enjoying this?
    Who knows, for all the distance, but I am as good as looking at you
        now, for all you cannot see me?

8. Ah, what can ever be more stately and admirable to me
        than mast-hemm'd Manhattan?
    River and sunset and scallop-edg'd waves of flood-tide?
    The sea-gulls oscillating their bodies, the hay-boat in the twilight,
        and the belated lighter?
    What gods can exceed these that clasp me by the hand, and with
        voices I love call me promptly and loudly by my nighest
        name as I approach?
    What is more subtle than this which ties me to the woman or man
        that looks in my face?
    Which fuses me into you now, and pours my meaning into you?

    We understand then do we not?
    What I promis'd without mentioning it, have you not accepted?
    What the study could not teach—what the preaching could not ac-
        complish is accomplish'd, is it not?

170

9. Flow on, river! flow with the flood-tide, and ebb with the ebb-tide!
Frolic on, crested and scallop-edg'd waves!
Gorgeous clouds of the sunset! drench with your splendor me,
    or the men and women generations after me!
Cross from shore to shore, countless crowds of passengers!
Stand up, tall masts of Mannahatta! stand up, beautiful hills of
    Brooklyn!
Throb, baffled and curious brain! throw out questions and answers!
Suspend here and everywhere, eternal float of solution!
Gaze, loving and thirsting eyes, in the house or street or public
    assembly!
Sound out, voices of young men! loudly and musically call me
    by my nighest name!
Live, old life! play the part that looks back on the actor or actress!
Play the old role, the role that is great or small according as one
    makes it!
Consider, you who peruse me, whether I may not in unknown ways
    be looking upon you;
Be firm, rail over the river, to support those who lean idly,
    yet haste with the hasting current;
Fly on, sea-birds! fly sideways, or wheel in large circles high in the
    air;
Receive the summer sky, you water, and faithfully hold it
    till all downcast eyes have time to take it from you!
Diverge, fine spokes of light, from the shape of my head,
    or any one's head, in the sunlit water!
Come on, ships from the lower bay! pass up or down,
    white-sail'd schooners, sloops, lighters!
Flaunt away, flags of all nations! be duly lower'd at sunset!
Burn high your fires, foundry chimneys! cast black shadows at
    nightfall! cast red and yellow light over the tops of the
    houses!
Appearances, now or henceforth, indicate what you are,
You necessary film, continue to envelop the soul,
About my body for me, and your body for you, be hung our divinest
    aromas,
Thrive, cities—bring your freight, bring your shows, ample and
    sufficient rivers,
Expand, being than which none else is perhaps more spiritual,
Keep your places, objects than which none else is more lasting.

You have waited, you always wait, you dumb, beautiful ministers,
We receive you with free sense at last, and are insatiate henceforward,
Not you any more shall be able to foil us, or withhold yourselves from us,
We use you, and do not cast you aside—we plant you permanently within us,
We fathom you not—we love you—there is perfection in you also,
You furnish your parts toward eternity,
Great or small, you furnish your parts toward the soul.

MANNAHATTA

I was asking for something specific and perfect for my city,
Whereupon lo! upsprang the aboriginal name.

Now I see what there is in a name, a word, liquid, sane, unruly,
    musical, self-sufficient,
I see that the word of my city is that word from of old,
Because I see that word nested in nests of water-bays, superb,
Rich, hemm'd thick all around with sailships and steamships,
    an island sixteen miles long, solid-founded,
Numberless crowded streets, high growths of iron, slender, strong,
    light, splendidly uprising toward clear skies,
Tides swift and ample, well-loved by me, toward sundown,
The flowing sea-currents, the little islands, larger adjoining islands,
    the heights, the villas,
The countless masts, the white shore-steamers, the lighters,
    the ferry-boats, the black sea-steamers well-model'd,
The down-town streets, the jobbers' houses of business, the houses of
        business of the ship-merchants and money-brokers, the river-
        streets,
Immigrants arriving, fifteen or twenty thousand in a week,
The carts hauling goods, the manly race of drivers of horses,
    the brown-faced sailors,
The summer air, the bright sun shining, and the sailing clouds aloft,
The winter snows, the sleigh-bells, the broken ice in the river,
    passing along up or down with the flood-tide or ebb-tide,
The mechanics of the city, the masters, well-form'd, beautiful-faced,
    looking you straight in the eyes,

172

Trottoirs throng'd, vehicles, Broadway, the women, the shops and
    shows,
A million people—manners free and superb—open voices—hospitality—
    the most courageous and friendly young men,
City of hurried and sparkling waters! city of spires and masts!
City nested in bays! my city!

I HEAR AMERICA SINGING

I hear America singing, the varied carols I hear,
Those of mechanics, each one singing his as it should be blithe and
    strong,
The carpenter singing his as he measures his plank or beam,
The mason singing his as he makes ready for work, or leaves off work,
The boatman singing what belongs to him in his boat, the deckhand
    singing on the steamboat deck,
The shoemaker singing as he sits on his bench, the hatter singing as he
    stands,
The wood-cutter's song, the ploughboy's on his way in the morning,
    or at noon intermission or at sundown,
The delicious singing of the mother, or of the young wife at work,
    or of the girl sewing or washing,
Each singing what belongs to him or her and to none else,
The day what belongs to the day—at night the party of young fellows,
    robust, friendly,
Singing with open mouths their strong melodious songs.

SONG OF MYSELF

1. I celebrate myself, and sing myself,
    And what I assume you shall assume,
    For every atom belonging to me as good belongs to you.

    I loafe and invite my soul,
    I lean and loafe at my ease observing a spear of summer grass.

    My tongue, every atom of my blood, form'd from this soil, this air,
    Born here of parents born here from parents the same,
        and their parents the same,

I, now thirty-seven years old in perfect health begin,
Hoping to cease not till death.

Creeds and schools in abeyance,
Retiring back a while sufficed at what they are, but never forgotten,
I harbor for good or bad, I permit to speak at every hazard,
Nature without check with original energy.

2. Houses and rooms are full of perfumes, the shelves are crowded
       with perfumes,
I breathe the fragrance myself and know it and like it,
The distillation would intoxicate me also, but I shall not let it.

The atmosphere is not a perfume, it has no taste of the distillation,
      it is odorless,
It is for my mouth forever, I am in love with it,
I will go to the bank by the wood and become undisguised and
      naked,
I am mad for it to be in contact with me. . . .

Have you reckon'd a thousand acres much? have you reckon'd the
      earth much?
Have you practis'd so long to learn to read?
Have you felt so proud to get at the meaning of poems?

Stop this day and night with me and you shall possess the origin
      of all poems,
You shall possess the good of the earth and sun, (there are mil-
      lions of suns left,)
You shall no longer take things at second or third hand, nor look
      through the eyes of the dead, nor feed on the spectres in
      books,
You shall not look through my eyes either, nor take things from
      me,
You shall listen to all sides and filter them from your self.

4. Trippers and askers surround me,
People I meet, the effect upon me of my early life or the ward and
      city I live in, or the nation,
The latest dates, discoveries, inventions, societies, authors old and
      new,
My dinner, dress, associates, looks, compliments, dues,
The real or fancied indifference of some man or woman I love,

174

The sickness of one of my folks or of myself, or ill-doing or loss
    or lack of money, or depressions or exaltations,
Battles, the horrors of fratricidal war, the fever of doubtful news,
    The fitful events;
These come to me days and nights and go from me again,
But they are not the Me myself.

Apart from the pulling and hauling stands what I am,
Stands amused, complacent, compassionating, idle, unitary,
Looks down, is erect, or bends an arm on an impalpable certain rest,
Looking with side-curved head curious what will come next,
Both in and out of the game and watching and wondering at it.

Backward I see in my own days where I sweated through fog
    with linguists and contenders,
I have no mockings or arguments, I witness and wait.

5. I believe in you my soul, the other I am must not abase itself to
    you,
And you must not be abased to the other.

Loafe with me on the grass, loose the stop from your throat,
Not words, not music or rhyme I want, not custom or lecture, not
        even the best,
Only the lull I like, the hum of your valvèd voice. . . .

Swiftly arose and spread around me the peace and knowledge
    that pass all the argument of the earth,
And I know that the hand of God is the promise of my own,
And I know that the spirit of God is the brother of my own,
And that all the men ever born are also my brothers,
    and the women my sisters and lovers,
And that a kelson of the creation is love,
And limitless are leaves stiff or drooping in the fields,
And brown ants in the little wells beneath them,
And mossy scabs of the worm fence, heap'd stones, elder,
    mullein and poke-weed.

6. A child said *What is the grass?* fetching it to me with full hands;
How could I answer the child? I do not know what it is any more
        than he.

I guess it must be the flag of my disposition, out of hopeful green
    stuff woven.

175

Or I guess it is the handkerchief of the Lord,
A scented gift and remembrancer designedly dropt,
Bearing the owner's name someway in the corners, that we may see
and remark, and say *Whose?*

Or I guess the grass is itself a child, the produced babe of the
vegetation.

Or I guess it is a uniform hieroglyphic,
And it means, Sprouting alike in broad zones and narrow zones,
Growing among black folks as among white,
Kanuck, Tuckahoe, Congressman, Cuff, I give them the same,
I receive them the same.

And now it seems to me the beautiful uncut hair of graves.

Tenderly will I use you curling grass,
It may be you transpire from the breasts of young men,
It may be if I had known them I would have loved them,
It may be you are from old people, or from offspring taken soon
out of their mothers' laps,
And here you are the mothers' laps.

This grass is very dark to be from the white heads of old mothers,
Darker than the colorless beards of old men,
Dark to come from under the faint red roofs of mouths.

O I perceive after all so many uttering tongues,
And I perceive they do not come from the roofs of mouths for
nothing.

I wish I could translate the hints about the dead young men and
women,
And the hints about old men and mothers, and the offspring taken
soon out of their laps.

What do you think has become of the young and old men?
And what do you think has become of the women and children?

They are alive and well somewhere,
The smallest sprout shows there is really no death,
And if ever there was it led forward life, and does not wait
at the end to arrest it,
And ceas'd the moment life appear'd.

176

All goes onward and outward, nothing collapses,
And to die is different from what any one supposed, and luckier.

9. The big doors of the country barn stand open'and ready,
The dried grass of the harvest-time loads the slow-drawn wagon,
The clear light plays on the brown gray and green intertinged,
The armfuls are pack'd to the sagging mow.

I am there, I help, I came stretch'd atop of the load,
I felt its soft jolts, one leg reclined on the other,
I jump from the cross-beams and seize the clover and timothy,
And roll head over heels and tangle my hair full of wisps.

12. The butcher-boy puts off his killing-clothes, or sharpens his knife
at the stall in the market,
I loiter enjoying his repartee and his shuffle and break-down.

Blacksmiths with grimed and hairy chests environ the anvil,
Each has his main-sledge, they are all out, there is a great heat in
the fire.

From the cinder-strew'd threshold I follow their movements,
The lithe sheer of their waists plays even with their massive arms,
Overhand the hammers swing, overhand so slow, overhand so sure,
They do not hasten, each man hits in his place.

13. The negro holds firmly the reins of his four horses, the block swags
underneath on its tied-over chain,
The negro that drives the long dray of the stone-yard, steady and
tall he stands pois'd on one leg on the string-piece,
His blue shirt exposes his ample neck and breast and loosens over
his hip-band,
His glance is calm and commanding, he tosses the slouch of his hat
away from his forehead,
The sun falls on his crispy hair and mustache, falls on the black
of his polish'd and perfect limbs.

I behold the picturesque giant and love him, and I do not stop
there,
I go with the team also.

In me the caresser of life wherever moving, backward as well as
forward sluing,
To niches aside and junior bending, not a person or object missing,
Absorbing all to myself and for this song.

177

Oxen that rattle the yoke and chain or halt in the leaty shade,
what is that you express in your eyes?
It seems to me more than all the print I have read in my life.

My tread scares the wood-drake and wood-duck on my distant
and day-long ramble,
They rise together, they slowly circle around.

I believe in those wing'd purposes,
And acknowledge red, yellow, white, playing within me,
And consider green and violet and the tufted crown intentional,
And do not call the tortoise unworthy because she is not something
else,
And the jay in the woods never studied the gamut, yet trills pretty
well to me,
And the look of the bay mare shames silliness out of me.

14. The wild gander leads his flock through the cool night,
Ya-honk he says, and sounds it down to me like an invitation,
The pert may suppose it meaningless, but I listening close,
Find its purpose and place up there toward the wintry sky.

The sharp-hoof'd moose of the north, the cat on the house-sill,
the chickadee, the prairie-dog,
The litter of the grunting sow as they tug at her teats,
The brood of the turkey-hen and she with her half-spread wings,
I see in them and myself the same old law.

The press of my foot to the earth springs a hundred affections,
They scorn the best I can do to relate them.

I am enamour'd of growing out-doors,
Of men that live among cattle or taste of the ocean or woods,
Of the builders and steerers of ships and the wielders of axes and
mauls, and the drivers of horses,
I can eat and sleep with them week in and week out.

What is commonest, cheapest, nearest, easiest, is Me,
Me going in for my chances, spending for vast returns,
Adorning myself to bestow myself on the first that will take me,
Not asking the sky to come down to my good will,
Scattering it freely forever.

16. I am of old and young, of the foolish as much as the wise,
Regardless of others, ever regardful of others,
Maternal as well as paternal, a child as well as a man,

178

Stuff'd with the stuff that is coarse and stuff'd with the stuff that is
fine,
One of the Nation of many nations, the smallest the same
and the largest the same,
A Southerner soon as a Northerner, a planter nonchalant and hos-
pitable down by the Oconee I live,
A Yankee bound my own way ready for trade, my joints the lim-
berest joints on earth and the sternest joints on earth,
A Kentuckian walking the vale of the Elkhorn in my deer-skin
leggings, a Louisianian or Georgian,
A boatman over lakes or bays or along coasts, a Hoosier, Badger,
Buckeye;
At home on Kanadian snow-shoes or up in the bush,
or with fishermen off Newfoundland,
At home in the fleet of ice-boats, sailing with the rest and tacking,
At home on the hills of Vermont or in the woods of Maine, or the
Texan ranch,
Comrade of Californians, comrade of free North-Westerners,
(loving their big proportions,)
Comrade of raftsmen and coalmen, comrade of all who shake hands
and welcome to drink and meat,
A learner with the simplest, a teacher of the thoughtfullest,
A novice beginning yet experient of myriads of seasons,
Of every hue and caste am I, of every rank and religion,
A farmer, mechanic, artist, gentleman, sailor, quaker,
Prisoner, fancy-man, rowdy, lawyer, physician, priest.

I resist any thing better than my own diversity,
Breathe the air but leave plenty after me,
And am not stuck up, and am in my place.

(The moth and the fish-eggs are in their place,
The bright suns I see and the dark suns I cannot see are in their
place,
The palpable is in its place and the impalpable is in its place.)

17. These are really the thoughts of all men in all ages and lands,
they are not original with me,
If they are not yours as much as mine they are nothing, or next to
nothing,
If they are not the riddle and the untying of the riddle they are
nothing,
If they are not just as close as they are distant they are nothing.

179

This is the grass that grows wherever the land is and the water is,
This the common air that bathes the globe.

18. With music strong I come, with my cornets and my drums,
I play not marches for accepted victors only, I play marches
for conquer'd and slain persons.

Have you heard that it was good to gain the day?
I also say it is good to fall, battles are lost in the same spirit
in which they are won.

I beat and pound for the dead,
I blow through my embouchures my loudest and gayest for them.

Vivas to those who have fail'd!
And to those whose war-vessels sank in the sea!
And to those themselves who sank in the sea!
And to all generals that lost engagements, and all overcome heroes!
And the numberless unknown heroes equal to the greatest heroes
known!

19. This is the meal equally set, this the meat for natural hunger,
It is for the wicked just the same as the righteous, I make appoint-
ments with all,
I will not have a single person slighted or left away, . . .

Do you guess I have some intricate purpose?
Well I have, for the Fourth-month showers have,
and the mica on the side of a rock has.

Do you take it I would astonish?
Does the daylight astonish? does the early redstart twittering
through the woods?
Do I astonish more than they?

This hour I tell things in confidence,
I might not tell everybody, but I will tell you.

20. Who goes there? hankering, gross, mystical, nude;
How is it I extract strength from the beef I eat?

What is a man anyhow? what am I? what are you?

All I mark as my own you shall offset it with your own,
Else it were time lost listening to me.

I do not snivel that snivel the world over,
That months are vacuums and the ground but wallow and filth.

180

Whimpering and truckling fold with powders for invalids,
   conformity goes to the fourth-remov'd,
I wear my hat as I please indoors or out.

Why should I pray? why should I venerate and be ceremonious?

Having pried through the strata, analyzed to a hair,
   counsel'd with doctors and calculated close,
I find no sweeter fat than sticks to my own bones.

In all people I see myself, none more and not one a barley-corn
      less,
And the good or bad I say of myself I say of them.

I know I am solid and sound,
To me the converging objects of the universe perpetually flow,
All are written to me, and I must get what the writing means.

I know I am deathless,
I know this orbit of mine cannot be swept by a carpenter's compass,
I know I shall not pass like a child's carlacue cut
   with a burnt stick at night.

I know I am august,
I do not trouble my spirit to vindicate itself or be understood,
I see that the elementary laws never apologize,
(I reckon I behave no prouder than the level I plant my house by,
      after all.)

I exist as I am, that is enough,
If no other in the world be aware I sit content,
And if each and all be aware I sit content.

One world is aware and by far the largest to me, and that is myself,
And whether I come to my own to-day or in ten thousand or ten
         million years,
I can cheerfully take it now, or with equal cheerfulness I can wait.

My foothold is tenon'd and mortis'd in granite,
I laugh at what you call dissolution,
And I know the amplitude of time.

21. I am the poet of the Body and I am the poet of the Soul,
The pleasures of heaven are with me and the pains of hell are with
      me,
The first I graft and increase upon myself, the latter I translate
   into a new tongue.

I am the poet of the woman the same as the man,
And I say it is as great to be a woman as to be a man,
And I say there is nothing greater than the mother of men.

I chant the chant of dilation or pride,
We have had ducking and deprecating about enough,
I show that size is only development.

Have you outstript the rest? are you the President?
It is a trifle, they will more than arrive there every one, and still
        pass on.

I am he that walks with the tender and growing night,
I call to the earth and sea half-held by the night.

Press close bare-bosom'd night—press close magnetic nourishing
        night!
Night of south winds—night of the large few stars!
Still nodding night—mad naked summer night.

Smile O voluptuous cool-breath'd earth!
Earth of the slumbering and liquid trees!
Earth of departed sunset—earth of the mountains misty-topt!
Earth of the vitreous pour of the full moon just tinged with blue!
Earth of shine and dark mottling the tide of the river!
Earth of the limpid gray of clouds brighter and clearer for my sake!
Far-swooping elbow'd earth—rich apple-blossom'd earth!
Smile, for your lover comes.

Prodigal, you have given me love—therefore I to you give love!
O unspeakable passionate love.

22. You sea! I resign myself to you also—I guess what you mean,
I behold from the beach your crooked inviting fingers,
I believe you refuse to go back without feeling of me,
We must have a turn together, I undress, hurry me out of sight of
        the land,
Cushion me soft, rock me in billowy drowse,
Dash me with amorous wet, I can repay you.

Sea of stretch'd ground-swells,
Sea breathing broad and convulsive breaths,
Sea of the brine of life and of unshovell'd yet always-ready graves,
Howler and scooper of storms, capricious and dainty sea,
I am integral with you, I too am of one phase and of all phases.

182

Partaker of influx and efflux I, extoller of hate and conciliation,
Extoller of amies and those that sleep in each others' arms.

I am he attesting sympathy,
(Shall I make my list of things in the house and skip the house
    that supports them?)

I am not the poet of goodness only, I do not decline to be
    the poet of wickedness also.

What blurt is this about virtue and about vice?
Evil propels me and reform of evil propels me, I stand indifferent,
My gait is no fault-finder's or rejecter's gait,
I moisten the roots of all that has grown. . . .

This minute that comes to me over the past decillions,
There is no better than it and now.

What behaved well in the past or behaves well to-day is not such a
    wonder,
The wonder is always and always how there can be a mean man or
    an infidel.

23. Endless unfolding of words of ages!
    And mine a word of the modern, the word En-Masse.

A word of the faith that never balks,
Here or henceforward it is all the same to me, I accept Time
    absolutely.

It alone is without flaw, it alone rounds and completes all,
That mystic baffling wonder alone completes all.

I accept Reality and dare not question it,
Materialism first and last imbuing.

Hurrah for positive science! long live exact demonstration!
Fetch stonecrop mixt with cedar and branches of lilac,
This is the lexicographer, this the chemist, this made a grammar
    of the old cartouches,
These mariners put the ship through dangerous unknown seas,
This is the geologist, this works with the scalpel, and this is a
    mathematician.

Gentlemen, to you the first honors always!
Your facts are useful, and yet they are not my dwelling,
I but enter by them to an area of my dwelling.

Less the reminders of properties told my words,
And more the reminders they of life untold, and of freedom
and extrication,
And make short account of neuters and geldings, and favor men
and women fully equipt,
And beat the gong of revolt, and stop with fugitives
and them that plot and conspire.

24. Walt Whitman, a kosmos, of Manhattan the son,
Turbulent, fleshy, sensual, eating, drinking and breeding,
No sentimentalist, no stander above men and women or apart from
them,
No more modest than immodest.

Unscrew the locks from the doors!
Unscrew the doors themselves from their jambs!

Whoever degrades another degrades me,
And whatever is done or said returns at last to me.

Through me the afflatus surging and surging, through me
the current and index.

I speak the pass-word primeval, I give the sign of democracy,
By God! I will accept nothing which all cannot have their counter-
part of on the same terms. . . .

31. I believe a leaf of grass is no less than the journey-work of the
stars,
And the pismire is equally perfect, and a grain of sand, and the
egg of the wren,
And the tree-toad is a chef-d'œuvre for the highest,
And the running blackberry would adorn the parlors of heaven,
And the narrowest hinge in my hand puts to scorn all machinery,
And the cow crunching with depress'd head surpasses any statue,
And a mouse is miracle enough to stagger sextillions of infidels.

I find I incorporate gneiss, coal, long-threaded moss, fruits, grains,
esculent roots,
And am stucco'd with quadrupeds and birds all over,
And have distanced what is behind me for good reasons,
But call any thing back again when I desire it.

In vain the speeding or shyness,
In vain the plutonic rocks send their old heat against my approach,

184

In vain the mastodon retreats beneath its own powder'd bones,
In vain objects stand leagues off and assume manifold shapes,
In vain the ocean settling in hollows and the great monsters lying
    low,
In vain the buzzard houses herself with the sky,
In vain the snake slides through the creepers and logs,
In vain the elk takes to the inner passes of the woods,
In vain the razor-bill'd auk sails far north to Labrador,
I follow quickly, I ascend to the nest in the fissure of the cliff.

32. I think I could turn and live with animals, they are so placid and
    self-contain'd,
I stand and look at them long and long.

They do not sweat and whine about their condition,
They do not lie awake in the dark and weep for their sins,
They do not make me sick discussing their duty to God,
Not one is dissatisfied, not one is demented with the mania of
    owning things,
Not one kneels to another, nor to his kind that lived thousands of
    years ago,
Not one is respectable or unhappy over the whole earth.

So they show their relations to me and I accept them,
They bring me tokens of myself, they evince them plainly in their
    possession.

I wonder where they get those tokens,
Did I pass that way huge times ago and negligently drop them?
Myself moving forward then and now and forever,
Gathering and showing more always and with velocity,
Infinite and omnigenous, and the like of these among them,
Not too exclusive toward the reachers of my remembrancers,
Picking out here one that I love, and now go with him on brotherly
    terms.

A gigantic beauty of a stallion, fresh and responsive to my caresses,
Head high in the forehead, wide between the ears,
Limbs glossy and supple, tail dusting the ground,
Eyes full of sparkling wickedness, ears finely cut, flexibly moving.

His nostrils dilate as my heels embrace him,
His well-built limbs tremble with pleasure as we race around and
    return.

I but use you a minute, then I resign you, stallion,
Why do I need your paces when I myself out-gallop them?
Even as I stand or sit passing faster than you. . . .

40. Flaunt of the sunshine I need not your bask—lie over!
You light surfaces only, I force surfaces and depths also.

Earth! you seem to look for something at my hands,
Say, old top-knot, what do you want?

Man or woman, I might tell how I like you, but cannot,
And might tell what it is in me and what it is in you, but cannot,

And might tell that pining I have, that pulse of my nights and
    days.

Behold, I do not give lectures or a little charity,
When I give I give myself. . . .

I seize the descending man and raise him with resistless will,
O despairer, here is my neck,
By God, you shall not go down! hang your whole weight upon me.

I dilate you with tremendous breath, I buoy you up,
Every room of the house do I fill with an arm'd force,
Lovers of me, bafflers of graves.

Sleep—I and they keep guard all night,
Not doubt, not decease shall dare to lay finger upon you,
I have embraced you, and henceforth possess you to myself,
And when you rise in the morning you will find what I tell you
    is so.

42. A call in the midst of the crowd,
My own voice, orotund sweeping and final.

Come my children,
Come my boys and girls, my women, household and intimates,
Now the performer launches his nerve,
    he has pass'd his prelude on the reeds within.

Easily written loose-finger'd chords—I feel the thrum of your
    climax and close.

My head slues round on my neck,
Music rolls, but not from the organ,
Folks are around me, but they are no household of mine.

186

Ever the hard unsunk ground,
Ever the eaters and drinkers, ever the upward and downward sun,
    ever the air and the ceaseless tides,
Ever myself and my neighbors, refreshing, wicked, real,
Ever the old inexplicable query, ever that thorn'd thumb,
    that breath of itches and thirsts,
Ever the vexer's *hoot! hoot!* till we find where the sly one hides
    and bring him forth,
Ever love, ever the sobbing liquid of life,
Ever the bandage under the chin, ever the trestles of death.

Here and there with dimes on the eyes walking,
To feed the greed of the belly the brains liberally spooning,
Tickets buying, taking, selling, but in to the feast never once going,
Many sweating, ploughing, thrashing, and then the chaff
    for payment receiving,
A few idly owning, and they the wheat continually claiming.

This is the city and I am one of the citizens,
Whatever interests the rest interests me, politics, wars, markets,
    newspapers, schools,
The mayor and councils, banks, tariffs, steamships, factories, stocks,
    stores, real estate and personal estate.

The little plentiful manikins skipping around in collars and tail'd
        coats,
I am aware who they are, (they are positively not worms or fleas,)
I acknowledge the duplicates of myself, the weakest and shallowest
    is deathless with me,
What I do and say the same waits for them,
Every thought that flounders in me the same flounders in them.

I know perfectly well my own egotism,
Know my omnivorous lines and must not write any less,
And would fetch you whoever you are flush with myself.

Not words of routine this song of mine,
But abruptly to question, to leap beyond yet nearer bring;
This printed and bound book—but the printer and the printing-
        office boy?
The well-taken photographs—but your wife or friend
    close and solid in your arms?
The black ship mail'd with iron, her mighty guns in her turrets—
    but the pluck of the captain and engineers?

In the houses the dishes and fare and furniture—but the host and
hostess, and the look out of their eyes?
The sky up there—yet here or next door, or across the way?
The saints and sages in history—but you yourself?
Sermons, creeds, theology—but the fathomless human brain,
And what is reason? and what is love? and what is life?

44. It is time to explain myself—let us stand up.

What is known I strip away,
I launch all men and women forward with me into the Unknown.

The clock indicates the moment—but what does eternity indicate?

We have thus far exhausted trillions of winters and summers,
There are trillions ahead, and trillions ahead of them.

Births have brought us richness and variety,
And other births will bring us richness and variety.

I do not call one greater and one smaller,
That which fills its period and place is equal to any.

Were mankind murderous or jealous upon you, my brother, my
sister?
.I am sorry for you, they are not murderous or jealous upon me,
All has been gentle with me, I keep no account with lamentation,
(What have I to do with lamentation?)

I am an acme of things accomplish'd, and I an encloser of things
to be.

My feet strike an apex of the apices of the stairs,
On every step bunches of ages, and larger bunches between the
steps,
All below duly travel'd, and still I mount and mount.

Rise after rise bow the phantoms behind me,
Afar down I see the huge first Nothing, I know I was even there,
I waited unseen and always, and slept through the lethargic mist,
And took my time, and took no hurt from the fetid carbon.

Long I was hugg'd close—long and long.

Immense have been the preparations for me,
Faithful and friendly the arms that have help'd me.

Cycles ferried my cradle, rowing and rowing like cheerful boatmen,
For room to me stars kept aside in their own rings,
They sent influences to look after what was to hold me.

Before I was born out of my mother generations guided me,
My embryo has never been torpid, nothing could overlay it.

For it the nebula cohered to an orb,
The long slow strata piled to rest it on,
Vast vegetables gave it sustenance,
Monstrous sauroids transported it in their mouths
    and deposited it with care.

All forces have been steadily employ'd to complete and delight me,
Now on this spot I stand with my robust soul.

46. I know I have the best of time and space, and was never measured
        and never will be measured.

I tramp a perpetual journey, (come listen all!)
My signs are a rain-proof coat, good shoes, and a staff cut from
        the woods,
No friend of mine takes his ease in my chair,
I have no chair, no church, no philosophy,
I lead no man to a dinner-table, library, exchange,
But each man and each woman of you I lead upon a knoll,
My left hand hooking you round the waist,
My right hand pointing to landscapes of continents and the public
        road.

Not I, not any one else can travel that road for you,
You must travel it for yourself.

It is not far, it is within reach,
Perhaps you have been on it since you were born and did not know,
Perhaps it is everywhere on water and on land.

Shoulder your duds dear son, and I will mine, and let us hasten
        forth,
Wonderful cities and free nations we shall fetch as we go.

If you tire, give me both burdens, and rest the chuff of your hand
        on my hip,
And in due time you shall repay the same service to me,
For after we start we never lie by again.

This day before dawn I ascended a hill and look'd at the crowded heaven,

And I said to my spirit, *When we become the enfolders of those orbs, and the pleasure and knowledge of every thing in them, shall we be fill'd and satisfied then?*

And my spirit said, *No, we but level that lift to pass and continue beyond.*

You are also asking me questions and I hear you,
I answer that I cannot answer, you must find out for yourself.

Sit a while dear son,
Here are biscuits to eat and here is milk to drink,
But as soon as you sleep and renew yourself in sweet clothes,
    I kiss you with a good-by kiss and open the gate for your egress hence.

Long enough have you dream'd contemptible dreams,
Now I wash the gum from your eyes,
You must habit yourself to the dazzle of the light and of every moment of your life.

Long have you timidly waded holding a plank by the shore,
Now I will you to be a bold swimmer,
To jump off in the midst of the sea, rise again, nod to me, shout, and laughingly dash with your hair.

47. I am the teacher of athletes,
He that by me spreads a wider breast than my own proves the width of my own,
He most honors my style who learns under it to destroy the teacher.

The boy I love, the same becomes a man not through derived power, but in his own right,
Wicked rather than virtuous out of conformity or fear,
Fond of his sweetheart, relishing well his steak,
Unrequited love or a slight cutting him worse than sharp steel cuts,
First-rate to ride, to fight, to hit the bull's eye, to sail a skiff,
    to sing a song or play on the banjo,
Preferring scars and the beard and faces pitted with small-pox over all latherers,
And those well-tann'd to those that keep out of the sun.

I teach straying from me, yet who can stray from me?
I follow you whoever you are from the present hour,
My words itch at your ears till you understand them.

190

I do not say these things for a dollar or to fill up the time
    while I wait for a boat,
(It is you talking just as much as myself, I act as the tongue of you,
Tied in your mouth, in mine it begins to be loosen'd.)

I swear I will never again mention love or death inside a house,
And I swear I will never translate myself at all, only to him or her
    who privately stays with me in the open air.

If you would understand me go to the heights or water-shore,
The nearest gnat is an explanation, and a drop or motion of waves
    a key,
The maul, the oar, the hand-saw, second my words.

No shutter'd room or school can commune with me,
But roughs and little children better than they.

The young mechanic is closest to me, he knows me well,
The woodman that takes his axe and jug with him shall take me
    with him all day,
The farm-boy ploughing in the field feels good at the sound of my
    voice,
In vessels that sail my words sail, I go with fishermen and seamen
    and love them.

The soldier camp'd or upon the march is mine,
On the night ere the pending battle many seek me, and I do not
    fail them,
On that solemn night (it may be their last) those that know me
    seek me.

My face rubs to the hunter's face when he lies down alone in his
    blanket,
The driver thinking of me does not mind the jolt of his wagon,
The young mother and old mother comprehend me,
The girl and the wife rest the needle a moment and forget where
    they are,
They and all would resume what I have told them.

48. I have said that the soul is not more than the body,
    And I have said that the body is not more than the soul,
    And nothing, not God, is greater to one than one's self is,
    And whoever walks a furlong without sympathy walks to his own
        funeral drest in his shroud,

191

And I or you pocketless of a dime may purchase the pick of the
earth,
And to glance with an eye or show a bean in its pod
confounds the learning of all times,
And there is no trade or employment but the young man following
it may become a hero,
And there is no object so soft but it makes a hub for the wheel'd
universe,
And I say to any man or woman, Let your soul stand cool and
composed before a million universes.

And I say to mankind, Be not curious about God,
For I who am curious about each am not curious about God,
(No array of terms can say how much I am at peace about God
and about death.)

I hear and behold God in every object, yet understand God not in
the least,
Nor do I understand who there can be more wonderful than
myself.

Why should I wish to see God better than this day?
I see something of God each hour of the twenty-four,
and each moment then,
In the faces of men and women I see God, and in my own face
in the glass,
I find letters from God dropt in the street, and every one
is sign'd by God's name,
And I leave them where they are, for I know that wheresoe'er I go,
Others will punctually come for ever and ever.

49. And as to you Death, and you bitter hug of mortality,
it is idle to try to alarm me.

To his work without flinching the accoucheur comes,
I see the elder-hand pressing, receiving, supporting,
I recline by the sills of the exquisite flexible doors,
And mark the outlet, and mark the relief and escape.

And as to you Corpse I think you are good manure,
but that does not offend me,
I smell the white roses sweet-scented and growing,
I reach to the leafy lips, I reach to the polish'd breasts of melons.

And as to you Life I reckon you are the leavings of many deaths,
(No doubt I have died myself ten thousand times before.)

192

I hear you whispering there O stars of heaven,
O suns—O grass of graves—O perpetual transfers and promotions,
If you do not say any thing how can I say any thing?

Of the turbid pool that lies in the autumn forest,
Of the moon that descends the steeps of the soughing twilight,
Toss, sparkles of day and dusk—toss on the black stems that decay
    in the muck,
Toss to the moaning gibberish of the dry limbs.

I ascend from the moon, I ascend from the night,
I perceive that the ghastly glimmer is noonday sunbeams reflected,
And debouch to the steady and central from the offspring great or
    small.

51. The past and present wilt—I have fill'd them, emptied them,
    And proceed to fill my next fold of the future.

Listener up there! what have you to confide to me?
Look in my face while I snuff the sidle of evening,
(Talk honestly, no one else hears you, and I stay only a minute
    longer.)

Do I contradict myself?
Very well then I contradict myself,
(I am large, I contain multitudes.)

I concentrate toward them that are nigh, I wait on the door-slab.

Who has done his day's work? who will soonest be through
    with his supper?
Who wishes to walk with me?

Will you speak before I am gone? will you prove already too late?

52. The spotted hawk swoops by and accuses me, he complains of my
    gab and my loitering.

I too am not a bit tamed, I too am untranslatable,
I sound my barbaric yawp over the roofs of the world.

The last scud of day holds back for me,
It flings my likeness after the rest and true as any on the shadow'd
    wilds,
It coaxes me to the vapor and the dusk.

193

I depart as air, I shake my white locks at the runaway sun,
I effuse my flesh in eddies, and drift it in lacy jags.

I bequeath myself to the dirt to grow from the grass I love,
If you want me again look for me under your boot-soles.

You will hardly know who I am or what I mean,
But I shall be good health to you nevertheless,
And filter and fibre your blood.

Failing to fetch me at first keep encouraged,
Missing me one place search another,
I stop somewhere waiting for you.

A SONG FOR OCCUPATIONS

1. A song for occupations!
   In the labor of engines and trades and the labor of fields I find the
         developments,
   And find the eternal meanings.

   Workmen and Workwomen!
   Were all educations practical and ornamental well display'd out of
         me, what would it amount to?
   Were I as the head teacher, charitable proprietor, wise statesman,
         what would it amount to?
   Were I to you as the boss employing and paying you, would that
         satisfy you?

   The learn'd, virtuous, benevolent, and the usual terms,
   A man like me and never the usual terms.

   Neither a servant nor a master I,
   I take no sooner a large price than a small price,
       I will have my own whoever enjoys me,
   I will be even with you and you shall be even with me.
   If you stand at work in a shop I stand as nigh as the nighest in the
         same shop,
   If you bestow gifts on your brother or dearest friend
       I demand as good as your brother or dearest friend,
   If your lover, husband, wife, is welcome by day or night,
       I must be personally as welcome,

If you become degraded, criminal, ill, then I become so for your
        sake,
If you remember your foolish and outlaw'd deeds,
    do you think I cannot remember my own foolish and outlaw'd
        deeds?
If you carouse at the table I carouse at the opposite side of the table,
If you meet some stranger in the streets and love him or her,
    why I often meet strangers in the street and love them.

Why what have you thought of yourself?
Is it you then that thought yourself less?
Is it you that thought the President greater than you?
Or the rich better off than you? or the educated wiser than you? . . .

2. Souls of men and women! it is not you I call unseen,
        unheard, untouchable and untouching,
    It is not you I go argue pro and con about, and to settle whether you
        are alive or no,
    I own publicly who you are, if nobody else owns.

    Grown, half-grown and babe, of this country and every country,
        in-doors and out-doors, one just as much as the other, I see,
    And all else behind or through them.

    The wife, and she is not one jot less than the husband,
    The daughter, and she is just as good as the son,
    The mother, and she is every bit as much as the father.

    Offspring of ignorant and poor, boys apprenticed to trades,
    Young fellows working on farms and old fellows working on farms,
    Sailor-men, merchant-men, coasters, immigrants,
    All these I see, but nigher and farther the same I see,
    None shall escape me and none shall wish to escape me.

    I bring what you much need yet always have,
    Not money, amours, dress, eating, erudition, but as good,
    I send no agent or medium, offer no representative of value,
        but offer the value itself.

    There is something that comes to one now and perpetually,
    It is not what is printed, preach'd, discussed, it eludes discussion
        and print,
    It is not to be put in a book, it is not in this book,
    It is for you whoever you are, it is no farther from you
        than your hearing and sight are from you,

It is hinted by nearest, commonest, readiest, it is ever provoked by
them.

You may read in many languages, yet read nothing about it,
You may read the President's message and read nothing about it
there,
Nothing in the reports from the State department or Treasury department, or in the daily papers or weekly papers,
Or in the census or revenue returns, prices current, or any accounts
of stock.

3. The sun and stars that float in the open air,
The apple-shaped earth and we upon it,
surely the drift of them is something grand,
I do not know what it is except that it is grand, and that it is happiness,
And that the enclosing purport of us here is not a speculation
or bon-mot or reconnoissance,
And that it is not something which by luck may turn out well for us,
and without luck must be a failure for us,
And not something which may yet be retracted in a certain con-
tingency.

The light and shade, the curious sense of body and identity,
the greed that with perfect complaisance devours all things,
The endless pride and outstretching of man, unspeakable joys and
sorrows,
The wonder every one sees in every one else he sees,
and the wonders that fill each minute of time forever,
What have you reckon'd them for, camerado?
Have you reckon'd them for your trade or farm-work?
or for the profits of your store?
Or to achieve yourself a position? or to fill a gentleman's leisure,
or a lady's leisure?

Have you reckon'd that the landscape took substance and form
that it might be painted in a picture?
Or men and women that they might be written of, and songs sung?
Or the attraction of gravity, and the great laws
and harmonious combinations and the fluids of the air,
as subjects for the savans?
Or the brown land and the blue sea for maps and charts?

196

Or the stars to be put in constellations and named fancy names?
Or that the growth of seeds is for agricultural tables,
    or agriculture itself?

Old institutions, these arts, libraries, legends, collections,
    and the practice handed along in manufactures,
    will we rate them so high?
Will we rate our cash and business high? I have no objection,
I rate them as high as the highest—then a child born of a woman
    and man I rate beyond all rate.

We thought our Union grand, and our Constitution grand,
I do not say they are not grand and good, for they are,
I am this day just as much in love with them as you,
Then I am in love with You, and with all my fellows upon the
    earth.

We consider bibles and religions divine—I do not say they are not
    divine,
I say they have all grown out of you, and may grow out of you still,
It is not they who give the life, it is you who give the life,
Leaves are not more shed from the trees, or trees from the earth,
    than they are shed out of you.

4. The sum of all known reverence I add up in you whoever you are,
    The President is there in the White House for you,
        it is not you who are here for him,
    The Secretaries act in their bureaus for you, not you here for them,
    The Congress convenes every Twelfth-month for you,
    Laws, courts, the forming of States, the charters of cities,
        the going and coming of commerce and mails, are all for you.

    List close my scholars dear,
    Doctrines, politics and civilization exurge from you,
    Sculpture and monuments and any thing inscribed anywhere are
        tallied in you,
    The gist of histories and statistics as far back as the records reach
        is in you this hour, and myths and tales the same,
    If you were not breathing and walking here, where would they
        all be?
    The most renown'd poems would be ashes,
        orations and plays would be vacuums.

                                                        197

All architecture is what you do to it when you look upon it,
(Did you think it was in the white or gray stone?
   or the lines of the arches and cornices?)

All music is what awakes from you when you are reminded
      by the instruments,
It is not the violins and the cornets, it is not the oboe nor the beat-
            ing drums, nor the score of the baritone singer singing his
            sweet romanza, nor that of the men's chorus, nor that of
            the women's chorus,
It is nearer and farther than they.

CITY OF ORGIES

City of orgies, walks and joys,
City whom that I have liv'd and sung in your midst
      will one day make you illustrious,
Not the pageants of you, not your shifting tableaus, your spectacles,
      repay me,
Not the interminable rows of your houses, nor the ships at the wharves,
Nor the processions in the streets, nor the bright windows with goods
      in them,
Nor to converse with learn'd persons, or bear my share in the soiree or
      feast;
Not those, but as I pass O Manhattan, your frequent and swift flash of
      eyes offering me love,
Offering response to my own—these repay me,
Lovers, continual lovers, only repay me.

FOR YOU, O DEMOCRACY

Come, I will make the continent indissoluble,
I will make the most splendid race the sun ever shone upon,
I will make divine magnetic lands,
            With the love of comrades,
            With the life-long love of comrades.

I will plant companionship thick as trees along all the rivers of America,
      and along the shores of the great lakes, and all over the prairies,
I will make inseparable cities with their arms about each other's necks,
            By the love of comrades,
            By the manly love of comrades.

198

For you these from me, O Democracy, to serve you ma femme!
For you, for you I am trilling these songs.

TO THE STATES

To the States or any one of them, or any city of the States, *Resist much,*
    obey little,
Once unquestioning obedience, once fully enslaved,
Once fully enslaved, no nation, state, city of this earth,
    ever afterward resumes its liberty.

SONG OF THE OPEN ROAD

1. Afoot and light-hearted I take to the open road,
     Healthy, free, the world before me,
     The long brown path before me leading wherever I choose.

     Henceforth I ask not good-fortune, I myself am good-fortune,
     Henceforth I whimper no more, postpone no more, need nothing,
     Done with indoor complaints, libraries, querulous criticisms,
     Strong and content I travel the open road.

     The earth, that is sufficient,
     I do not want the constellations any nearer,
     I know they are very well where they are,
     I know they suffice for those who belong to them.

     (Still here I carry my old delicious burdens,
     I carry them, men and women, I carry them with me wherever I go,
     I swear it is impossible for me to get rid of them,
     I am fill'd with them, and I will fill them in return.)

3. You air that serves me with breath to speak!
     You objects that call from diffusion my meanings and give them
         shape!
     You light that wraps me and all things in delicate equable showers!
     You paths worn in the irregular hollows by the roadsides!
     I believe you are latent with unseen existences, you are so dear
         to me.

You flagg'd walks of the cities! you strong curbs at the edges!
You ferries! you planks and posts of wharves! you timber-lined
    sides! you distant ships!
You rows of houses! you window-pierc'd façades! you roofs!
You porches and entrances! you copings and iron guards!
You windows whose transparent shells might expose so much!
You doors and ascending steps! you arches!
You gray stones of interminable pavements! you trodden crossings!
From all that has touch'd you I believe you have imparted to
    yourselves, and now would impart the same secretly to me,
From the living and the dead you have peopled your impassive
    surfaces, and the spirits thereof would be evident and
    amicable with me.

4. The earth expanding right hand and left hand,
   The picture alive, every part in its best light,
   The music falling in where it is wanted, and stopping where it is
       not wanted,
   The cheerful voice of the public road, the gay fresh sentiment of
       the road.

   O highway I travel, do you say to me, *Do not leave me?*
   Do you say, *Venture not—if you leave me you are lost?*
   Do you say, *I am already prepared, I am well-beaten and undenied,
       adhere to me?*

   O public road, I say back I am not afraid to leave you, yet I love you,
   You express me better than I can express myself,
   You shall be more to me than my poem.

   I think heroic deeds were all conceiv'd in the open air, and all free
       poems also,
   I think I could stop here myself and do miracles,
   I think whatever I shall meet on the road I shall like,
       and whoever beholds me shall like me,
   I think whoever I see must be happy.

5. From this hour I ordain myself loos'd of limits and imaginary lines,
   Going where I list, my own master total and absolute,
   Listening to others, considering well what they say,
   Pausing, searching, receiving, contemplating,
   Gently, but with undeniable will, divesting myself of the holds
       that would hold me.

200

I inhale great draughts of space,
The east and the west are mine, and the north and the south are
      mine.

I am larger, better than I thought,
I did not know I held so much goodness.

All seems beautiful to me,
I can repeat over to men and women, You have done such good to me
      I would do the same to you,
I will recruit for myself and you as I go,
I will scatter myself among men and women as I go,
I will toss a new gladness and roughness among them,
Whoever denies me it shall not trouble me,
Whoever accepts me he or she shall be blessed and shall bless me.

6. Now if a thousand perfect men were to appear it would not amaze
      me,
Now if a thousand beautiful forms of women appear'd
      it would not astonish me.

Now I see the secret of the making of the best persons,
It is to grow in the open air and to eat and sleep with the earth.

Here a great personal deed has room,
(Such a deed seizes upon the hearts of the whole race of men,
Its effusion of strength and will overwhelms law and mocks all
      authority and all argument against it.)

Here is the test of wisdom,
Wisdom is not finally tested in schools,
Wisdom cannot be pass'd from one having it to another not having
      it,
Wisdom is of the soul, is not susceptible of proof, is its own proof,
Applies to all stages and objects and qualities and is content,
Is the certainty of the reality and immortality of things,
      and the excellence of things;
Something there is in the float of the sight of things
      that provokes it out of the soul.

Now I re-examine philosophies and religions,
They may prove well in lecture-rooms, yet not prove at all
      under the spacious clouds and along the landscape and flowing
      currents.

201

Here is realization,
Here is a man tallied—he realizes here what he has in him,
The past, the future, majesty, love—if they are vacant of you,
    you are vacant of them.

Only the kernel of every object nourishes;
Where is he who tears off the husks for you and me?
Where is he that undoes stratagems and envelopes for you and me?

Here is adhesiveness, it is not previously fashion'd, it is apropos;
Do you know what it is as you pass to be loved by strangers?
Do you know the talk of those turning eye-balls?

9. Allons! whoever you are come travel with me!
Traveling with me you find what never tires.

The earth never tires,
The earth is rude, silent, incomprehensible at first,
    Nature is rude and incomprehensible at first,
Be not discouraged, keep on, there are divine things well envelop'd,
I swear to you there are divine things more beautiful
    than words can tell.

Allons! we must not stop here,
However sweet these laid-up stores, however convenient this
    dwelling we cannot remain here,
However shelter'd this port and however calm these waters
    we must not anchor here,
However welcome the hospitality that surrounds us
    we are permitted to receive it but a little while.

11. Listen! I will be honest with you,
I do not offer the old smooth prizes, but offer rough new prizes,
These are the days that must happen to you:
You shall not heap up what is call'd riches,
You shall scatter with lavish hand all that you earn or achieve,
You but arrive at the city to which you were destin'd, you hardly
    settle yourself to satisfaction before you are call'd by an
    irresistible call to depart,
You shall be treated to the ironical smiles and mockings
    of those who remain behind you,
What beckonings of love you receive you shall only answer
    with passionate kisses of parting,

202

You shall not allow the hold of those who spread their reach'd hands toward you.

12. Allons! after the great Companions, and to belong to them!
They too are on the road—they are the swift and majestic men—
    they are the greatest women,
Enjoyers of calms of seas and storms of seas,
Sailors of many a ship, walkers of many a mile of land,
Habitués of many distant countries, habitués of far-distant dwell-
    ings,
Trusters of men and women, observers of cities, solitary toilers,
Pausers and contemplators of tufts, blossoms, shells of the shore,
Dancers at wedding-dances, kissers of brides, tender helpers of
    children, bearers of children,
Soldiers of revolts, standers by gaping graves, lowerers-down of
    coffins,
Journeyers over consecutive seasons, over the years, the curious years
    each emerging from that which preceded it,
Journeyers as with companions, namely their own diverse phases,
Forth-steppers from the latent unrealized baby-days,
Journeyers gayly with their own youth, journeyers with their bearded
    and well-grain'd manhood,
Journeyers with their womanhood, ample, unsurpass'd, content,
Journeyers with their own sublime old age of manhood or woman-
    hood,
Old age, calm, expanded, broad with the haughty breadth of the
    universe,
Old age, flowing free with the delicious near-by freedom of death.

13. Allons! to that which is endless as it was beginningless,
To undergo much, tramps of days, rests of nights,
To merge all in the travel they tend to, and the days and nights
    they tend to,
Again to merge them in the start of superior journeys,
To see nothing anywhere but what you may reach it and pass it,
To conceive no time, however distant, but what you may reach it
    and pass it,
To look up or down no road but it stretches and waits for you,
    however long but it stretches and waits for you,
To see no being, not God's or any, but you also go thither,
To see no possession but you may possess it,
    enjoying all without labor or purchase, abstracting the feast
    yet not abstracting one particle of it,

To take the best of the farmer's farm and the rich man's elegant
  villa, and the chaste blessings of the well-married couple,
  and the fruits of orchards and flowers of gardens,
To take to your use out of the compact cities as you pass through,
To carry buildings and streets with you afterward wherever you go,
To gather the minds of men out of their brains as you encounter
  them, to gather the love out of their hearts,
To take your lovers on the road with you, for all that
  you leave them behind you,
To know the universe itself as a road, as many roads,
  as roads for traveling souls.

All parts away for the progress of souls,
All religion, all solid things, arts, governments—all that was or is
  apparent upon this globe or any globe, falls into niches
  and corners before the procession of souls along the grand
  roads of the universe.

Of the progress of the souls of men and women along the grand
  roads of the universe, all other progress is the needed
  emblem and sustenance.

Forever alive, forever forward,
Stately, solemn, sad, withdrawn, baffled, mad, turbulent, feeble,
  dissatisfied,
Desperate, proud, fond, sick, accepted by men, rejected by men,
They go! they go! I know that they go, but I know not where they
  go,
But I know that they go toward the best—toward something great.

Whoever you are, come forth! or man or woman come forth!
You must not stay sleeping and dallying there in the house,
  though you built it, or though it has been built for you.

Out of the dark confinement! out from behind the screen!
It is useless to protest, I know all and expose it.

Behold through you as bad as the rest,
Through the laughter, dancing, dining, supping, of people,
204

Inside of dresses and ornaments, inside of those wash'd and trimm'd faces,
Behold a secret silent loathing and despair.

No husband, no wife, no friend, trusted to hear the confession,
Another self, a duplicate of every one, skulking and hiding it goes,
Formless and wordless through the streets of the cities,
    polite and bland in the parlors,
In the cars of railroads, in steamboats, in the public assembly,
Home to the houses of men and women, at the table,
    in the bedroom, everywhere,
Smartly attired, countenance smiling, form upright,
    death under the breast-bones, hell under the skull-bones,
Under the broadcloth and gloves, under the ribbons and artificial flowers,
Keeping fair with the customs, speaking not a syllable of itself,
Speaking of any thing else but never of itself.

14. Allons! through struggles and wars!
The goal that was named cannot be countermanded.

Have the past struggles succeeded?
What has succeeded? yourself? your nation? Nature?
Now understand me well—it is provided in the essence of things
    that from any fruition of success, no matter what,
    shall come forth something to make a greater struggle necessary.

My call is the call of battle, I nourish active rebellion,
He going with me must go well arm'd,
He going with me goes often with spare diet, poverty,
    angry enemies, desertions.

15. Allons! the road is before us!
It is safe—I have tried it—my own feet have tried it well—be not detain'd!
Let the paper remain on the desk unwritten, and the book on the shelf unopen'd!
Let the tools remain in the workshop! let the money remain unearn'd!
Let the school stand! mind not the cry of the teacher!
Let the preacher preach in his pulpit! let the lawyer plead in the court, and the judge expound the law.

Camerado, I give you my hand!
I give you my love more precious than money,
I give you myself before preaching or law;
Will you give me yourself? will you come travel with me?
Shall we stick by each other as long as we live?

ONCE I PASS'D THROUGH A POPULOUS CITY

Once I pass'd through a populous city imprinting my brain for future use,
    with its shows, architecture, customs, traditions,
Yet now of all that city I remember only a woman I casually met there
    who detain'd me for love of me,
Day by day and night by night we were together—
    all else has long been forgotten by me,
I remember I say only that woman who passionately clung to me,
Again we wander, we love, we separate again,
Again she holds me by the hand, I must not go,
I see her close beside me with silent lips sad and tremulous.

OUT OF THE CRADLE ENDLESSLY ROCKING

Out of the cradle endlessly rocking,
Out of the mocking-bird's throat, the musical shuttle,
Out of the Ninth-month midnight,
Over the sterile sands and the fields beyond, where the child
    leaving his bed wander'd alone, bareheaded, barefoot,
Down from the shower'd halo,
Up from the mystic play of shadows twining and twisting
    as if they were alive,
Out from the patches of briers and blackberries,
From the memories of the bird that chanted to me,
From your memories sad brother, from the fitful risings
    and fallings I heard,
From under that yellow half-moon late-risen and swollen as if with
    tears,
From those beginning notes of yearning and love there in the mist,
From the thousand responses of my heart never to cease,
From the myriad thence-arous'd words,
From the word stronger and more delicious than any,

206

From such as now they start the scene revisiting,
As a flock, twittering, rising, or overhead passing,
Borne hither, ere all eludes me, hurriedly,
A man, yet by these tears a little boy again,
Throwing myself on the sand, confronting the waves,
I, chanter of pains and joys, uniter of here and hereafter,
Taking all hints to use them, but swiftly leaping beyond them,
A reminiscence sing.

Once Paumanok,
When the lilac-scent was in the air and Fifth-month grass was growing,
Up this seashore in some briers,
Two feather'd guests from Alabama, two together,
And their nest, and four light-green eggs spotted with brown,
And every day the he-bird to and fro near at hand,
And every day the she-bird crouch'd on her nest, silent, with bright eyes,
And every day I, a curious boy, never too close, never disturbing them,
Cautiously peering, absorbing, translating.

Shine! shine! shine!
Pour down your warmth, great sun!
While we bask, we two together.

Two together!
Winds blow south, or winds blow north,
Day come white, or night come black,
Home, or rivers and mountains from home,
Singing all time, minding no time,
While we two keep together.

Till of a sudden,
May-be kill'd, unknown to her mate,
One forenoon the she-bird crouch'd not on the nest,
Nor return'd that afternoon, nor the next,
Nor ever appear'd again.

And thenceforward all summer in the sound of the sea,
And at night under the full of the moon in calmer weather,
Over the hoarse surging of the sea,
Or flitting from brier to brier by day,
I saw, I heard at intervals the remaining one, the he-bird,
The solitary guest from Alabama.

207

Blow! blow! blow!
Blow up sea-winds along Paumanok's shore;
I wait and I wait till you blow my mate to me.

Yes, when the stars glisten'd,
All night long on the prong of a moss-scallop'd stake,
Down almost amid the slapping waves,
Sat the lone singer wonderful causing tears.

He call'd on his mate,
He pour'd forth the meanings which I of all men know.

Yes my brother I know,
The rest might not, but I have treasur'd every note,
For more than once dimly down to the beach gliding,
Silent, avoiding the moonbeams, blending myself with the shadows,
Recalling now the obscure shapes, the echoes,
    the sounds and sights after their sorts,
The white arms out in the breakers tirelessly tossing,
I, with bare feet, a child, the wind wafting my hair,
Listen'd long and long.

Listen'd to keep, to sing, now translating the notes,
Following you my brother.

Soothe! soothe! soothe!
Close on its wave soothes the wave behind,
And again another behind embracing and lapping, every one close,
But my love soothes not me, not me.

Low hangs the moon, it rose late,
It is lagging—O I think it is heavy with love, with love.

O madly the sea pushes upon the land,
With love, with love.

O night! do I not see my love fluttering out among the breakers?
What is that little black thing I see there in the white?

Loud! loud! loud!
Loud I call to you, my love!
High and clear I shoot my voice over the waves,
Surely you must know who is here, is here,
You must know who I am, my love.

208

Low-hanging moon!
What is that dusky spot in your brown yellow?
O it is the shape, the shape of my mate!
O moon do not keep her from me any longer.

Land! land! O land!
Whichever way I turn, O I think you could give me my mate
*   back again if you only would,*
For I am almost sure I see her dimly whichever way I look.

O rising stars!
Perhaps the one I want so much will rise, will rise with some of you.

O throat! O trembling throat!
Sound clearer through the atmosphere!
Pierce the woods, the earth,
Somewhere listening to catch you must be the one I want.

Shake out carols!
Solitary here, the night's carols!
Carols of lonesome love! death's carols!
Carols under that lagging, yellow, waning moon!
O under that moon where she droops almost down into the sea!
O reckless despairing carols.

But soft! sink low!
Soft! let me just murmur,
And do you wait a moment you husky-nois'd sea,
For somewhere I believe I heard my mate responding to me,
So faint, I must be still, be still to listen,
But not altogether still, for then she might not come immediately to me.

Hither my love!
Here I am! here!
With this just-sustain'd note I announce myself to you,
This gentle call is for you my love, for you.

Do not be decoy'd elsewhere,
That is the whistle of the wind, it is not my voice,
That is the fluttering, the fluttering of the spray,
Those are the shadows of leaves.

O darkness! O in vain!
O I am very sick and sorrowful.

209

O brown halo in the sky near the moon, drooping upon the sea!
O troubled reflection in the sea!
O throat! O throbbing heart!
And I singing uselessly, uselessly all the night.

O past! O happy life! O songs of joy!
In the air, in the woods, over fields,
Loved! loved! loved! loved! loved!
But my mate no more, no more with me!
We two together no more.

The aria sinking,
All else continuing, the stars shining,
The winds blowing, the notes of the bird continuous echoing,
With angry moans the fierce old mother incessantly moaning,
On the sands of Paumanok's shore gray and rustling,
The yellow half-moon enlarged, sagging down, drooping,
    the face of the sea almost touching,
The boy ecstatic, with his bare feet the waves,
    with his hair the atmosphere dallying,
The love in the heart long pent, now loose, now at last tumultuously
    bursting,
The aria's meaning, the ears, the soul, swiftly depositing,
The strange tears down the cheeks coursing,
The colloquy there, the trio, each uttering,
The undertone, the savage old mother incessantly crying,
To the boy's soul's questions sullenly timing, some drown'd secret hiss-
    ing,
To the outsetting bard.

Demon or bird! (said the boy's soul,)
Is it indeed toward your mate you sing? or is it really to me?
For I, that was a child, my tongue's use sleeping, now I have heard you,
Now in a moment I know what I am for, I awake,
And already a thousand singers, a thousand songs,
    clearer, louder and more sorrowful than yours,
A thousand warbling echoes have started to life within me, never to die.

O you singer solitary, singing by yourself, projecting me,
O solitary me listening, never more shall I cease perpetuating you,
Never more shall I escape, never more the reverberations,
Never more the cries of unsatisfied love be absent from me,
Never again leave me to be the peaceful child I was before
    what there in the night,

210

By the sea under the yellow and sagging moon,
The messenger there arous'd, the fire, the sweet hell within,
The unknown want, the destiny of me.

O give me the clue! (it lurks in the night here somewhere,)
O if I am to have so much, let me have more!

A word then, (for I will conquer it,)
The word final, superior to all,
Subtle, sent up—what is it?—I listen;
Are you whispering it, and have been all the time, you sea-waves?
Is that it from your liquid rims and wet sands?

Whereto answering, the sea,
Delaying not, hurrying not,
Whisper'd me through the night, and very plainly before daybreak,
Lisp'd to me the low and delicious word death,
And again death, death, death, death,
Hissing melodious, neither like the bird nor like my arous'd child's
        heart,
But edging near as privately for me rustling at my feet,
Creeping thence steadily up to my ears and laving me softly all over,
Death, death, death, death, death.

Which I do not forget,
But fuse the song of my dusky demon and brother,
That he sang to me in the moonlight on Paumanok's gray beach,
With the thousand responsive songs at random,
My own songs awaked from that hour,
And with them the key, the word up from the waves,
The word of the sweetest song and all songs,
That strong and delicious word which, creeping to my feet,
(Or like some old crone rocking the cradle,
        swathed in sweet garments, bending aside,)
The sea whisper'd me.

STARTING FROM PAUMANOK

1. Starting from fish-shape Paumanok where I was born,
    Well-begotten, and rais'd by a perfect mother,
    After roaming many lands, lover of populous pavements,
    Dweller in Mannahatta my city, or on southern savannas,

211

Or a soldier camp'd or carrying my knapsack and gun, or a miner
    in California,
Or rude in my home in Dakota's woods, my diet meat, my drink
    from the spring,
Or withdrawn to muse and meditate in some deep recess,
Far from the clank of crowds intervals passing rapt and happy,
Aware of the fresh free giver the flowing Missouri,
    aware of mighty Niagara,
Aware of the buffalo herds grazing the plains, the hirsute
    and strong-breasted bull,
Of earth, rocks, Fifth-month flowers experienced, stars, rain,
    snow, my amaze,
Having studied the mocking-bird's tones and the flight of the
    mountain-hawk,
And heard at dawn the unrivall'd one, the hermit thrush
    from the swamp-cedars,
Solitary, singing in the West, I strike up for a New World.

4. Take my leaves America, take them South and take them North,
Make welcome for them everywhere, for they are your own
    offspring,
Surround them East and West, for they would surround you,
And you precedents, connect lovingly with them, for they connect
    lovingly with you.

I conn'd old times,
I sat studying at the feet of the great masters,
Now if eligible O that the great masters might return and study
    me.

In the name of these States shall I scorn the antique?
Why these are the children of the antique to justify it.

6. The soul,
Forever and forever—longer than soil is brown and solid—
    longer than water ebbs and flows.

I will make the poems of materials, for I think they are to be
    the most spiritual poems,
And I will make the poems of my body and of mortality,
For I think I shall then supply myself with the poems of my soul
    and of immortality.

212

I will make a song for these States that no one State may under
any circumstances be subjected to another State,
And I will make a song that there shall be comity by day and by
night between all the States, and between any two of them,
And I will make a song for the ears of the President, full of
weapons with menacing points,
And behind the weapons countless dissatisfied faces;
And a song make I of the One form'd out of all,
The fang'd and glittering One whose head is over all,
Resolute warlike One including and over all,
(However high the head of any else that head is over all.)

I will acknowledge contemporary lands,
I will trail the whole geography of the globe and salute courteously
every city large and small,
And employments! I will put in my poems that with you is heroism
upon land and sea,
And I will report all heroism from an American point of view.

I will sing the song of companionship,
I will show what alone must finally compact these,
I believe these are to found their own ideal of manly love,
indicating it in me,
I will therefore let flame from me the burning fires that were
threatening to consume me,
I will lift what has too long kept down those smouldering fires,
I will give them complete abandonment,
I will write the evangel-poem of comrades and of love,
For who but I should understand love with all its sorrow and joy?
And who but I should be the poet of comrades?

10. Know you, solely to drop in the earth the germs of a greater
religion,
The following chants each for its kind I sing.

My comrade!
For you to share with me two greatnesses, and a third one rising
inclusive and more resplendent,
The greatness of Love and Democracy, and the greatness of
Religion. . . .

O such themes—equalities! O divine average!
Warblings under the sun, usher'd as now, or at noon, or setting,

213

Strains musical flowing through ages, now reaching hither,
I take to your reckless and composite chords, add to them,
　　and cheerfully pass them forward.

13.　Was somebody asking to see the soul?
See, your own shape and countenance, persons, substances, beasts,
　　the trees, the running rivers, the rocks and sands.

All hold spiritual joys and afterwards loosen them;
How can the real body ever die and be buried?

Of your real body and any man's or woman's real body,
Item for item it will elude the hands of the corpse-cleaners
　　and pass to fitting spheres,
Carrying what has accrued to it from the moment of birth
　　to the moment of death.

Not the types set up by the printer return their impression,
　　the meaning, the main concern,
Any more than a man's substance and life or a woman's substance
　　and life return in the body and the soul,
Indifferently before death and after death.

Behold, the body includes and is the meaning, the main concern,
　　and includes and is the soul;
Whoever you are, how superb and how divine is your body,
　　or any part of it!

14.　Whoever you are, to you endless announcements!

Daughter of the lands did you wait for your poet?
Did you wait for one with a flowing mouth and indicative hand?

Toward the male of the States, and toward the female of the States,
Exulting words, words to Democracy's lands.

Interlink'd, food-yielding lands!
Land of coal and iron! land of gold! land of cotton, sugar, rice!
Land of wheat, beef, pork! land of wool and hemp!
　　land of the apple and the grape!
Land of the pastoral plains, the grass-fields of the world!
　　land of those sweet-air'd interminable plateaus!
Land of the herd, the garden, the healthy house of adobie!
Lands where the north-west Columbia winds,
　　and where the south-west Colorado winds!

Land of the eastern Chesapeake! land of the Delaware!
Land of Ontario, Erie, Huron, Michigan!
Land of the Old Thirteen! Massachusetts land!
    land of Vermont and Connecticut!
Land of the ocean shores! land of sierras and peaks!
Land of boatmen and sailors! fishermen's land!
Inextricable lands! the clutch'd together! the passionate ones!
The side by side! the elder and younger brothers! the bony-limb'd!
The great women's land! the feminine! the experienced sisters
    and the inexperienced sisters!
Far breath'd land! Arctic braced! Mexican breez'd! the diverse! the
        compact!
The Pennsylvanian! the Virginian! the double Carolinian!
O all and each well-loved by me! my intrepid nations!
    O I at any rate include you all with perfect love!
I cannot be discharged from you! not from one any sooner than
        another!
O death! O for all that, I am yet of you unseen this hour
    with irrepressible love,
Walking New England, a friend, a traveler,
Splashing my bare feet in the edge of the summer ripples on
        Paumanok's sands,
Crossing the prairies, dwelling again in Chicago, dwelling in every
        town,
Observing shows, births, improvements, structures, arts,
Listening to orators and oratresses in public halls,
Of and through the States as during life, each man and woman
        my neighbor,
The Louisianian, the Georgian, as near to me, and I as near to him
        and her,
The Mississippian and Arkansian yet with me, and I yet with any
        of them,
Yet upon the plains west of the spinal river, yet in my house of
        adobie,
Yet returning eastward, yet in the Seaside State or in Maryland,
Yet Kanadian cheerily braving the winter, the snow and ice wel-
        come to me,
Yet a true son either of Maine or of the Granite State,
    or the Narragansett Bay State, or the Empire State,
Yet sailing to other shores to annex the same,
    yet welcoming every new brother,

Hereby applying these leaves to the new ones from the hour
    they unite with the old ones,
Coming among the new ones myself to be their companion and
    equal, coming personally to you now,
Enjoining you to acts, characters, spectacles, with me.

15.   With me with firm holding, yet haste, haste on.

For your life adhere to me,
(I may have to be persuaded many times before I consent to give
    myself really to you, but what of that?
Must not Nature be persuaded many times?)

No dainty dolce affettuoso I,
Bearded, sun-burnt, grey-neck'd, forbidding, I have arrived,
To be wrestled with as I pass for the solid prizes of the universe,
For such I afford whoever can persevere to win them.

18.   See, steamers steaming through my poems,
See, in my poems immigrants continually coming and landing,
See, in arriere, the wigwam, the trail, the hunter's hut, the flat-boat,
    the maize-leaf, the claim, the rude fence, and the backwoods
    village,
See, on the one side the Western Sea and on the other the Eastern
    Sea, how they advance and retreat upon my poems as upon
    their own shores,
See, pastures and forests in my poems—see, animals wild and
    tame—see, beyond the Kaw, countless herds of buffalo
    feeding on short curly grass,
See, in my poems, cities, solid, vast, inland, with paved streets,
    with iron and stone edifices, ceaseless vehicles, and commerce,
See, the many-cylinder'd steam printing-press—see, the electric tele-
    graph stretching across the continent,
See, through Atlantica's depths pulses American, Europe reaching,
    pulses of Europe duly return'd,
See, the strong and quick locomotive as it departs,
    panting, blowing the steam-whistle,
See, ploughmen ploughing farms—see, miners digging mines—
    see, the numberless factories,
See, mechanics busy at their benches with tools—see from among
    them superior judges, philosophs, Presidents, emerge, drest
    in working dresses,

See, lounging through the shops and fields of the States,
    me well-belov'd, close-held by day and night,
Hear the loud echoes of my songs there—read the hints come at
    last.

19. O camerado close! O you and me at last, and us two only.

O a word to clear one's path ahead endlessly!
O something ecstatic and undemonstrable! O music wild!
O now I triumph—and you shall also;
O hand in hand—O wholesome pleasure—O one more desirer and
    lover!
O to haste firm holding—to haste, haste on with me.

TO A FOIL'D EUROPEAN REVOLUTIONAIRE

Courage yet, my brother or my sister!
Keep on—Liberty is to be subserv'd whatever occurs;
That is nothing that is quell'd by one or two failures, or any number
    of failures,
Or by the indifference or ingratitude of the people, or by any unfaith-
    fulness,
Or the show of the tushes of power, soldiers, cannon, penal statutes.

What we believe in waits latent forever through all the continents,
Invites no one, promises nothing, sits in calmness and light,
    is positive and composed, knows no discouragement,
Waiting patiently, waiting its time.

(Not songs of loyalty alone are these,
But songs of insurrection also,
For I am the sworn poet of every dauntless rebel the world over,
And he going with me leaves peace and routine behind him,
And stakes his life to be lost at any moment.)

The battle rages with many a loud alarm and frequent advance and
    retreat,
The infidel triumphs, or supposes he triumphs,
The prison, scaffold, garrote, handcuffs, iron necklace
    and lead-balls do their work,
The named and unnamed heroes pass to other spheres,

217

The great speakers and writers are exiled, they lie sick in distant lands,
The cause is asleep, the strongest throats are choked with their own
blood,
The young men droop their eyelashes toward the ground when they
meet;
But for all this Liberty has not gone out of the place,
  nor the infidel enter'd into full possession.

When liberty goes out of a place it is not the first to go,
  nor the second or third to go,
It waits for all the rest to go, it is the last.

When there are no more memories of heroes and martyrs,
And when all life and all the souls of men and women are discharged
  from any part of the earth,
Then only shall liberty or the idea of liberty be discharged
  from that part of the earth,
And the infidel come into full possession.

Then encourage European revolter, revoltress!
For till all ceases neither must you cease.

I do not know what you are for, (I do not know what I am for myself,
  nor what any thing is for,)
But I will search carefully for it even in being foil'd,
In defeat, poverty, misconception, imprisonment—for they too are great.

Did we think victory great?
So it is—but now it seems to me, when it cannot be help'd,
  that defeat is great,
And that death and dismay are great.

BY BLUE ONTARIO'S SHORE

1. By blue Ontario's shore,
    As I mused of these warlike days and of peace return'd,
      and the dead that return no more,
    A Phantom gigantic superb, with stern visage accosted me,
    Chant me the poem, it said, *that comes from the soul of America,*
      chant me the carol of victory,
    And strike up the marches of Libertad, marches more powerful yet,
    And sing me before you go the song of the throes of Democracy.

(Democracy, the destin'd conqueror, yet treacherous lip-smiles
    everywhere,
And death and infidelity at every step.)

2. A Nation announcing itself,
    I myself make the only growth by which I can be appreciated,
    I reject none, accept all, then reproduce all in my own forms.

    A breed whose proof is in time and deeds,
    What we are we are, nativity is answer enough to objections,
    We wield ourselves as a weapon is wielded.

    We are powerful and tremendous in ourselves,
    We are executive in ourselves, we are sufficient in the variety of
        ourselves,
    We are the most beautiful to ourselves and in ourselves,
    We stand self-pois'd in the middle, branching thence over the
        world,
    From Missouri, Nebraska, or Kansas, laughing attacks to scorn.

    Nothing is sinful to us outside of ourselves,
    Whatever appears, whatever does not appear,
        we are beautiful or sinful in ourselves only.

    (O Mother—O Sisters dear!
    If we are lost, no victor else has destroy'd us,
    It is by ourselves we go down to eternal night.)

3. Have you thought there could be but a single supreme?
    There can be any number of supremes—one does not countervail
        another any more than one eyesight countervails another,
        or one life countervails another.

    All is eligible to all,
    All is for individuals, all is for you,
    No condition is prohibited, not God's or any.

    All comes by the body, only health puts you rapport with the
        universe.

    Produce great Persons, the rest follows.

4. Piety and conformity to them that like,
    Peace, obesity, allegiance, to them that like,
    I am he who tauntingly compels men, women, nations,
    Crying, Leap from your seats and contend for your lives!

219

I am he who walks the States with a barb'd tongue,
    questioning every one I meet,
Who are you that wanted only to be told what you knew before?
Who are you that wanted only a book to join you in your nonsense?

(With pangs and cries as thine own O bearer of many children,
These clamors wild to a race of pride I give.)

O lands, would you be freer than all that has ever been before?
If you would be freer than all that has been before, come listen
    to me.

Fear grace, elegance, civilization, delicatesse,
Fear the mellow sweet, the sucking of honey-juice,
Beware the advancing mortal ripening of Nature,
Beware what precedes the decay of the ruggedness of states and
    men.

5. Ages, precedents, have long been accumulating undirected mate-
        rials,
    America brings builders, and brings its own styles.

The immortal poets of Asia and Europe have done their work
        and pass'd to other spheres,
A work remains, the work of surpassing all they have done.

America, curious toward foreign characters, stands by its own at
        all hazards,
Stands removed, spacious, composite, sound, initiates the true use
        of precedents,
Does not repel them or the past or what they have produced under
        their forms,
Takes the lesson with calmness, perceives the corpse slowly borne
        from the house,
Perceives that it waits a little while in the door, that it was fittest
        for its days,
That its life has descended to the stalwart and well-shaped heir
        who approaches,
And that he shall be fittest for his days.

Any period one nation must lead,
One land must be the promise and reliance of the future.

These States are the amplest poem,
Here is not merely a nation but a teeming Nation of nations,

220

Here the doings of men correspond with the broadcast doings
    of the day and night,
Here is what moves in magnificent masses careless of particulars,
Here are the roughs, beards, friendliness, combativeness, the soul
    loves,
Here the flowing trains, here the crowds, equality, diversity, the
    soul loves.

8. Others take finish, but the Republic is ever constructive and ever
    keeps vista,
Others adorn the past, but you O days of the present, I adorn you,
O days of the future I believe in you—I isolate myself for your
    sake,
O America because you build for mankind I build for you,
O well-beloved stone-cutters, I lead them who plan with decision
    and science,
Lead the present with friendly hand toward the future.

(Bravas to all impulses sending sane children to the next age!
But damn that which spends itself with no thought of the stain,
    pains, dismay, feebleness, it is bequeathing.)

9. I listened to the Phantom by Ontario's shore,
I heard the voice arising demanding bards,
By them all native and grand, by them alone can these States be
    fused into the compact organism of a Nation.

To hold men together by paper and seal or by compulsion is no
    account,
That only holds men together which aggregates all in a living
    principle, as the hold of the limbs of the body or the
    fibres of plants.

Of all races and eras these States with veins full of poetical stuff
    most need poets, and are to have the greatest, and use them
    the greatest,
Their Presidents shall not be their common referee so much
    as their poets shall.

(Soul of love and tongue of fire!
Eye to pierce the deepest deeps and sweep the world!
Ah Mother, prolific and full in all besides, yet how long barren,
    barren?)

10. Of these States the poet is the equable man,
      Not in him but off from him things are grotesque, eccentric,
          fail of their full returns,
      Nothing out of its place is good, nothing in its place is bad,
      He bestows on every object or quality its fit proportion, neither
          more nor less,
      He is the arbiter of the diverse, he is the key,
      He is the equalizer of his age and land,
      He supplies what wants supplying, he checks what wants checking,
      In peace out of him speaks the spirit of peace, large, rich, thrifty,
          building populous towns, encouraging agriculture, arts, com-
          merce, lighting the study of man, the soul, health, immortality,
          government,
      In war he is the best backer of the war,
        he fetches artillery as good as the engineer's,
        he can make every word he speaks draw blood,
      The years straying toward infidelity he withholds by his steady
          faith,
      He is no arguer, he is judgment, (Nature accepts him absolutely,)
      He judges not as the judge judges but as the sun falling round a
          helpless thing,
      As he sees the farthest he has the most faith,
      His thoughts are the hymns of the praise of things,
      In the dispute on God and eternity he is silent,
      He sees eternity less like a play with a prologue and denouement,
      He sees eternity in men and women,
        he does not see men and women as dreams or dots.

      For the great Idea, the idea of perfect and free individuals,
      For that, the bard walks in advance, leader of leaders,
      The attitude of him cheers up slaves and horrifies foreign despots.

      Without extinction is Liberty, without retrograde is Equality,
      They live in the feelings of young men and the best women,
      (Not for nothing have the indomitable heads of the earth
          been always ready to fall for Liberty.)

11. For the great Idea,
      That, O my brethren, that is the mission of poets.

      Songs of stern defiance ever ready,
      Songs of the rapid arming and the march,
      The flag of peace quick-folded, and instead the flag we know,
      Warlike flag of the great Idea.

222

(Angry cloth I saw there leaping!
I stand again in leaden rain your flapping folds saluting,
I sing you over all, flying beckoning through the fight—
O the hard-contested fight!
The cannons ope their rosy-flashing muzzles—the hurtled balls
scream,
The battle-front forms amid the smoke—
the volleys pour incessant from the line,
Hark, the ringing word *Charge!*—
now the tussle and the furious maddening yells,
Now the corpses tumble curl'd upon the ground,
Cold, cold in death, for precious life of you,
Angry cloth I saw there leaping.)

13. Rhymes and rhymers pass away,
poems distill'd from poems pass away,
The swarms of reflectors and the polite pass, and leave ashes,
Admirers, importers, obedient persons, make but the soil of liter-
ature,
America justifies itself, give it time, no disguise can deceive it
or conceal from it, it is impassive enough,
Only toward the likes of itself will it advance to meet them,
If its poets appear it will in due time advance to meet them,
there is no fear of mistake,
(The proof of a poet shall be sternly deferr'd till his country ab-
sorbs him as affectionately as he has absorb'd it.)

He masters whose spirit masters, he tastes sweetest who results
sweetest in the long run,
The blood of the brawn beloved of time is unconstraint;
In the need of songs, philosophy, an appropriate native grand-
opera, shipcraft, any craft,
He or she is greatest who contributes the greatest original practical
example.

Already a nonchalant breed, silently emerging, appears on the
streets,
People's lips salute only doers, lovers, satisfiers, positive knowers,
There will shortly be no more priests, I say their work is done,
Death is without emergencies here, but life is perpetual emergen-
cies here,
Are your body, days, manners, superb? after death you shall be
superb,

Justice, health, self-esteem, clear the way with irresistible power;
How dare you place any thing before a man?

14. Fall behind me States!
A man before all—myself, typical, before all.

Give me the pay I have served for,
Give me to sing the songs of the great Idea, take all the rest,
I have loved the earth, sun, animals, I have despised riches,
I have given alms to every one that ask'd, stood up for the stupid
    and crazy, devoted my income and labor to others,
Hated tyrants, argued not concerning God, had patience and indul-
    gence toward the people, taken off my hat to nothing
    known or unknown,
Gone freely with powerful uneducated persons and with the young,
    and with the mothers of families,
Read these leaves to myself in the open air, tried them by trees,
    stars, rivers,
Dismiss'd whatever insulted my own soul or defiled my body,
Claim'd nothing to myself which I have not carefully claim'd for
    others on the same terms,
Sped to the camps, and comrades found and accepted from every
    State,
(Upon this breast has many a dying soldier lean'd to breathe his
    last,
This arm, this hand, this voice, have nourish'd, rais'd, restored,
To life recalling many a prostrate form;)
I am willing to wait to be understood by the growth of the taste of
    myself,
Rejecting none, permitting all.

(Say O Mother, have I not to your thought been faithful?
Have I not through life kept you and yours before me?)

15. I swear I begin to see the meaning of these things,
It is not the earth, it is not America who is so great,
It is I who am great or to be great, it is You up there, or any one,
It is to walk rapidly through civilizations, governments, theories,
Through poems, pageants, shows, to form individuals.

Underneath all, individuals,
I swear nothing is good to me now that ignores individuals,
The American compact is altogether with individuals,

224

The only government is that which makes minute of individuals,
The whole theory of the universe is directed unerringly
    to one single individual—namely to You.

(Mother! with subtle sense severe, with the naked sword in your
    hand,
I saw you at last refuse to treat but directly with individuals.)

17.   O I see flashing that this America is only you and me,
    Its power, weapons, testimony, are you and me,
    Its crimes, lies, thefts, defections, are you and me,
    Its Congress is you and me, the officers, capitols, armies, ships, are
        you and me,
    Its endless gestations of new States are you and me,
    The war, (that war so bloody and grim, the war I will henceforth
        forget), was you and me,
    Natural and artificial are you and me,
    Freedom, language, poems, employments, are you and me,
    Past, present, future, are you and me.

I dare not shirk any part of myself,
Not any part of America good or bad,
Not to build for that which builds for mankind,
Not to balance ranks, complexions, creeds, and the sexes,
Not to justify science nor the march of equality,
Nor to feed the arrogant blood of the brawn belov'd of time.

I am for those that have never been master'd,
For men and women whose tempers have never been master'd,
For those whom laws, theories, conventions, can never master.

I am for those who walk abreast with the whole earth,
Who inaugurate one to inaugurate all.

I will not be outfaced by irrational things,
I will penetrate what it is in them that is sarcastic upon me,
I will make cities and civilizations defer to me,
This is what I have learnt from America—it is the amount, and it
    I teach again.

(Democracy, while weapons were everywhere aim'd at your breast,
I saw you serenely give birth to immortal children,
    saw in dreams your dilating form,
Saw you with spreading mantle covering the world.)

18. I will confront these shows of the day and night,
I will know if I am to be less than they,
I will see if I am not as majestic as they,
I will see if I am not as subtle and real as they,
I will see if I am to be less generous than they,
I will see if I have no meaning, while the houses and ships have
     meaning,
I will see if the fishes and birds are to be enough for themselves,
    and I am not to be enough for myself.

I match my spirit against yours you orbs, growths, mountains,
     brutes,
Copious as you are I absorb you all in myself, and become the
     master myself,
America isolated yet embodying all, what is it finally except myself?
These States, what are they except myself?

I know now why the earth is gross, tantalizing, wicked, it is for my
     sake,
I take you specially to be mine, you terrible, rude forms.

(Mother, bend down, bend close to me your face,
I know not what these plots and wars and deferments are for,
I know not fruition's success, but I know that through war and
     crime your work goes on, and must yet go on.)

20. O my rapt verse, my call, mock me not!
Not for the bards of the past, not to invoke them have I launch'd
     you forth,
Not to call even those lofty bards here by Ontario's shores,
Have I sung so capricious and loud my savage song.

Bards for my own land only I invoke,
(For the war, the war is over, the field is clear'd,)
Till they strike up marches henceforth triumphant and onward,
To cheer O Mother your boundless expectant soul.

Bards of the great Idea! bards of the peaceful inventions!
    (for the war, the war is over!)
Yet bards of latent armies, a million soldiers waiting ever-ready,
Bards with songs as from burning coals or the lightning's fork'd
     stripes!
Ample Ohio's, Kanada's bards—bards of California!
    inland bards—bards of the war!
You by my charm I invoke.

226

SONG OF THE BROAD-AXE

1. Weapon shapely, naked, wan,
   Head from the mother's bowels drawn,
   Wooded flesh and metal bone, limb only one and lip only one,
   Gray-blue leaf by red-heat grown, helve produced from a little seed
           sown,
   Resting the grass amid and upon,
   To be lean'd and to lean on.

   Strong shapes and attributes of strong shapes, masculine trades,
       sights and sounds,
   Long varied train of an emblem, dabs of music,
   Fingers of the organist skipping staccato over the keys of the great
       organ.

2. Welcome are all earth's lands, each for its kind,
   Welcome are lands of pine and oak,
   Welcome are lands of the lemon and fig,
   Welcome are lands of gold,
   Welcome are lands of wheat and maize, welcome those of the
           grape,
   Welcome are lands of sugar and rice,
   Welcome the cotton-lands, welcome those of the white potato
       and sweet potato,
   Welcome are mountains, flats, sands, forests, prairies,
   Welcome the rich borders of rivers, table-lands, openings,
   Welcome the measureless grazing-lands, welcome the teeming soil
       of orchards, flax, honey, hemp;
   Welcome just as much the other more hard-faced lands,
   Lands rich as lands of gold or wheat and fruit lands,
   Lands of mines, lands of the manly and rugged ores,
   Lands of coal, copper, lead, tin, zinc,
   Lands of iron—lands of the make of the axe.

4. Muscle and pluck forever!
   What invigorates life invigorates death,
   And the dead advance as much as the living advance,
   And the future is no more uncertain than the present,
   For the roughness of the earth and of man encloses as much
       as the delicatesse of the earth and of man,
   And nothing endures but personal qualities.

What do you think endures?

Do you think a great city endures?

Or a teeming manufacturing state? or a prepared constitution? or the best built steamships?

Or hotels of granite and iron? or any chef-d'œuvres of engineering, forts, armaments?

Away! these are not to be cherish'd for themselves,

They fill their hour, the dancers dance, the musicians play for them,

The show passes, all does well enough of course,

All does very well till one flash of defiance.

A great city is that which has the greatest men and women,

If it be a few ragged huts it is still the greatest city in the whole world.

5. The place where a great city stands is not the place of stretch'd wharves, docks, manufactures, deposits of produce merely,

Nor the place of ceaseless salutes of new-comers or the anchor-lifters of the departing,

Nor the place of the tallest and costliest buildings or shops selling goods from the rest of the earth,

Nor the place of the best libraries and schools, nor the place where money is plentiest,

Nor the place of the most numerous population.

Where the city stands with the brawniest breed of orators and bards,

Where the city stands that is belov'd by these, and loves them in return and understands them,

Where no monuments exist to heroes but in the common words and deeds,

Where thrift is in its place, and prudence is in its place,

Where the men and women think lightly of the laws,

Where the slave ceases, and the master of slaves ceases,

Where the populace rise at once against the never-ending audacity of elected persons,

Where fierce men and women pour forth as the sea to the whistle of death pours its sweeping and unript waves,

Where outside authority enters always after the precedence of inside authority,

Where the citizen is always the head and ideal,

228

and President, Mayor, Governor and what not, are agents for
        pay,
Where children are taught to be laws to themselves, and to depend
        on themselves,
Where equanimity is illustrated in affairs,
Where speculations on the soul are encouraged,
Where women walk in public processions in the streets
        the same as the men,
Where they enter the public assembly and take places the same as
        the men;
Where the city of the faithfulest friends stands,
Where the city of the cleanliness of the sexes stands,
Where the city of the healthiest fathers stands,
Where the city of the best-bodied mothers stands,
There the great city stands.

9.   (America! I do not vaunt my love for you,
     I have what I have.)

The axe leaps!
The solid forest gives fluid utterances,
They tumble forth, they rise and form,
Hut, tent, landing, survey,
Flail, plough, pick, crowbar, spade,
Shingle, rail, prop, wainscot, jamb, lath, panel, gable,
Citadel, ceiling, saloon, academy, organ, exhibition-house, library,
Cornice, trellis, pilaster, balcony, window, turret, porch,
Hoe, rake, pitchfork, pencil, wagon, staff, saw, jack-plane, mallet,
        wedge, rounce,
Chair, tub, hoop, table, wicket, vane, sash, floor,
Work-box, chest, string'd instrument, boat, frame, and what not,
Capitols of States, and capitol of the nation of States,
Long stately rows in avenues, hospitals for orphans or for the poor
        or sick,
Manhattan steamboats and clippers taking the measure of all seas.

The shapes arise!
Shapes of the using of axes anyhow, and the users and all that
        neighbors them,
Cutters down of wood and haulers of it to the Penobscot or Ken-
        nebec,
Dwellers in cabins among the California mountains or by the little
        lakes, or on the Columbia,

Dwellers south on the banks of the Gila or Rio Grande,
	friendly gatherings, the characters and fun,
Dwellers along the St. Lawrence, or north in Kanada,
	or down by the Yellowstone, dwellers on coasts and off coasts,
Seal-fishers, whalers, arctic seamen breaking passages through the
	ice.

The shapes arise!
Shapes of factories, arsenals, foundries, markets,
Shapes of the two-threaded tracks of railroads,
Shapes of the sleepers of bridges, vast frameworks, girders, arches,
Shapes of the fleets of barges, tows, lake and canal craft, river craft,
Ship-yards and dry-docks along the Eastern and Western seas,
	and in many a bay and by-place,
The live-oak kelsons, the pine planks, the spars,
	the hackmatack-roots for knees,
The ships themselves on their ways, the tiers of scaffolds,
	the workmen busy outside and inside,
The tools lying around, the great auger and little auger, the adze,
	bolt, line, square, gouge, and bead-plane.

12.	The main shapes arise!
Shapes of Democracy total, result of centuries,
Shapes ever projecting other shapes,
Shapes of turbulent manly cities,
Shapes of the friends and home-givers of the whole earth,
Shapes bracing the earth and braced with the whole earth.

O MAGNET-SOUTH

O magnet-south! O glistening perfumed South! my South!
O quick mettle, rich blood, impulse and love! good and evil! O all dear
	to me!
O dear to me my birth-things—all moving things and the trees
	where I was born—the grains, plants, rivers,
Dear to me my own slow sluggish rivers where they flow, distant,
	over flats of silvery sands or through swamps,
Dear to me the Roanoke, the Savannah, the Altamahaw, the Pedee,
	the Tombigbee, the Santee, the Coosa and the Sabine,
O pensive, far away wandering, I return with my soul
	to haunt their banks again,

230

Again in Florida I float on transparent lakes, I float on the Okeechobee,
   I cross the hummock-land or through pleasant openings or dense
      forests,
I see the parrots in the woods, I see the papaw-tree and the blossoming
      titi;
Again, sailing in my coaster on deck, I coast off Georgia, I coast up the
         Carolinas,
I see where the live-oak is growing, I see where the yellow-pine,
   the scented bay-tree, the lemon and orange, the cypress,
   the graceful palmetto,
I pass rude sea-headlands and enter Pamlico sound through an inlet,
   and dart my vision inland;
O the cotton plant! the growing fields of rice, sugar, hemp!
The cactus guarded with thorns, the laurel-tree with large white flowers,
The range afar, the richness and barrenness,
   the old woods charged with mistletoe and trailing moss,
The piney odor and the gloom, the awful natural stillness,
   (here in these dense swamps the freebooter carries his gun,
   and the fugitive has his conceal'd hut;)
O the strange fascination of these half-known half-impassable swamps,
   infested by reptiles, resounding with the bellow of the alligator,
   the sad noises of the night-owl and the wild-cat,
   and the whirr of the rattlesnake,
The mocking-bird, the American mimic, singing all the forenoon,
   singing through the moon-lit night,
The humming-bird, the wild turkey, the raccoon, the opossum;
A Kentucky corn-field, the tall, graceful, long-leav'd corn, slender,
   flapping, bright green, with tassels, with beautiful ears
   each well-sheath'd in its husk;
O my heart! O tender and fierce pangs, I can stand them not, I will
      depart;
O to be a Virginian where I grew up! O to be a Carolinian!
O longings irrepressible! O I will go back to old Tennessee
   and never wander more.

FULL OF LIFE NOW

Full of life now, compact, visible,
I, forty years old the eighty-third year of the States,
To one a century hence or any number of centuries hence,
To you yet unborn these, seeking you.

When you read these I that was visible am become invisible,
Now it is you, compact, visible, realizing my poems, seeking me,
Fancying how happy you were if I could be with you and become your
      comrade;
Be it as if I were with you. (Be not too certain but I am now with you.)

MIRACLES

Why, who makes much of a miracle?
As to me I know of nothing else but miracles,
Whether I walk the streets of Manhattan,
Or dart my sight over the roofs of houses toward the sky,
Or wade with naked feet along the beach just in the edge of the water,
Or stand under trees in the woods, . . .
Or sit at table at dinner with the rest,
Or look at strangers opposite me riding in the car,
Or watch honey-bees busy around the hive of a summer forenoon,
Or animals feeding in the fields,
Or birds, or the wonderfulness of insects in the air,
Or the wonderfulness of the sundown, or of stars shining so quiet and
      bright,
Or the exquisite delicate thin curve of the new moon in spring;
These with the rest, one and all, are to me miracles,
The whole referring, yet each distinct and in its place.

To me every hour of the light and dark is a miracle,
Every cubic inch of space is a miracle,
Every square yard of the surface of the earth is spread with the same,
Every foot of the interior swarms with the same.

To me the sea is a continual miracle,
The fishes that swim—the rocks—the motion of the waves—
    the ships with men in them,
What stranger miracles are there?

THIS COMPOST

1. Something startles me where I thought I was safest,
   I withdraw from the still woods I loved,
   I will not go now on the pastures to walk,

232

I will not strip the clothes from my body to meet my lover the sea,
I will not touch my flesh to the earth as to other flesh to renew me.

O how can it be that the ground itself does not sicken?
How can you be alive you growths of spring?
How can you furnish health you blood of herbs, roots, orchards,
    grain?
Are they not continually putting distemper'd corpses within you?
Is not every continent work'd over and over with sour dead?

Where have you disposed of their carcasses?
Those drunkards and gluttons of so many generations?
Where have you drawn off all the foul liquid and meat?
I do not see any of it upon you to-day, or perhaps I am deceiv'd,
I will run a furrow with my plough, I will press my spade through
    the sod and turn it up underneath,
I am sure I shall expose some of the foul meat.

2. Behold this compost! behold it well!
Perhaps every mite has once form'd part of a sick person—yet
    behold!
The grass of spring covers the prairies,
The bean bursts noiselessly through the mould in the garden,
The delicate spear of the onion pierces upward,
The apple-buds cluster together on the apple-branches,
The resurrection of the wheat appears with pale visage out of its
    graves,
The tinge awakes over the willow-tree and the mulberry-tree,
The he-birds carol mornings and evenings while the she-birds sit on
    their nests,
The young of poultry break through the hatch'd eggs,
The new-born of animals appear, the calf is dropt from the cow,
    the colt from the mare,
Out of its little hill faithfully rise the potato's dark green leaves,
Out of its hill rises the yellow maize-stalk, the lilacs bloom in the
    dooryards,
The summer growth is innocent and disdainful above all those strata
    of sour dead. . . .

Now I am terrified at the Earth, it is that calm and patient,
It grows such sweet things out of such corruptions,
It turns harmless and stainless on its axis,
    with such endless successions of diseas'd corpses,

233

It distills such exquisite winds out of such infused fetor,
It renews with such unwitting looks its prodigal, annual, sumptuous
  crops,
It gives such divine materials to men, and accepts such leavings
  from them at last.

ONE'S-SELF I SING

One's-self I sing, a simple separate person,
Yet utter the word Democratic, the word En-Masse.

Of physiology from top to toe I sing,
Not physiognomy alone nor brain alone is worthy for the Muse,
  I say the Form complete is worthier far,
The Female equally with the Male I sing.

Of Life immense in passion, pulse, and power,
Cheerful, for freest action form'd under the laws divine,
The Modern Man I sing.

WHOEVER YOU ARE HOLDING ME NOW IN HAND

Whoever you are holding me now in hand,
Without one thing all will be useless,
I give you fair warning before you attempt me further,
I am not what you supposed, but far different.

Who is he that would become my follower?
Who would sign himself a candidate for my affections?

The way is suspicious, the result uncertain, perhaps destructive,
You would have to give up all else, I alone would expect to be
  your sole and exclusive standard,
Your novitiate would even then be long and exhausting,
The whole past theory of your life and all conformity to the lives
  around you would have to be abandon'd,
Therefore release me now before troubling yourself any further,
  let go your hand from my shoulders,
Put me down and depart on your way.

234

Or else by stealth in some wood for trial,
Or back of a rock in the open air,
(For in any roof'd room of a house I emerge not, nor in company,
And in libraries I lie as one dumb, a gawk, or unborn, or dead,)
But just possibly with you on a high hill, first watching lest any person
    for miles around approach unawares,
Or possibly with you sailing at sea, or on the beach of the sea
    or some quiet island,
Here to put your lips upon mine I permit you,
With the comrade's long-dwelling kiss or the new husband's kiss,
For I am the new husband and I am the comrade.

Or if you will, thrusting me beneath your clothing,
Where I may feel the throbs of your heart or rest upon your hip,
Carry me when you go forth over land or sea;
For thus merely touching you is enough, is best,
And thus touching you would I silently sleep and be carried eternally.

But these leaves conning you con at peril,
For these leaves and me you will not understand,
They will elude you at first and still more afterward, I will certainly
    elude you,
Even while you should think you had unquestionably caught me, behold!
Already you see I have escaped from you.

For it is not for what I have put into it that I have written this book,
Nor is it by reading it you will acquire it,
Nor do those know me best who admire me and vauntingly praise me,
Nor will the candidates for my love (unless at most a very few) prove
    victorious,
Nor will my poems do good only, they will do just as much evil, per-
    haps more,
For all is useless without that which you may guess at many times and
    not hit, that which I hinted at;
Therefore release me and depart on your way.

NOT THE PILOT

Not the pilot has charge himself to bring his ship into port,
    though beaten back and many times baffled;
Not the pathfinder penetrating inland weary and long,

235

By deserts parch'd, snows chill'd, rivers wet,
    perseveres till he reaches his destination,
More than I have charged myself, heeded or unheeded,
    to compose a march for these States,
For a battle-call, rousing to arms if need be, years, centuries hence.

AS I PONDER'D IN SILENCE

As I ponder'd in silence,
Returning upon my poems, considering, lingering long,
A Phantom arose before me with distrustful aspect,
Terrible in beauty, age, and power,
The genius of poets of old lands,
As to me directing like flame its eyes,
With finger pointing to many immortal songs,
And menacing voice, *What singest thou?* it said,
Know'st thou not there is but one theme for ever-enduring bards?
And that is the theme of War, the fortune of battles,
The making of perfect soldiers.

Be it so, then I answer'd,
I too haughty Shade also sing war, and a longer and greater one than
    any,
Waged in my book with varying fortune, with flight, advance and
    retreat, victory deferr'd and wavering,
(Yet methinks certain, or as good as certain, at the last,) the field the
    world,
For life and death, for the Body and for the eternal Soul,
Lo, I too am come, chanting the chant of battles,
I above all promote brave soldiers.

EIGHTEEN SIXTY-ONE

Arm'd year—year of the struggle,
No dainty rhymes or sentimental love verses for you terrible year,
Not you as some pale poetling seated at a desk lisping cadenzas piano,
But as a strong man erect, clothed in blue clothes, advancing,
    carrying a rifle on your shoulder,

236

With well-gristled body and sunburnt face and hands,
  with a knife in the belt at your side,
As I heard you shouting loud, your sonorous voice ringing
  across the continent,
Your masculine voice O year, as rising amid the great cities,
Amid the men of Manhattan I saw you as one of the workmen,
  the dwellers in Manhattan,
Or with large steps crossing the prairies out of Illinois and Indiana,
Rapidly crossing the West with springy gait and descending the Alle-
    ghanies,
Or down from the great lakes or in Pennsylvania,
  or on deck along the Ohio river,
Or southward along the Tennessee or Cumberland rivers,
  or at Chattanooga on the mountain top,
Saw I your gait and saw I your sinewy limbs clothed in blue,
  bearing weapons, robust year,
Heard your determin'd voice launch'd forth again and again,
Year that suddenly sang by the mouths of the round-lipp'd cannon,
I repeat you, hurrying, crashing, sad, distracted year.

O CAPTAIN! MY CAPTAIN!

O Captain! my Captain! our fearful trip is done,
The ship has weather'd every rack, the prize we sought is won,
The port is near, the bells I hear, the people all exulting,
While follow eyes the steady keel, the vessel grim and daring;
        But O heart! heart! heart!
          O the bleeding drops of red,
            Where on the deck my Captain lies,
              Fallen cold and dead.

O Captain! my Captain! rise up and hear the bells;
Rise up—for you the flag is flung—for you the bugle trills,
For you bouquets and ribbon'd wreaths—for you the shores a-crowding,
For you they call, the swaying mass, their eager faces turning;
        Here Captain! dear father!
          This arm beneath your head!
            It is some dream that on the deck,
              You've fallen cold and dead.

237

My Captain does not answer, his lips are pale and still,
My father does not feel my arm, he has no pulse nor will,
The ship is anchor'd safe and sound, its voyage closed and done,
From fearful trip the victor ship comes in with object won;
        Exult O shores, and ring O bells!
          But I with mournful tread,
            Walk the deck my Captain lies,
            Fallen cold and dead.

WHEN LILACS LAST IN THE DOORYARD BLOOM'D

1. When lilacs last in the dooryard bloom'd,
    And the great star early droop'd in the western sky in the night,
    I mourn'd, and yet shall mourn with ever-returning spring.

    Ever-returning spring, trinity sure to me you bring,
    Lilac blooming perennial and drooping star in the west,
    And thought of him I love.

2. O powerful western fallen star!
    O shades of night—O moody, tearful night!
    O great star disappear'd—O the black murk that hides the star!
    O cruel hands that hold me powerless—O helpless soul of me!
    O harsh surrounding cloud that will not free my soul.

3. In the dooryard fronting an old farm-house near the white-wash'd
      palings,
    Stands the lilac-bush tall-growing with heart-shaped leaves of rich
      green,
    With many a pointed blossom rising delicate, with the perfume
      strong I love,
    With every leaf a miracle—and from this bush in the dooryard,
    With delicate-color'd blossoms and heart-shaped leaves of rich green,
    A sprig with its flower I break.

4. In the swamp in secluded recesses,
    A shy and hidden bird is warbling a song.

    Solitary the thrush,
    The hermit withdrawn to himself, avoiding the settlements,
    Sings by himself a song.

Song of the bleeding throat,
Death's outlet song of life, (for well dear brother I know,
If thou wast not granted to sing thou would'st surely die.)

5. Over the breast of the spring, the land, amid cities,
   Amid lanes and through old woods, where lately the violets peep'd
       from the ground, spotting the gray debris,
   Amid the grass in the fields each side of the lanes, passing the
       endless grass,
   Passing the yellow-spear'd wheat, every grain from its shroud
       in the dark-brown fields uprisen,
   Passing the apple-tree blows of white and pink in the orchards,
   Carrying a corpse to where it shall rest in the grave,
   Night and day journeys a coffin.

6. Coffin that passes through lanes and streets,
   Through day and night with the great cloud darkening the land,
   With the pomp of the inloop'd flags with the cities draped in
       black,
   With the show of the States themselves as of crape-veil'd women
       standing,
   With processions long and winding and the flambeaus of the
       night,
   With the countless torches lit, with the silent sea of faces
       and the unbared heads,
   With the waiting depot, the arriving coffin, and the sombre faces,
   With dirges through the night, with the thousand voices
       rising strong and solemn,
   With all the mournful voices of the dirges pour'd around the
       coffin,
   The dim-lit churches and the shuddering organs—
       where amid these you journey,
   With the tolling tolling bells' perpetual clang,
   Here, coffin that slowly passes,
   I give you my sprig of lilac.

7. (Nor for you, for one alone,
   Blossoms and branches green to coffins all I bring,
   For fresh as the morning, thus would I chant a song for you
       O sane and sacred death.

   All over bouquets of roses,
   O death, I cover you over with roses and early lilies,

But mostly and now the lilac that blooms the first,
Copious I break, I break the sprigs from the bushes,
With loaded arms I come, pouring for you,
For you and the coffins all of you O death.)

8. O western orb sailing the heaven,
Now I know what you must have meant as a month since I walk'd,
As I walk'd in silence the transparent shadowy night,
As I saw you had something to tell as you bent to me night after
    night,
As you droop'd from the sky low down as if to my side,
    (while the other stars all look'd on,)
As we wander'd together the solemn night, (for something
    I know not what kept me from sleep,)
As the night advanced, and I saw on the rim of the west
    how full you were of woe,
As I stood on the rising ground in the breeze in the cool trans-
    parent night,
As I watch'd where you pass'd and was lost
    in the netherward black of the night,
As my soul in its trouble dissatisfied sank, as where you sad orb,
Concluded, dropt in the night, and was gone.

9. Sing on there in the swamp,
O singer bashful and tender, I hear your notes, I hear your call,
I hear, I come presently, I understand you,
But a moment I linger, for the lustrous star has detain'd me,
The star my departing comrade holds and detains me.

10. O how shall I warble myself for the dead one there I loved?
And how shall I deck my song for the large sweet soul that has
    gone?
And what shall my perfume be for the grave of him I love?

Sea-winds blown from east and west,
Blown from the Eastern sea and blown from the Western sea,
    till there on the prairies meeting,
These and with these and the breath of my chant,
I'll perfume the grave of him I love.

11. O what shall I hang on the chamber walls?
And what shall the pictures be that I hang on the walls,
To adorn the burial-house of him I love?

240

Pictures of growing spring and farms and homes,

With the Fourth-month eve at sundown, and the gray smoke lucid
and bright,

With floods of the yellow gold of the gorgeous, indolent, sinking
sun, burning, expanding the air,

With the fresh sweet herbage under foot, and the pale green
leaves of the trees prolific,

In the distance the flowing glaze, the breast of the river,
with a wind-dapple here and there,

With ranging hills on the banks, with many a line against the sky,
and shadows,

And the city at hand with dwellings so dense, and stacks of
chimneys,

And all the scenes of life and the workshops,
and the workmen homeward returning.

12. Lo, body and soul—this land,

My own Manhattan with spires, and the sparkling and hurrying
tides, and the ships,

The varied and ample land, the South and the North in the light,
Ohio's shores and flashing Missouri,

And ever the far-spreading prairies cover'd with grass and corn.

Lo, the most excellent sun so calm and haughty,

The violet and purple morn with just-felt breezes,

The gentle soft-born measureless light,

The miracle spreading bathing all, the fulfill'd noon,

The coming eve delicious, the welcome night and the stars,

Over my cities shining all, enveloping man and land.

13. Sing on, sing on you gray-brown bird,

Sing from the swamps, the recesses, pour your chant from the
bushes,

Limitless out of the dusk, out of the cedars and pines.

Sing on dearest brother, warble your reedy song,

Loud human song, with voice of uttermost woe.

O liquid and free and tender!

O wild and loose to my soul—O wondrous singer!

You only I hear—yet the star holds me, (but will soon depart,)

Yet the lilac with mastering odor holds me.

241

14. Now while I sat in the day and look'd forth,
      In the close of the day with its light and the fields of spring,
         and the farmers preparing their crops,
      In the large unconscious scenery of my land with its lakes and
         forests,
      In the heavenly aerial beauty, (after the perturb'd winds and the
         storms,)
      Under the arching heavens of the afternoon swift passing,
         and the voices of children and women,
      The many-moving sea-tides, and I saw the ships how they sail'd,
      And the summer approaching with richness, and the fields all busy
         with labor,
      And the infinite separate houses, how they all went on,
         each with its meals and minutia of daily usages,
      And the streets how their throbbings throbb'd, and the cities pent—
         lo, then and there,
      Falling upon them all and among them all, enveloping me with
         the rest,
      Appear'd the cloud, appear'd the long black trail,
      And I knew death, its thought, and the sacred knowledge of death.

      Then with the knowledge of death as walking one side of me,
      And the thought of death close-walking the other side of me,
      And I in the middle as with companions,
         and as holding the hands of companions,
      I fled forth to the hiding receiving night that talks not,
      Down to the shores of the water, the path by the swamp in the
         dimness,
      To the solemn shadowy cedars and ghostly pines so still.

      And the singer so shy to the rest receiv'd me,
      The gray-brown bird I know receiv'd us comrades three,
      And he sang the carol of death, and a verse for him I love.

      From deep secluded recesses,
      From the fragrant cedars and the ghostly pines so still,
      Came the carol of the bird.

      And the charm of the carol rapt me,
      As I held as if by their hands my comrades in the night,
      And the voice of my spirit tallied the song of the bird.

      Come lovely and soothing death,
      Undulate round the world, serenely arriving, arriving,

242

In the day, in the night, to all, to each,
Sooner or later delicate death.

Prais'd be the fathomless universe,
For life and joy, and for objects and knowledge curious,
And for love, sweet love—but praise! praise! praise!
For the sure-enwinding arms of cool-enfolding death.

Dark mother always gliding near with soft feet,
Have none chanted for thee a chant of fullest welcome?
Then I chant it for thee, I glorify thee above all,
I bring thee a song that when thou must indeed come, come un-
        falteringly.

Approach strong deliveress,
When it is so, when thou hast taken them I joyously sing the dead,
Lost in the loving floating ocean of thee,
Laved in the flood of thy bliss O death.

From me to the glad serenades,
Dances for thee I propose saluting thee, adornments and feastings
        for thee,
And the sights of the open landscape and the high-spread sky are
        fitting,
And life and the fields, and the huge and thoughtful night.

The night in silence under many a star,
The ocean shore and the husky whispering wave whose voice I
        know,
And the soul turning to thee O vast and well-veil'd death,
And the body gratefully nestling close to thee.

Over the tree-tops I float thee a song,
Over the rising and sinking waves, over the myriad fields and the
        prairies wide,
Over the dense-pack'd cities all and the teeming wharves and ways,
I float this carol with joy, with joy to thee O death.

15. To the tally of my soul,
    Loud and strong kept up the gray-brown bird,
    With pure deliberate notes spreading filling the night.

    Loud in the pines and cedars dim,
    Clear in the freshness moist and the swamp-perfume,
    And I with my comrades there in the night.

243

While my sight that was bound in my eyes unclosed,
As to long panoramas of visions.

And I saw askant the armies,
I saw as in noiseless dreams hundreds of battle-flags,
Borne through the smoke of the battles and pierc'd with missiles I
      saw them,
And carried hither and yon through the smoke, and torn and
      bloody,
And at last but a few shreds left on the staffs, (and all in silence,)
And the staffs all splinter'd and broken.

I saw battle-corpses, myriads of them,
And the white skeletons of young men, I saw them,
I saw the debris and debris of all the slain soldiers of the war,
But I saw they were not as was thought,
They themselves were fully at rest, they suffer'd not,
The living remain'd and suffer'd, the mother suffer'd,
And the wife and the child and the musing comrade suffer'd,
And the armies that remain'd suffer'd.

16. Passing the visions, passing the night,
Passing, unloosing the hold of my comrades' hands,
Passing the song of the hermit bird and the tallying song of my
      soul,
Victorious song, death's outlet song, yet varying ever-altering song,
As low and wailing, yet clear the notes, rising and falling, flooding
      the night,
Sadly sinking and fainting, as warning and warning,
    and yet again bursting with joy,
Covering the earth and filling the spread of the heaven,
As that powerful psalm in the night I heard from recesses,
Passing, I leave thee lilac with heart-shaped leaves,
I leave thee there in the door-yard, blooming, returning with spring.

I cease from my song for thee,
From my gaze on thee in the west, fronting the west, communing
      with thee,
O comrade lustrous with silver face in the night.

Yet each to keep and all, retrievements out of the night,
The song, the wondrous chant of the gray-brown bird,
And the tallying chant, the echo arous'd in my soul,

With the lustrous and drooping star with the countenance full of
    woe,
With the holders holding my hand nearing the call of the bird,
Comrades mine and I in the midst, and their memory ever to keep,
    for the dead I loved so well,
For the sweetest, wisest soul of all my days and lands—
    and this for his dear sake,
Lilac and star and bird twined with the chant of my soul,
There in the fragrant pines and the cedars dusk and dim.

SHUT NOT YOUR DOORS

Shut not your doors to me proud libraries,
For that which was lacking on all your well-fill'd shelves,
    yet needed most, I bring,
Forth from the war emerging, a book I have made,
The words of my book nothing, the drift of it every thing,
A book separate, not link'd with the rest nor felt by the intellect,
But you ye untold latencies will thrill to every page.

I HEAR IT WAS CHARGED AGAINST ME

I hear it was charged against me that I sought to destroy institutions,
But really I am neither for nor against institutions,
(What indeed have I in common with them?
    or what with the destruction of them?)
Only I will establish in the Mannahatta and in every city
    of these States inland and seaboard,
And in the fields and woods, and above every keel little or large
    that dents the water,
Without edifices or rules or trustees or any argument,
The institution of the dear love of comrades.

I DREAM'D IN A DREAM

I dream'd in a dream I saw a city invincible to the attacks
    of the whole of the rest of the earth,
I dream'd that was the new city of Friends,

Nothing was greater there than the quality of robust love, it led the rest,
It was seen every hour in the actions of the men of that city,
And in all their looks and words.

OUT OF THE ROLLING OCEAN THE CROWD

Out of the rolling ocean the crowd came a drop gently to me,
Whispering, *I love you, before long I die,*
I have travel'd a long way merely to look on you to touch you,
For I could not die till I once look'd on you,
For I fear'd I might afterward lose you.

Now we have met, we have look'd, we are safe,
Return in peace to the ocean my love,
I too am part of that ocean my love, we are not so much separated,
Behold the great rondure, the cohesion of all, how perfect!
But as for me, for you, the irresistible sea is to separate us,
As for an hour carrying us diverse, yet cannot carry us diverse forever;
Be not impatient—a little space—know you I salute the air,
      the ocean and the land,
Every day at sundown for your dear sake my love.

SOMETIMES WITH ONE I LOVE

Sometimes with one I love I fill myself with rage
      for fear I effuse unreturn'd love,
But now I think there is no unreturn'd love,
      the pay is certain one way or another,
(I loved a certain person ardently and my love was not return'd,
Yet out of that I have written these songs.)

QUICKSAND YEARS

Quicksand years that whirl me I know not whither,
Your schemes, politics, fail, lines give way, substances mock and elude
      me,
Only the theme I sing, the great and strong-possess'd soul, eludes not,
One's-self must never give way—that is the final substance—
      that out of all is sure,

246

Out of politics, triumphs, battles, life, what at last finally remains?
When shows break up what but One's-Self is sure?

AH POVERTIES, WINCINGS, AND SULKY RETREATS

Ah poverties, wincings, and sulky retreats,
Ah you foes that in conflict have overcome me,
(For what is my life or any man's life but a conflict with foes,
    the old, the incessant war?)
You degradations, you tussle with passions and appetites,
You smarts from dissatisfied friendships, (ah wounds the sharpest of
    all!)
You toil of painful and choked articulations, you meannesses,
You shallow tongue-talks at tables, (my tongue the shallowest of any;)
You broken resolutions, you racking angers, you smother'd ennuis!
Ah think not you finally triumph, my real self has yet to come forth,
It shall yet march forth o'ermastering, till all lies beneath me,
It shall yet stand up the soldier of ultimate victory.

YEARS OF THE MODERN

Years of the modern! years of the unperform'd!
Your horizon rises, I see it parting away for more august dramas,
I see not America only, not only Liberty's nation but other nations
    preparing,
I see tremendous entrances and exits, new combinations, the solidarity
    of races,
I see that force advancing with irresistible power on the world's stage,
(Have the old forces, the old wars, played their parts?
    are the acts suitable to them closed?)
I see Freedom, completely arm'd and victorious and very haughty,
    with Law on one side and Peace on the other,
A stupendous trio all issuing forth against the idea of caste;
What historic denouements are these we so rapidly approach?
I see men marching and countermarching by swift millions,
I see the frontiers and boundaries of the old aristocracies broken,
I see the landmarks of European kings removed,
I see this day the People beginning their landmarks, (all others give
    way;)

247,

Never were such sharp questions ask'd as this day,
Never was average man, his soul, more energetic, more like a God,
Lo, how he urges and urges, leaving the masses no rest!
His daring foot is on land and sea everywhere,
    he colonizes the Pacific, the archipelagoes,
With the steamship, the electric telegraph, the newspaper,
    the wholesale engines of war,
With these and the world-spreading factories
    he interlinks all geography, all lands;
What whispers are these O lands, running ahead of you, passing under
    the seas?
Are all nations communing? is there going to be but one heart to the
    globe?
Is humanity forming en-masse? for lo, tyrants tremble, crowns grow
    dim,
The earth, restive, confronts a new era, perhaps a general divine war,
No one knows what will happen next, such portents fill the days and
    nights;
Years prophetical! the space ahead as I walk, as I vainly try to pierce it,
    is full of phantoms,
Unborn deeds, things soon to be, project their shapes around me,
This incredible rush and heat, this strange ecstatic fever of dreams O
    years!
Your dreams O years, how they penetrate through me!
    (I know not whether I sleep or wake;)
The perform'd America and Europe grow dim, retiring in shadow be-
    hind me,
The unperform'd, more gigantic than ever, advance, advance upon me.

PASSAGE TO INDIA

1. Singing my days,
    Singing the great achievements of the present,
    Singing the strong light works of engineers,
    Our modern wonders, (the antique ponderous Seven outvied,)
    In the Old World the east the Suez canal,
    The New by its mighty railroad spann'd,
    The seas inlaid with eloquent gentle wires;
    Yet first to sound, and ever sound, the cry with thee O soul,
    The Past! the Past! the Past!

248

The Past—the dark unfathom'd retrospect!
The teeming gulf—the sleepers and the shadows!
The past—the infinite greatness of the past!
For what is the present after all but a growth out of the past?
(As a projectile form'd, impell'd, passing a certain line, still keeps
     on,
So the present, utterly form'd, impell'd by the past.)

2. Passage O soul to India!
Eclaircise the myths Asiatic, the primitive-fables.
Not you alone proud truths of the world,
Nor you alone ye facts of modern science,
But myths and fables of eld, Asia's, Africa's fables,
The far-darting beams of the spirit, the unloos'd dreams,
The deep diving bibles and legends,
The daring plots of the poets, the elder religions;
O you temples fairer than lilies pour'd over by the rising sun!
O you fables spurning the known, eluding the hold of the known,
    mounting to heaven!
You lofty and dazzling towers, pinnacled, red as roses,
    burnish'd with gold!
Towers of fables immortal fashion'd from mortal dreams!
You too I welcome and fully the same as the rest!
You too with joy I sing.

Passage to India!
Lo, soul, seest thou not God's purpose from the first?
The earth to be spann'd, connected by network,
The races, neighbors, to marry and be given in marriage,
The oceans to be cross'd, the distant brought near,
The lands to be welded together.

A worship new I sing,
You captains, voyagers, explorers, yours,
You engineers, you architects, machinists, yours,
You, not for trade or transportation only,
But in God's name, and for thy sake O soul.

3. Passage to India!
Lo soul for thee of tableaus twain,
I see in one the Suez canal initiated, open'd,
I see the procession of steamships, the Empress Eugenie's leading
    the band,

I mark from on deck the strange landscape, the pure sky,
  the level sand in the distance,
I pass swiftly the picturesque groups, the workmen gather'd,
The gigantic dredging machines.

In one again, different, (yet thine, all thine, O soul, the same,)
I see over my own continent the Pacific railroad surmounting every
  barrier,
I see continual trains of cars winding along the Platte
  carrying freight and passengers,
I hear the locomotives rushing and roaring, and the shrill steam-
  whistle,
I hear the echoes reverberate through the grandest scenery in the
  world,
I cross the Laramie plains, I note the rocks in grotesque shapes, the
  buttes,
I see the plentiful larkspur and wild onions, the barren,
  colorless, sage-deserts,
I see in glimpses afar or towering immediately above me the great
  mountains, I see the Wind river and the Wahsatch moun-
  tains,
I see the Monument mountain and the Eagle's Nest, I pass the
  Promontory, I ascend the Nevadas,
I scan the noble Elk mountain and wind around its base,
I see the Humboldt range, I thread the valley and cross the river,
I see the clear waters of lake Tahoe, I see forests of majestic pines,
Or crossing the great desert, the alkaline plains, I behold enchanting
  mirages of waters and meadows,
Marking through these and after all, in duplicate slender lines,
Bridging the three or four thousand miles of land travel,
Tying the Eastern to the Western sea,
The road between Europe and Asia.

(Ah Genoese thy dream! thy dream!
Centuries after thou art laid in thy grave,
The shore thou foundest verifies thy dream.)

4. Passage to India!
Struggles of many a captain, tales of many a sailor dead,
Over my mood stealing and spreading they come,
Like clouds and cloudlets in the unreach'd sky.

250

Along all history, down the slopes,
As a rivulet running, sinking now, and now again to the surface
     rising,
A ceaseless thought, a varied train—lo, soul, to thee, thy sight, they
     rise,
The plans, the voyages again, the expeditions;
Again Vasco da Gama sails forth,
Again the knowledge gain'd, the mariner's compass,
Lands found and nations born, thou born America,
For purpose vast, man's long probation fill'd,
Thou rondure of the world at last accomplish'd.

5. O vast Rondure, swimming in space,
    Cover'd all over with visible power and beauty,
    Alternate light and day and the teeming spiritual darkness,
    Unspeakable high processions of sun and moon and countless stars
         above,
    Below, the manifold grass and waters, animals, mountains, trees,
    With inscrutable purpose, some hidden prophetic intention,
    Now first it seems my thought begins to span thee.

Down from the gardens of Asia descending radiating,
Adam and Eve appear, then their myriad progeny after them,
Wandering, yearning, curious, with restless explorations,
With questionings, baffled, formless, feverish, with never-happy
     hearts,
With that sad incessant refrain, Wherefore unsatisfied soul?
     and Whither O mocking life?

Ah who shall soothe these feverish children?
Who justify these restless explorations?
Who speak the secret of impassive earth?
Who bind it to us? what is this separate Nature so unnatural?
What is this earth to our affections? (unloving earth,
     without a throb to answer ours,
Cold earth, the place of graves.)

Yet soul be sure the first intent remains, and shall be carried out,
Perhaps even now the time has arrived.

After the seas are all cross'd, (as they seem already cross'd,)
After the great captains and engineers have accomplish'd their work,
After the noble inventors, after the scientists, the chemist,
     the geologist, ethnologist,

251

Finally shall come the poet worthy that name,
The true son of God shall come singing his songs.

Then not your deeds only O voyagers, O scientists and inventors,
    shall be justified,
All these hearts as of fretted children shall be sooth'd,
All affection shall be fully responded to, the secret shall be told,
All these separations and gaps shall be taken up and hook'd
    and link'd together,
The whole earth, this cold, impassive, voiceless earth,
    shall be completely justified,
Trinitas divine shall be gloriously accomplish'd and compacted
    by the true son of God, the poet,
(He shall indeed pass the straits and conquer the mountains,
He shall double the cape of Good Hope to some purpose,)
Nature and Man shall be disjoin'd and diffused no more,
The true son of God shall absolutely fuse them.

6. Year at whose wide-flung door I sing!
    Year of the purpose accomplish'd!
    Year of the marriage of continents, climates and oceans!
    (No mere doge of Venice now wedding the Adriatic,)
    I see O year in you the vast terraqueous globe given and giving all,
    Europe to Asia, Africa join'd, and they to the New World,
    The lands, geographies, dancing before you, holding a festival gar-
        land,
    As brides and bridegrooms hand in hand.

Passage to India!
Cooling airs from Caucasus far, soothing cradle of man,
The river Euphrates flowing, the past lit up again.

Lo soul, the retrospect brought forward,
The old, most populous, wealthiest of earth's lands,
The streams of the Indus and the Ganges and their many affluents,
(I my shores of America walking to-day behold, resuming all,)
The tale of Alexander on his warlike marches suddenly dying,
On one side China and on the other side Persia and Arabia,
To the south the great seas and the bay of Bengal,
The flowing literatures, tremendous epics, religions, castes,
Old occult Brahma interminably far back, the tender and junior
    Buddha,
Central and southern empires and all their belongings, possessors,

252

The wars of Tamerlane, the reign of Aurungzebe,
The traders, rulers, explorers, Moslems, Venetians, Byzantium,
    the Arabs, Portuguese,
The first travelers famous yet, Marco Polo, Batouta the Moor,
Doubts to be solv'd, the map incognita, blanks to be fill'd,
The foot of man unstay'd, the hands never at rest,
Thyself O soul that will not brook a challenge.

The mediæval navigators rise before me,
The world of 1492, with its awaken'd enterprise,
Something swelling in humanity now like the sap of the earth in
    spring,
The sunset splendor of chivalry declining.

And who art thou sad shade?
Gigantic, visionary, thyself a visionary,
With majestic limbs and pious beaming eyes,
Spreading around with every look of thine a golden world,
Enhuing it with gorgeous hues.

As the chief histrion,
Down to the footlights walks in some great scena,
Dominating the rest I see the Admiral himself,
(History's type of courage, action, faith,)
Behold him sail from Palos leading his little fleet,
His voyage behold, his return, his great fame,
His misfortunes, calumniators, behold him a prisoner, chain'd,
Behold his dejection, poverty, death.

(Curious in time I stand, noting the efforts of heroes,
Is the deferment long? bitter the slander, poverty, death?
Lies the seed unreck'd for centuries in the ground? lo, to God's due
    occasion,
Uprising in the night, it sprouts, blooms,
And fills the earth with use and beauty.)

7. Passage indeed O soul to primal thought,
Not lands and seas alone, thy own clear freshness,
The young maturity of brood and bloom,
To realms of budding bibles.

O soul, repressless, I with thee and thou with me,
Thy circumnavigation of the world begin,
Of man, the voyage of his mind's return,

To reason's early paradise,
Back, back to wisdom's birth, to innocent intuitions,
Again with fair creation.

8. O we can wait no longer,
We too take ship O soul,
Joyous we too launch out on trackless seas,
Fearless for unknown shores on waves of ecstasy to sail,
Amid the wafting winds, (thou pressing me to thee, I thee to me,
        O soul,)
Caroling free, singing our song of God,
Chanting our chant of pleasant exploration.

With laugh and many a kiss,
(Let others deprecate, let others weep for sin, remorse, humiliation,)
O soul thou pleasest me, I thee.

Ah more than any priest O soul we too believe in God,
But with the mystery of God we dare not dally.

O soul thou pleasest me, I thee,
Sailing these seas or on the hills, or waking in the night,
Thoughts, silent thoughts, of Time and Space and Death, like waters
        flowing,
Bear me indeed as through the regions infinite,
Whose air I breathe, whose ripples hear, lave me all over,
Bathe me O God in thee, mounting to thee,
I and my soul to range in range of thee.

O Thou transcendent,
Nameless, the fibre and the breath,
Light of the light, shedding forth universes, thou centre of them,
Thou mightier centre of the true, the good, the loving,
Thou moral, spiritual fountain—affection's source—thou reservoir,
(O pensive soul of me—O thirst unsatisfied—waitest not there?
Waitest not haply for us somewhere there the Comrade perfect?)
Thou pulse—thou motive of the stars, suns, systems,
That, circling, move in order, safe, harmonious,
Athwart the shapeless vastnesses of space,
How should I think, how breathe a single breath, how speak, if, out
        of myself,
I could not launch, to those, superior universes?

254

Swiftly I shrivel at the thought of God,
At Nature and its wonders, Time and Space and Death,
But that I, turning, call to thee O soul, thou actual Me,
And lo, thou gently masterest the orbs,
Thou matest Time, smilest content at Death,
And fillest, swellest full the vastnesses of Space.

Greater than stars or suns,
Bounding O soul thou journeyest forth;
What love than thine and ours could wider amplify?
What aspirations, wishes, outvie thine and ours O soul?
What dreams of the ideal? what plans of purity, perfection, strength?
What cheerful willingness for others' sake to give up all?
For others' sake to suffer all?

Reckoning ahead O soul, when thou, the time achiev'd,
The seas all cross'd, weather'd the capes, the voyage done,
Surrounded, copest, frontest God, yieldest, the aim attain'd,
As fill'd with friendship, love complete, the Elder Brother found,
The Younger melts in fondness in his arms.

9. Passage to more than India!
Are thy wings plumed indeed for such far flights?
O soul, voyagest thou indeed on voyages like those?
Disportest thou on waters such as those?
Soundest below the Sanscrit and the Vedas?
Then have thy bent unleash'd.

Passage to you, your shores, ye aged fierce enigmas!
Passage to you, to mastership of you, ye strangling problems!
You, strew'd with the wrecks of skeletons, that, living,
        never reach'd you.

Passage to more than India!
O secret of the earth and sky!
Of you O waters of the sea! O winding creeks and rivers!
Of you O woods and fields! of you strong mountains of my land!
Of you O prairies! of you gray rocks!
O morning red! O clouds! O rain and snows!
O day and night, passage to you!

O sun and moon and all you stars! Sirius and Jupiter!
Passage to you!

255

Passage, immediate passage! the blood burns in my veins!
Away O soul! hoist instantly the anchor!
Cut the hawsers—haul out—shake out every sail!
Have we not stood here like trees in the ground long enough?
Have we not grovel'd here long enough, eating and drinking like
        mere brutes?
Have we not darken'd and dazed ourselves with books long enough?

Sail forth—steer for the deep waters only,
Reckless O soul, exploring, I with thee, and thou with me,
For we are bound where mariner has not yet dared to go,
And we will risk the ship, ourselves and all.

O my brave soul!
O farther farther sail!
O daring joy, but safe! are they not all the seas of God?
O farther, farther, farther sail!

PRAYER OF COLUMBUS

A batter'd, wreck'd old man,
Thrown on this savage shore, far, far from home,
Pent by the sea and dark rebellious brows, twelve dreary months,
Sore, stiff with many toils, sicken'd and nigh to death,
I take my way along the island's edge,
Venting a heavy heart.

I am too full of woe?
Haply I may not live another day;
I cannot rest O God, I cannot eat or drink or sleep,
Till I put forth myself, my prayer, once more to Thee,
Breathe, bathe myself once more in Thee, commune with Thee,
Report myself once more to Thee.

Thou knowest my years entire, my life,
My long and crowded life of active work, not adoration merely;
Thou knowest the prayers and vigils of my youth,
Thou knowest my manhood's solemn and visionary meditations,
Thou knowest how before I commenced I devoted all to come to Thee,
Thou knowest I have in age ratified all those vows and strictly kept them,
Thou knowest I have not once lost nor faith nor ecstasy in Thee,

256

In shackles, prison'd, in disgrace, repining not,
Accepting all from Thee, as duly come from Thee.

All my emprises have been fill'd with Thee,
My speculations, plans, begun and carried on in thoughts of Thee,
Sailing the deep or journeying the land for Thee;
Intentions, purports, aspirations mine, leaving results to Thee.

O I am sure they really came from Thee,
The urge, the ardor, the unconquerable will,
The potent, felt, interior command, stronger than words,
A message from the Heavens whispering to me even in sleep,
These sped me on.

By me and these the work so far accomplish'd,
By me earth's elder cloy'd and stifled lands uncloy'd, unloos'd,
By me the hemispheres rounded and tied, the unknown to the known.

The end I know not, it is all in Thee,
Or small or great I know not—haply what broad fields, what lands,
Haply the brutish measureless human undergrowth I know,
Transplanted there may rise to stature, knowledge worthy Thee,
Haply the swords I know may there indeed be turn'd to reaping-tools,
Haply the lifeless cross I know, Europe's dead cross, may bud and blos-
          som there.

One effort more, my altar this bleak sand;
That Thou O God my life hast lighted,
With ray of light, steady, ineffable, vouchsafed of Thee,
Light rare untellable, lighting the very light,
Beyond all signs, descriptions, languages;
For that O God, be it my latest word, here on my knees,
Old, poor, and paralyzed, I thank Thee.

My terminus near,
The clouds already closing in upon me,
The voyage balk'd, the course disputed, lost,
I yield my ships to Thee.

My hands, my limbs grow nerveless,
My brain feels rack'd, bewilder'd,
Let the old timbers part, I will not part,
I will cling fast to Thee, O God, though the waves buffet me,
Thee, Thee at least I know.

Is it the prophet's thought I speak, or am I raving?
What do I know of life? what of myself?
I know not even my own work past or present,
Dim ever-shifting guesses of it spread before me,
Of newer better worlds, their mighty parturition,
Mocking, perplexing me.

And these things I see suddenly, what mean they?
As if some miracle, some hand divine unseal'd my eyes,
Shadowy vast shapes smile through the air and sky,
And on the distant waves sail countless ships,
And anthems in new tongues I hear saluting me.

SONG OF THE UNIVERSAL

1. Come said the Muse,
    Sing me a song no poet yet has chanted,
    Sing me the universal.

    In this broad earth of ours,
    Amid the measureless grossness and the slag,
    Enclosed and safe within its central heart,
    Nestles the seed perfection.

    By every life a share or more or less,
    None born but it is born, conceal'd or unconceal'd the seed is
        waiting.

2. Lo! keen-eyed towering science,
    As from tall peaks the modern overlooking,
    Successive absolute fiats issuing.

    Yet again, lo! the soul, above all science,
    For it has history gather'd like husks around the globe,
    For it the entire star-myriads roll through the sky.

    In spiral routes by long detours,
    (As a much-tacking ship upon the sea,)
    For it the partial to the permanent flowing,
    For it the real to the ideal tends.

    For it the mystic evolution,
    Not the right only justified, what we call evil also justified.

258

Forth from their masks, no matter what,
From the huge festering trunk, from craft and guile and tears,
Health to emerge and joy, joy universal.

Out of the bulk, the morbid and the shallow,
Out of the bad majority, the varied countless frauds of men and
        states,
Electric, antiseptic yet, cleaving, suffusing all,
Only the good is universal.

3. Over the mountain-growths disease and sorrow,
An uncaught bird is ever hovering, hovering,
High in the purer, happier air.

From imperfection's murkiest cloud,
Darts always forth one ray of perfect light,
One flash of heaven's glory.

To fashion's, custom's discord,
To the mad Babel-din, the deafening orgies,
Soothing each lull a strain is heard, just heard,
From some far shore the final chorus sounding.

O the blest eyes, the happy hearts,
That see, that know the guiding thread so fine,
Along the mighty labyrinth.

4. And thou America,
For the scheme's culmination, its thought and its reality,
For these (not for thyself) thou has arrived.

Thou too surroundest all,
Embracing carrying welcoming all, thou too by pathways broad and
        new,
To the ideal tendest.

The measur'd faiths of other lands, the grandeurs of the past,
Are not for thee, but grandeurs of thine own,
Deific faiths and amplitudes, absorbing, comprehending all,
All eligible to all.

All, all for immortality,
Love like the light silently wrapping all,
Nature's amelioration blessing all,
The blossoms, fruits of ages, orchards divine and certain,
Forms, objects, growths, humanities, to spiritual images ripening.

Give me O God to sing that thought,
Give me, give him or her I love this quenchless faith,
In Thy ensemble, whatever else withheld withhold not from us,
Belief in plan of Thee enclosed in Time and Space,
Health, peace, salvation universal.

Is it a dream?
Nay but the lack of it the dream,
And failing it life's lore and wealth a dream,
And all the world a dream.

A CLEAR MIDNIGHT

This is thy hour O Soul, thy free flight into the wordless,
Away from books, away from art, the day erased, the lesson done,
Thee fully forth emerging, silent, gazing,
       pondering the themes thou lovest best,
Night, sleep, death and the stars.

TO RICH GIVERS

What you give me I cheerfully accept,
A little sustenance, a hut and garden, a little money,
       as I rendezvous with my poems,
A traveler's lodging and breakfast as I journey through the States,—
       why should I be ashamed to own such gifts? why to advertise for
           them?
For I myself am not one who bestows nothing upon man and woman,
For I bestow upon any man or woman the entrance
       to all the gifts of the universe.

SPIRIT THAT FORM'D THIS SCENE
Written in Platte Cañon, Colorado

Spirit that form'd this scene,
These tumbled rock-piles grim and red,
These reckless heaven-ambitious peaks,
These gorges, turbulent-clear streams, this naked freshness,

260

These formless wild arrays, for reasons of their own,
I know thee, savage spirit—we have communed together,
Mine too such wild arrays, for reasons of their own;
Was't charged against my chants they had forgotten art?
To fuse within themselves its rules precise and delicatesse?
The lyrist's measur'd beat, the wrought-out temple's grace—
    column and polish'd arch forgot?
But thou that revelest here—spirit that form'd this scene,
They have remember'd thee.

A NOISELESS PATIENT SPIDER

A noiseless patient spider,
I mark'd where on a little promontory it stood isolated,
Mark'd how to explore the vacant vast surrounding,
It launch'd forth filament, filament, filament, out of itself,
Ever unreeling them, ever tirelessly speeding them.

And you O my soul where you stand,
Surrounded, detached, in measureless oceans of space,
Ceaselessly musing, venturing, throwing, seeking the spheres to connect
    them,
Till the bridge you will need be form'd, till the ductile anchor hold,
Till the gossamer thread you fling catch somewhere, O my soul.

SO LONG!

To conclude, I announce what comes after me.

I remember I said before my leaves sprang at all,
I would raise my voice jocund and strong with reference to consumma-
    tions.

When America does what was promis'd,
When through these States walk a hundred millions of superb persons,
When the rest part away for superb persons and contribute to them,
When breeds of the most perfect mothers denote America,
Then to me and mine our due fruition.

261

I have press'd through in my own right,
I have sung the body and the soul, war and peace have I sung,
    and the songs of life and death,
And the songs of birth, and shown that there are many births.

I have offer'd my style to every one, I have journey'd with confident
    step;
While my pleasure is yet at the full I whisper, So long!
And take the young woman's hand and the young man's hand for the
    last time.

I announce natural persons to arise,
I announce justice triumphant,
I announce uncompromising liberty and equality,
I announce the justification of candor and the justification of pride.

I announce that the identity of these States is a single identity only,
I announce the Union more and more compact, indissoluble,
I announce splendors and majesties to make all the previous politics
    of the earth insignificant.

I announce adhesiveness, I say it shall be limitless, unloosen'd,
I say you shall yet find the friend you were looking for.

I announce a man or woman coming, perhaps you are the one,
    (So long!)
I announce the great individual, fluid as Nature, chaste,
    affectionate, compassionate, fully arm'd.

I announce a life that shall be copious, vehement, spiritual, bold,
I announce an end that shall lightly and joyfully meet its translation.

I announce myriads of youths, beautiful, gigantic, sweet-blooded,
I announce a race of splendid and savage old men.

O thicker and faster—(So long!)
O crowding too close upon me,
I foresee too much, it means more than I thought,
It appears to me I am dying.

Hasten throat and sound your last,
Salute me—salute the days once more. Peal the old cry once more.

Screaming electric, the atmosphere using,
At random glancing, each as I notice absorbing,

Swiftly on, but a little while alighting,
Curious envelop'd messages delivering,
Sparkles hot, seed ethereal down in the dirt dropping,
Myself unknowing, my commission obeying, to question it never daring,
To ages and ages yet the growth of the seed leaving,
To troops out of the war arising, they the tasks I have set promulging,
To women certain whispers of myself bequeathing,
    their affection me more clearly explaining,
To young men my problems offering—no dallier I—
    I the muscle of their brains trying,
So I pass, a little time vocal, visible, contrary,
Afterward a melodious echo, passionately bent for,
    (death making me really undying,)
The best of me then when no longer visible, for toward that
    I have been incessantly preparing.

What is there more, that I lag and pause and crouch extended
    with unshut mouth?
Is there a single final farewell?

My songs cease, I abandon them,
From behind the screen where I hid I advance personally solely to you.

Camerado, this is no book,
Who touches this touches a man,
(Is it night? are we here together alone?)
It is I you hold and who holds you,
I spring from the pages into your arms—decease calls me forth. . . .

Dear friend whoever you are take this kiss,
I give it especially to you, do not forget me,
I feel like one who has done work for the day to retire awhile,
I receive now again of my many translations, from my avataras ascend-
        ing, while others doubtless await me,
An unknown sphere more real than I dream'd, more direct,
    darts awakening rays about me, So long!
Remember my words, I may again return,
I love you, I depart from materials,
I am as one disembodied, triumphant, dead.

Poets to come! orators, singers, musicians to come!
Not to-day is to justify me and answer what I am for,
But you, a new brood, native, athletic, continental, greater than before
      known,
Arouse! for you must justify me.

I myself but write one or two indicative words for the future,
I but advance a moment only to wheel and hurry back in the darkness.

I am a man who, sauntering along without fully stopping,
    turns a casual look upon you and then averts his face,
Leaving it to you to prove and define it,
Expecting the main things from you.

264

SUGGESTED READINGS

For those readers who may wish to tally Whitman's poems with the story of his life, excerpts from "Leaves of Grass" to be read in connection with each chapter of this book are listed below. Many of them are included in the Selection printed above. In some instances only that portion of a poem is noted which is appropriate to the text. Occasionally Whitman used the same title for more than one poem. In those cases, the section of "Leaves of Grass" in which the particular poem is to be found is given in parentheses.

READINGS

CHAPTER ONE.   STARTING FROM PAUMANOK
  Paumanok
  Old Salt Kossabone
  There Was a Child Went Forth
  Song of Myself, sec. 9
  Faces, sec. 5

CHAPTER TWO.   DROPPED IN THE STREET
  To the Man-of-War Bird
  From Montauk Point
  The Wallabout Martyrs
  Song of Myself, sec. 6, 14, 48

CHAPTER THREE.   A FONT OF TYPE
  Mannahatta (From Noon to Starry Night)
  I Hear America Singing
  In Cabin'd Ships at Sea
  For You O Democracy
  Crossing Brooklyn Ferry, sec. 8, 9
  Song of Myself, sec. 2
  City of Orgies
  By Blue Ontario's Shore, sec. 18

BIBLIOGRAPHY

I. WALT WHITMAN'S WRITINGS

The Complete Writings, issued under the supervision of his literary executors, R. M. Bucke, Thomas Harned & Horace L. Traubel, with additional bibliographical and critical material prepared by Oscar Lovell Triggs. New York, 1902. 10 vols.

Since the appearance of these volumes, a number of Whitman's prose writings have been published, so that this edition is no longer complete. It includes his most important letters, notably those to Peter Doyle and to his mother, but others appear elsewhere. It also contains a biography by his literary executors.

Leaves of Grass, including variorum readings, prefaces, and rejected poems, ed. by Emory Holloway. Garden City, 1919. 3 vols. in 1.

An inclusive edition of all of Whitman's poems prepared by the foremost Whitman scholar.

Complete Prose Works. New York, 1904.

A handy volume, authorized by Whitman's literary executors. Contains only some of the journalistic writings and none of his correspondence.

Complete Poetry & Selected Prose and Letters, ed. by Emory Holloway. New York, 1938.

The best volume for the general reader. It is furnished with a bibliographical chronology and useful notes.

The Uncollected Poetry and Prose, ed. by Emory Holloway. New York, 1921. 2 vols.

Contains among other things a number of early manuscripts, carefully edited. Throws a good deal of light on Whitman's literary development.

Calamus, ed. by R. M. Bucke, Boston, 1897.

Whitman's letters to his friend Peter Doyle, the car

conductor, covering the period from the Civil War down to Whitman's death.

The Wound Dresser, ed. by R. M. Bucke. Boston, 1898.
Whitman's letters to his mother, written during the war.

Diary in Canada, ed. by W. S. Kennedy. Boston, 1904.
Whitman's notes on his trip to Canada in 1880.

An American Primer, ed. by H. L. Traubel. Boston, 1904.
A sketch for a lecture that Whitman planned to deliver, the first published pages from his "barrel of lectures," and interesting as an expression of his views on literature.

Walt Whitman's Workshop, ed. by C. S. Furness. Cambridge, 1928.
Drafts of lectures and other hitherto unpublished manuscripts, with an introduction and notes by the editor. Valuable for the light thrown on the development of the poet's ideas and on his conception of his mission.

The Gathering of the Forces, ed. by Cleveland Rodgers and John Black. New York, 1920. 2 vols.
Hitherto uncollected pieces from the *Brooklyn Eagle*. Useful for a study of Whitman's political and social thinking.

A Childhood Reminiscence, ed. by Thomas O. Mabott and Rollo G. Silver. Seattle, 1930.
First draft of the poem, "Out of the Cradle Endlessly Rocking."

I Sit and Look Out, editorials from the *Brooklyn Daily Times*, selected and edited by Emory Holloway and Vernoliam Schwarz. New York, 1932.
Valuable for a presentation of Whitman's opinions on political and social matters in the period before the Civil War.

270

II. MEMOIRS

Burroughs, John. Notes on Walt Whitman as Poet and Person. New York, 1867.
Reminiscences of the war years by the naturalist who was a close friend of the poet to the end of his life.

Carpenter, Edward. Days with Walt Whitman, with some notes on his life and work. London, 1906.
Chiefly interesting for a report of the English writer's visits to the poet in 1877 and 1884. Contains also an account of the relations between Whitman and Emerson.

Conway, Moncure. Walt Whitman (Fortnightly Review, Nov. 15, 1866).
Account of Conway's visit to Whitman, as Emerson's envoy.

Donaldson, Thomas. Walt Whitman the Man. New York, 1896.
Intimate glimpses of Whitman in Camden, 1873-92, by a friend who first met him in Washington in 1862.

Hartmann, Sadakichi. Conversations with Walt Whitman. New York, 1895.
Brief account of a few interchanges between the poet and a young German-Japanese student in 1894 and 1890.

Johnson, John and J. W. Wallace. Visits to Walt Whitman in 1890-91. London, 1918.
Reminiscences by two admirers from Lancashire who visited not only the poet, but also his first printer, one of his pilot chums, and other friends of his.

Keller, Elizabeth L. Walt Whitman in Mickle Street. New York, 1921.
The story of Whitman's last illness written twenty-five years after the event by a woman who helped nurse him. Curious, if not wholly reliable, and obviously

271

intended as a defense of Whitman's housekeeper, Mrs. Davis.

Kennedy, W. S. Reminiscences of Walt Whitman, London, 1896.
Interesting memoirs containing a number of letters and diary entries, together with an appreciation of Whitman as the universal poet of humanity.

Merrill, Stuart. Walt Whitman. Canada, 1922.
Brief account of Whitman's address on Lincoln in 1887, as it impressed a young American poet.

Smith, Logan Pearsall. Unforgotten Years. Boston, 1939.
Lively reminiscences of visits to and from Whitman in his last years when the accomplished essayist who wrote this account was a young man.

Traubel, H. L. With Walt Whitman in Camden; July 16, 1888-Jan. 20, 1889. Boston, 1906-14. 3 vols.
Detailed and intimate account of these years in a Boswellian style by the man who was Whitman's disciple and one of his literary executors. Interspersed with numerous letters.

III. BIOGRAPHIES

Arvin, Newton. Whitman. New York, 1938.
A valuable study of the political, social, and intellectual currents of Whitman's day as they affected his life and work.

Baily, John. Walt Whitman. New York, 1926.
Interesting estimate of the poet's work.

Barrus, Clara. Whitman and Burroughs, Comrades. Boston, 1931.
A carefully documented study, especially valuable for its many quotations from contemporary sources: diaries, letters, and records of conversations.

Bazalgette, Leon. Walt Whitman, the Man and his
Work. New York, 1920.
An enthusiastic study by a French admirer.

Bucke, R. M. Walt Whitman. Philadelphia, 1883.
An authorized biography, written by one of Whit-
man's intimates during the poet's lifetime, and based
on his own testimony and that of other close friends.
The second part of the book is a critical estimate of
Whitman's work emphasizing its moral import. Con-
tains the text of W. D. O'Connor's vindication of
Whitman: The Good Gray Poet.

Holloway, Emory. Whitman, an Interpretation in Narra-
tive. New York, 1926.
The standard biography, written by the leading Whitman scholar.

Masters, Edgar Lee. Whitman. New York, 1937.
The most recent full-length biography of Whitman
by the American poet whose own work and background help him to an understanding of his great
confrère.

Perry, Bliss. Walt Whitman, his life and work. Boston,
1906.
Admirable brief biography by a sensitive and witty
scholar.

Platt, Isaac H. Walt Whitman. Boston, 1904.
Short enthusiastic account, prepared with the help of
Whitman's literary executors.

Skinner, C. H. M. Walt Whitman as an Editor (*Atlantic
Monthly,* Nov. 1903).
Brief account by a personal friend of Whitman's
journalistic activities.

Traubel, H. L., R. M. Bucke and Thomas B. Harned. In
re Walt Whitman. Philadelphia, 1893.
Valuable collection of essays on the poet, including

among other papers, W. D. O'Connor's vindication of him: The Good Gray Poet; A Woman's Estimate of Walt Whitman by Mrs. Gilchrist; Robert Ingersoll's address on Whitman; accounts of his birthday dinner in Camden and of his last illness and death; a report by one of the attending physicians; tributes by foreign admirers.

INDEX

275

277

278